D1127269

*Femininity & the
Creative Imagination*

Femininity
& the Creative
Imagination

A Study of Henry James, Robert Musil
& Marcel Proust

by Lisa Appignanesi

BARNES & NOBLE
BOOKS
10 East 53d St., New York 10022
(a division of Harper & Row Publishers, Inc.)

Published in the U.S.A. by
Barnes & Noble Books
Harper & Row, Publishers, Inc.
10 East 53rd Street
New York

ISBN 06-490190-4

© 1973 Vision Press, London

MCMLXXIII

Acknowledgments

My sincerest thanks go to Professors Anthony K. Thorlby and Eduard Goldstuecker for their patience, encouragement and critical insight; to Christine Bernard for her superlative editorial skills; and finally to Richard whose midnight tirades on literature, capitalism, woman and the western world have roused me both to anger and inspiration.

Acknowledgments are also due to the late Mr. George Scott Moncrieff and Chatto and Windus Ltd. for permission to quote from Marcel Proust's *Remembrance of Things Past*; to Eithne Wilkins, Ernst Kaiser and Martin Secker & Warburg Ltd. for permission to quote from Robert Musil's *The Man Without Qualities* and to Mrs. Roslyn Targ and the Musil Estate for other quotations from Robert Musil's work; and finally to Routledge & Kegan Paul Ltd. for permission to quote from Erich Neumann's *The Origins and History of Consciousness, Amor and Psyche,* and *The Great Mother.*

Note on Texts

Except when otherwise stated, all Henry James's works are quoted in the standard New York Edition of *The Novels and Tales of Henry James* which appeared both in the USA and the UK between 1907 and 1909.

For the section on Robert Musil, I have used as an initial source the *Gesammelte Werke in Einzelausgaben* edited by Adolf Frisé, including the ninth printing of *Der Mann ohne Eigenschaften,* which incorporates many of the textual corrections suggested by Wilhelm Bausinger. Translations are my own, except for Books One, Two and part of Three of *The Man Without Qualities,* for which I have used the Eithne Wilkins and Ernst Kaiser three-volume paperback edition published by Panther in 1968.

For the section on Marcel Proust, I have used the C. F. Scott Moncrieff translation of *A la recherche du temps perdu* in the twelve-volume Chatto and Windus edition, which includes *Le temps retrouvé,* translated by Stephen Hudson. Where the Scott Moncrieff translation differs significantly from the present definitive Gallimard edition of *A la recherche . . .* I have done my own translation.

Volume and page references for these works are generally included in parentheses following the quotation.

Abbreviations used in the Robert Musil section:

MOE   *Der Mann ohne Eigenschaften*
PD   *Prosa Dramen Späte Briefe*
TB   *Tagebücher, Aphorismen, Essays und Reden*
MWQ   *The Man Without Qualities*

Contents

Femininity: Definitions and Perspectives

Literary critics repeatedly use the word 'feminine' to describe a writer, his vision, or his characters. It is often suggested that Henry James and Marcel Proust are 'feminine' writers, in contrast to the purely masculine Hemingway. Though George Eliot is personally said to have a strong 'masculine' side, yet her male characters are thought to be 'too feminine'. Wedekind's Lulu, Strindberg's Miss Julie, or Norman Mailer's 'Great Bitch' are all quoted as being embodiments of the 'feminine' principle. So too, somewhat paradoxically, are Dostoievski's golden-hearted whore, Sonya, in *Crime and Punishment* and Joyce's faithful-faithless Molly Bloom. Strangely enough, the recurrent usage of this term 'feminine' has made it none the less elusive; for when the term is employed, it is rarely defined and it often appears not to refer directly to woman characters or to women at all. Clearly then, we are dealing with something more general than the word female or woman denotes. In fact, we are involved with a principle of diverse connotations which suggests some essential 'feminine' quality.

If we emphasize the abstract aspect of this principle by designating it as *femininity*, we put two implications into relief. Femininity is a term which implies, on the one hand, consciousness of feminine properties and on the other, assumptions about these properties which may not be entirely definite. In short, the difficulty lies precisely in the principle's evocative power. In the writers to be studied here, as well as in other writers of this epoch, we discover both this consciousness and these assumptions.

The evocative power of the term femininity makes it a word which is generally, if somewhat vaguely, understood—even though little effort is made to decipher what exactly it means. As such it constitutes what Roland Barthes calls a 'myth': a statement which bears no *direct* relationship to the object it describes (woman) and evokes a range of suggestions which is culturally determined.[1]

This study then, is about the 'myth of femininity'. Through a comparative inquiry into the works of Henry James, Robert Musil and Marcel Proust, it will seek firstly to isolate a basic pattern underlying femininity; and secondly, describe the place of this myth of femininity—the arrangement of this pattern—within the creative imagination of the three authors concerned. If a certain comparable pattern can be found in these three writers' understanding of femininity, then one can postulate that femininity bears a more general, critical relationship to literary creativity in that loosely defined historical period which is generally called 'modern', but perhaps cannot much longer be called such.

It is perhaps necessary here to define my approach a little further. By a study of femininity I do not mean that I am looking for archetypal female figures—such as Lilith, Eve, Cressida or Circe—as they may or may not appear in the works of various authors.[2] Nor is this to be a psychoanalytic study which seeks to reveal a feminine character structure in the authors themselves on the basis of biographical data. Finally, when I say 'femininity', I do not mean 'woman' as a sociologically defined being (although, of course, feminine characteristics are most often evident in female figures!).

What is interesting here is the dual focus regarding the feminine of many writers of this period. On the one hand in their work they illuminate the constituent factors of the myth of femininity—and an analysis of this artistic reflection of woman should tangentially help to clarify what it is in the wider cultural image of woman which can and perhaps needs to be changed. On the other, they seem to identify creativity, some intrinsic aspect of the fiction-making process, and sometimes even their own status as artists, with the feminine.

This link between femininity and creativity is not new in litera-

---

[1] Roland Barthes, *Mythologies* (Paris, 1957). See especially the section entitled 'Le mythe est une parole', pp. 215–217.

[2] I am not, for instance, attempting a study in the manner of Northrop Frye.

ture. Goethe provides us with an early intimation of this link in his 'the eternal feminine draws us onward' which is perhaps the first post neo-classical intuition of creativity being something other than imitation. But in the period we are concerned with here, let us say roughly from 1850 onward, this identification seems to be stressed time and again. Baudelaire, fascinated by lesbianism, woman complete within her own sex, stated that *'la femme est fatalement suggestive'* and constructed an entire sphere of symbolic and imaginative possibilities—ranging from elevated beauty to the corruption of the charnel house—around the female. His prose poem, 'Le Thyrce', where he speaks of the duality of creative genius, gives us an indication of the central role femininity played in his art, and how he consciously equated the feminine principle with the arabesque, the suggestive and imaginative element.

The high priestess presiding over the secular mystery of Stéphane Mallarmé's symbolic art is the dancing figure of Salomé; and it is somehow fitting to find that Mallarmé, for a while, edited and almost single-handedly wrote a woman's fashion magazine entitled *La dernière mode*. Théophile Gautier in his *Le roman de la momie* and in *Mademoiselle de Maupin* imbues woman with that mystery which for him constituted the essence of art. The major receptacles of James's vision are female figures. Musil, throughout his life, contemplated writing a biography in the first person, taking on the form and spirit of a woman. James Joyce, who has set down the myth of the artist's development for our century and who has found the matter of his art in the inner workings of the artistic consciousness, intimates in *A Portrait of the Artist as a Young Man* that the individual's development into an artist is triggered, in the last analysis, by the feminine figure. Indeed femininity is constantly linked to creativity in Joyce's art. Stephen rejects the enclosing mother—church and country—for the transformative and liberating figure of the young bird-girl, the symbol of art, only to return, himself metamorphosed in the book of night and unconsciousness, to the Mother : the glorified *Magna Mater,* Anna Livia Plurabelle, who is a supreme creative force. Joyce's artistic trajectory finds its beginning (leave-taking), middle (transformation) and end (homecoming), in figures of femininity.

But it is in the so-called 'father of realism', perhaps more accurately, the father of modern litrature, Gustave Flaubert, that the first radical statement about the feminization of art is found. It is Flaubert, the epitome of the modern artist, who—with his insistence on the *mot juste,* his conscious manipulation of the craft of writing, his total involvement with art rather than life—suggests an equation between the feminine and the artist in his famous remark, *'Madame Bovary, c'est moi'.* We are further reminded by Sartre that Flaubert 'during his trip to the Orient dreamed of writing the story of a mystic virgin, living in the Netherlands, consumed by dreams, a woman who would have been the symbol of Flaubert's own cult of art'.[3] This according to Sartre implies the artistic transformation of masculine modes of acting or proceeding into feminine ones and 'la féminisation de l'expérience'.

Now Flaubert's dreaming mystic virgin who becomes a symbol for hs art, like Mallarmé's Salomé and Baudelaire's *'femme fatalement suggestive'* evidently bears no direct relationship to woman as such, but is rather the distilled essence of woman – woman mediated through culture and through literary tradition and transformed into a myth of femininity. Culture has provided the artist with this myth and in this period it seems to act as a particularly deep reservoir of creative mystery. Hence, this so-called feminization of literature.

At the same time, and this needs to be emphasized, although Flaubert, for example, works with the suggestiveness of the myth, when he sets out to depict woman in his realistic fictional canvas, he casts a critical focus on the myth and illuminates it, as well as woman's actual place in society. Madame Bovary is Flaubert to the extent that she incorporates certain attributes that are generally considered to belong to the artist. She is a daydreamer, a continual wanderer in the realms of fantasy and she is one of the few members of her *petit bourgeois* society to have any imagination. Insofar as her dreams, her imaginings, have a romantic centre, and have to do with an idealization of passion and love, Flaubert is playing along with the stock assumptions of the feminine myth. However, what he reveals most succinctly through the course of the novel is that Madame Bovary's romantic fantasies—whether they take on religious or purely sexual overtones—have been fed to her by her own culture, its literature, its vision of woman. And when she attempts to live out these fantasies implicit in her society, that very society victimizes her, destroys her. Madame Bovary emerges as the first female victim of cultural feedback. Flaubert has utilized the feminine myth and self-critically illuminated it.

[3] Jean-Paul Sartre, *Search for a Method* (New York, 1963), pp. 140–150.

Now why is it that the feminine seems to cast its aura with particular predominance over this period of literature? Why this linking of the artist or his art with femininity; this feminization of the literary process at this particular historical moment?

Before this can be answered it is necessary to make some initial forages into the tangled undergrowth of the feminine myth so that a primary understanding of this artistic correlative of the fact of woman can be reached. To provide a basic topography for this exploration, it is useful to turn to certain writers outside the field of fiction. The fact that the majority of these non-fictional writers are psychoanalytical need not deflect us from our purpose, for psychoanalytical thinkers attempt an unravelling of mystery which is not dissimilar from our own. They too search for the latent content beneath a manifest statement, character or culture.

It is, of course, in the Vienna of the turn of the century that we first find a direct attempt to illuminate scientifically the whole complex of unspoken concepts which make up the so-called 'feminine principle'. The hypothesis of human bisexuality, a theory essential to the clarification of the feminine principle, was first posited here.

> . . . Man and woman are like two substances which are distributed among living individuals in varying mixed proportions, without the coefficient of one substance ever vanishing. In experience, one might say, there is neither man nor woman, only masculine and feminine.[4]

This hypothesis of human bisexuality is commonly attributed to Otto Weininger, the youthful Viennese philosopher who committed suicide in the early years of this century.[5] Every human being, regardless of sexual differentiation, is composed of masculine and feminine characteristics. This concept is familiar to us in descriptions of George Sand and George Eliot as having a strongly 'masculine' side; of suggestions that Proust and James are 'feminine' writers, and so on. Such statements, as has already been suggested, sound

---

[4] Otto Weininger, *Geschlecht und Charakter* (Wien and Leipsig, 1904), p. 10. My translation.

[5] Freud points out that although in lay circles the concept of bisexuality is attributed to Weininger, he was not the first to enunciate this hypothesis. See Sigmund Freud, 'Drei Abhandlungen zur Sexualtheorie', *Gesammelte Werke*, V, 27–145, p. 43. I use Weininger as the source for this concept precisely because the drama of his early suicide brought his book to the attention of many. Furthermore, his analyses of masculinity and femininity are echoed in the work of Musil as well as other German writers of the period.

meaningful because of the evocative power of the terms masculinity and femininity, but what is actually meant by these terms is rarely defined. Weininger, however, attempted a description of the masculine and feminine principles.[6] Since I propose to study only the feminine component of the concept of bisexuality, it is on Weininger's ideas on femininity that I shall concentrate.

For Weininger, then, the feminine side of personality is completely subsumed by sexuality. The 'feminine' woman lives in a constant devotion to sexual matters, intrinsically linked to her reproductive function. Unlike the male, who is something more than sexual, the female has no consciousness and hence no control over her sexual side. For her thinking and feeling are identical; for the male they are in constant opposition. Unconsciousness is feminine and for Weininger it is linked with the condition of fusion, of unity between subject and object. Thus, the masculine being will be conscious of the tension between private and public values, 'solitude and community'. The feminine being, because of her undivided nature, will experience no conflict of this kind. Furthermore, because of her basic unconsciousness, the feminine being does not recognize the importance of the laws of morality and is incapable of true ethical action. Weininger, in the paternalistic tradition of his epoch, favours the masculine side of the human duality. It is in the masculine consciousness and intellect that he sees the individual's ultimate liberation. Masculinity is the seat of all higher human endeavour, of all philosophical and artistic achievement.

The rationalistic prejudice of Weininger's time is here; but here also is the basic dichotomy of human make-up. Femininity is linked to unconsciousness, sexuality and the state of unity. Masculinity represents intellect, consciousness, and a tendency to separateness, to alienation of subject from object. We have here the beginnings of a definition of femininity—albeit one clouded by a personal as well as a social bias.

In order to move from the particular to the general, that is from

[6] Weininger's description of the feminine may in effect do nothing to demystify the myth of femininity in a wider social context. Because of his deeply rooted misogyny his analysis appears to be intensely one-sided and hence far from a scientific objectivity. He refers to many of the age-old prejudices against femininity. But in spite of this, his attempt at illumination, at revealing the veiled content of human make-up, makes his analysis interesting. If we try to remove the emotional bias from his statements—that which makes them in Barthe's sense, myth—we discover certain ideas relevant to this study.

a psychologically-based to a historically-oriented vision, we turn now to J. J. Bachofen, the nineteenth century Swiss classical scholar and thinker, who broadly anticipates Weininger's postulates, but here within a larger cultural and anthropological context.[7]

Where Weininger draws on observation of individual behaviour, Bachofen turns to the behaviour of entire epochs for his formulations. However, the result is similar. While it is impossible to present the whole scope of Bachofen's theories in a few lines, there are a few salient points relevant to this present argument.

Bachofen states that in the dawn of mankind, human beings lived in a state of unlimited hetaerism where procreation was rampant and knew no law beyond the raw forces of nature. This first phase of human existence Bachofen places under the divinity of the goddess Aphrodite. Following upon this first phase is the matriarchal state, ruled by Demeter and characterised by matrimony and agriculture. Here Bachofen finds the bare rudiments of jurisprudence.

These two initial stages of human development are essentially feminine. They are followed by what Bachofen understands to be the greatest revolutionary triumph of mankind: the change which gave birth to Western civilisation. The matriarchal tie between mother and child, that is, the visible material tie, gave way to the invisible, apparently non-material and hence spiritual link of paternalism. In this overcoming of *mater*iality and the natural world by the forces of the spirit, Bachofen sees the birth of all philosophical and intellectual possibility.

It is not difficult to see the link between Bachofen and Weininger. For both thinkers femininity is directly related to sexuality: the chaotic state of hetaerism taken to the individual level, becomes an image for Weininger's feminine unconsciousness with its lack of moral responsibility. Civilisation comes about with the recognition of a spiritual paternal tie. Masculinity, for Weininger and Bachofen, acts as a force which liberates humanity from mere materialism. It

[7] Johann Jakob Bachofen, *Das Mutterrecht* (Stuttgart, 1861). This is the main work in question here and it is most easily available in the Alfred Kröner Verlag edition, edited by Rudolf Marx and entitled *Mutterrecht und Urreligion* (Stuttgart, 1926). Bachofen's views are important here to an understanding of the 'myth of femininity' as it emerged in the modern period: we find his theories appearing in Musil's work, and they gained a certain notoriety in the Munich group, 'Die Kosmiker'. Also, his structured view of human development is reapplied in partial form to individual development by such writers as Erich Neumann.

effects a positive change which enables man to live by cultural and spiritual values.

Weininger and Bachofen present two similar paths toward an understanding of the feminine myth. Their definitions of femininity as a negative quantity lead directly to another exponent of a culture oriented towards rationalism and masculinity: Sigmund Freud. The traditional Freudian description of femininity is once again a paternalist one, and it has invoked criticism from many quarters, most notably from Simone de Beauvoir. Thus femininity implies passivity, while masculinity implies activity—'the universal opposition between activity and passivity, masculinity and femininity'.[8] Furthermore, Freud, like Weininger, finds a lack of a higher, independent, moral sense in the feminine being. 'I cannot evade the notion (though I hesitate to give it expression) that for women the level of what is ethically normal is different from what it is in men. Their superego is never so inexorable, so impersonal, so independent of its emotional origins as we require it to be in men.'[9]

Helen Deutsch, a follower of Freud who has made femininity the major focus of her writings, has modified Freud's equation of femininity with passivity by showing that the prime feminine characteristic is an *interiorization of sensibility*. Passivity, here, attains a positive rather than a negative value.

. . . The boy's more active sexuality leads to a stronger turn towards reality and toward conquering the outside world than is the case with the young girl. Hence an important psychologic (sic) difference between the sexes: man's attention is principally directed outward and woman's inward. The typical trait of adolescence that we discussed before—keen observation of one's own psychological processes—is as a rule more intense in the girl than in the boy. Preoccupation with her own mind continues in the woman's later life and determines two important and distinctive feminine characteristics, namely woman's greater intuition and greater subjectivity in assimilating and appreciating the life processes.[10]

[8] Sigmund Freud, 'Female Sexuality', *Collected Papers* (London, 1956), vol. V, pp. 252–272.

[9] Sigmund Freud, 'Some Psychic Consequences of the Anatomical Distinction Between the Sexes', *The Complete Psychological Works*, 23 vols. (London, 1953–1966), vol. XIX, pp. 257–258.

[10] Helen Deutsch, *The Psychology of Women*, 2 vols. (New York, 1944), I, p. 130.

Helen Deutsch further states: 'If we replace the expression "turn toward passivity" by "activity directed inward", the term "feminine passivity" acquires a more vital content . . ."[11] From its association with passivity, femininity thus becomes linked with the concept of an interiorization of life processes and sensibility. This particular psychoanalytical description of femininity is a central one and should be kept in mind.

For another kind of psychoanalytic statement, we turn to C. G. Jung who tells us in his *Symbols of Transformation* that Goethe's 'realm of the mothers' has some connections with the womb, which frequently symbolizes the creative aspect of the unconscious.[12] The feminine principle is, for Jung, the anima, 'the unconscious source of all creativity', and the 'personification of the collective unconscious' from which poetic symbols, myths, archetypes stem. The creativity which Jung speaks of is of course more general than artistic creativity and it includes the entire sphere of human action. It should, however, be noted that for Jung the artist's powers of symbolization derive from this collective and creative unconscious which is feminine.

Jung further recounts that in the neo-Platonist doctrines of Plotinus, the 'world-soul' is compared to the moon and hence is essentially a feminine force. This world-soul has a 'tendency towards separation and divisibility; the sine qua non of all change, creation and reproduction. It is an 'unending All of life and wholly energy'.[13] We have already seen how, for Weininger and Bachofen, femininity bore a direct relationship to unconsciousness. (Bachofen calls this the instinctual and hetaeric state.) Here the dimension of creativity is added to the unconscious—a point worth remembering throughout this study.

Another partial definition of femininity comes to us from existentialism and the existential psychologists. David Holbrook in an article on R. D. Laing sees being, the 'I AM' quality, as primarily that of the feminine element. This view is perhaps an outgrowth of the Freudian position, but here the paternalistic preference for activity—the masculine side of the human duality—is attacked. Our society, points out Mr. Holbrook, 'attaches the problem of identity

---

[11] Helen Deutsch, Ip. 190.
[12] C. G. Jung, *Symbols of Transformation*, The Collected Works (London, 1953), vol. V, p. 125.
[13] Ibid., p. 138.

to *doing* and *becoming*: to acquisitiveness, prowess, having and making' rather than allowing us to 'complete our processes of growth, in terms of *being,* by human contact, by love and sympathy, by creativity and modes of the "feminine element" '.[14] Being, here, is best achieved and expressed by personal relationship and creativity.

In a more astringent tone Jean-Paul Sartre writes: 'The obscenity of the feminine sex is that of everything which "gapes open". It is an "appeal to being" as all holes are.'[15] Femininity, here, is a call to being, and it may have still broader associations with the existentialist conception of the 'openness of being'. It is the gaping hole, the abyss, which calls the individual out of himself, so that he can return to a 'being in himself', *En-soi-Pour-soi*.

There would seem to be a certain number of contradictions in the non-literary thinkers here examined, but there is also some general agreement. For Weininger, from whom we derived the concept of bisexuality, Bachofen and Jung, femininity is directly related to the unconscious, while masculinity governs consciousness and the intellect. Jung finds this unconsciousness to be creative, a principle of energy and change. Freud, on the other hand, equates femininity with passivity. This passivity is qualified to mean a tendency to inwardness or interiorization by Helen Deutsch, which would seem to tie up with David Holbrook's personalistic 'modes of the feminine element'.

These various psychoanalytical insights into femininity could be divided into two essentially related groups. The first would link the feminine principle with an interiorization of life processes and sensibility; a turning inward to an examination of self and being. The second would tie femininity to unconsciousness, creative or destructive depending on the particular ideological orientation—but basically an irrationality which pays no heed to the socially determined ethical norm. If these initial descriptions of femininity are brought back into the orbit of literature, it begins to be apparent why literature takes on what has been called a feminine orientation in the period we are here concerned with and how an examination of the concept of femininity in various writers of this period can provide a fruitful critical method.

Critics have observed in the literature of the latter half of the

[14] David Holbrook, 'R. D. Laing and the Death Circuit', *Encounter* XXXI, 2, August 1968, p. 39.
[15] Jean-Paul Sartre, *Being and Nothingness* (London, 1957), p. 613.

nineteenth century an increasing interiorization of literature. Roland
Barthes notes the development of a *conscience malheureuse,* a tragic
awareness in the artist as he becomes alienated from society and increasingly self-conscious about his own inner workings and the
creative process.

> We shall see, for example,, that the ideological unity of the bour-
> geoisie gave rise to a single mode of writing, and that in the bour-
> geois periods (classical and romantic), literary form could not be
> divided because consciousness was not; whereas as soon as the
> writer ceased to be a witness to the universal, to become the incar-
> nation of a tragic awareness (around 1850), his first gesture was
> to choose the commitment of his form, either by adopting or
> rejecting the writing of his past. Classical writing therefore dis-
> integrated, and the whole of literature from Flaubert to the present
> day became the problematics of language.
> . . . literary form develops a second order power, independent of
> its economy and euphemistic charm; it fascinates the reader, it
> strikes him as exotic, it enthralls him, it acquires a weight. Litera-
> ture is no longer felt as a socially privileged mode of transaction,
> but as a language having body and hidden depth, existing both
> as dream and menace.[16]

(In this second paragraph of Barthes', one could almost substitute
femininity—as embodied by Wedekind's Lulu or Baudelaire's poeti-
cized mistress—for literature.)

Literature in the period Barthes mentions goes in search of itself
both in poetry and prose. Once again Flaubert and French literary
history provide a model to be repeated with less striking clarity
elsewhere. The failure of the 1848 revolution in France, as Flaubert
reveals so clearly in *L'Education sentimentale,* resulted in the loss
of faith in the possibility of social action and the greater loss of
faith in the potential for literature and ideas to play any significant
role in social action. Disillusionment with external social and political activity, with any form of all-embracing ideology or religion,
set in. It is telling that Flaubert, looking back on the revolutionary
period from the vantage point of 1869, calls his book about that
period a sentimental education. Thereby he re-emphasizes his dis-
affection with all forms of outwardly oriented activity and points

[16] Roland Barthes, *Writing Degree Zero* (London, 1967), pp. 8-9.

the way to the Second Empire, the monotonous, empty and petty world of Madame Bovary, the feminized Flaubert, whose interests can only be directed inward. As Flaubert admits in a letter to George Sand :

> I lack a firm, comprehensive outlook on life. . . . The words religion or Catholicism, on the one hand, and progress, fraternity and democracy, on the other, no longer meet the intellectual demands of the present. The new dogma of equality, which radicalism preaches, is refuted by physiology and history in practice. I see no possibility today either of finding a new principle or of respecting old principles. Thus I seek in vain for the ideal on which everything else depends.

This confession is accompanied by another : 'I try hard to think correctly in order to write correctly. But writing is my goal, I do not conceal it.'

This disenchantment with a sphere of endeavour which ranges beyond the self and beyond art is re-echoed in the journals of the Brothers Goncourt who find in art the only meaningful form of activity. Having summed up the course of recent politics in several pithy phrases, they conclude : '. . . All this, in the long run, brings disillusionment, an aversion to all belief, a tolerance of any power, an indifference to political passion which I find in my literary colleagues, in Flaubert as well as myself. Hence no cause is worth dying for, any government can be lived with, nothing but art may be believed in, and literature is the only confession.'

Artistic activity becomes the only viable form of engagement and the artist becomes *une conscience malheureuse,* pondering Malarmé's blank page, the problems of craft and of the internal organization of the self. A self-conscious preoccupation with artistic problems encircles the examination of all that exists within the various strata of the human personality. To look at this preoccupation as self-indulgent immersion in a vacuum is to miss the agony of these writers. For them, art is the only realm left in which one can still assemble one's wits in order to make some coherent assessment of the state of values. Thus the effort of writing correctly, of writing well, constitutes a victory of integrity over incoherence.

Sometimes the techniques of the realist, who seeks to see everything as it actually is, are applied to individual psychology. Harry Levin speaks of this process, in relation to Proust, as the 'rediscovery of self through the modalities of art'. More and more, the entire novelistic canvas is subsumed by the subjective glance, by the I's conception of time and space. Literature undertakes a journey toward the interior and simultaneously one finds that content and style are heightened to a pitch of esotericism. One has only here to think of the poetic projects of the *Symbolistes* and those poets influenced by them, of Joyce, the late Henry James, of Virginia Woolf and the Surrealists, to see this process at work.

Now does this impulse of literature toward the conscious creation and use of mystery—which accompanies its interiorization—relate in any way to our initial definitions of femininity? Certainly unconsciousness, the irrational with which we have seen femininity to be equated, presents the greatest mystery in a scientized, secularized epoch: an unknown, a polar otherness. In a world which claims to function by rational and scientific modes, a world denuded of mythopoeic forms, it is not surprising that the artist should attempt to search out some form of myth or mystery. Marx himself underlines the dependence of art on mythology and pinpoints the difficulty (or perhaps the impossibility) of artistic creation in a world totally demythologized, rendered prosaic by technology.

> We know that Greek mythology is not only the arsenal of Greek art, but also its basis. Is the conception of nature and of social relations which underlies Greek imagination and therefore Greek [art] possible when there are self-acting mules, railways, locomotives and electric telegraphs? . . . At any rate [Greek art presupposes] a mythology; on no account however a social development which precludes a mythological attitude toward nature, i.e., any attitude to nature which might give rise to myth; a society therefore demanding from the artist an imagination independent of mythology.
>
> Regarded from another aspect: is Achilles possible when powder and shot have been invented? And is the Illiad possible at all when the printing press and even printing machines exist? Is it not inevitable that with the emergence of the press bar the singing and the telling and the muse cease, that is, the conditions necessary for epic poetry disappear?[17]

If the conditions for the making of epic poetry—and under *epos* one can include the novel—seem to have disappeared in the concre-

[17] Karl Marx, *Critique of Political Economy*, pp. 216–217.

tized and explicit social values of the period we are speaking of, then it becomes essential that the artist find some sphere where there is still a mythical residue which can provide the metaphorical possibilities necessary for the making of art. This mythical residue finds its most justifiable sociological and historical form in this epoch in the otherness of femininity. To reduce this process for a moment to a simplification : since it is men who run the world of politics, business and the mundane extensions of technology which appear to have exhausted mystery, then it is in woman that the possibilities of another order, a new resolution, a new way of viewing reality must reside. Thus the artist turns to the feminine, the mystery she still represents, and uses it as a meditational core for his art.

It is necessary here not to succumb to the classistic temptation and see myth as a fixed pattern : merely a series of narratives about gods, or to bring things closer to our own interests, a series of fabulations or superstitions around woman. Myth, after all, constitutes any attempt by man to see himself coherently in a world that he does not feel he has entirely made. As such it must be regarded as a dynamic process. Myth continues whether it is centred on Olympus or transferred to the mystery of commodities or the dialectics of estrangement. And one myth illuminates the contents of its predecessor, but only to replace it in an ongoing process. Thus, if artists in this period revitalize the feminine myth, it serves to illuminate what has led to a dead end, a petrified standstill in the preceding or ongoing conceptualization of the world. And further, this myth points to its own transformation : in that, insofar as it still constitutes mystery, the unknown, it opens the way to futurity, a new resolution of values, a new conceptualization of man's place in the universe. The myth and mystery of femininity provide a suggestive core, a meditational pattern in the artist's quest for a new configuration of reality.

One can perhaps begin to see why the term feminine has been applied to literature which in its *most extreme forms* seems to exist at a great remove from the world of rational, ideological or technological pursuits, or a socially defined reality. It is art which is distinctly separate, wholly alienated from common daily reality; art which may see life from a depersonalized position as a static object to be described, not as a complex process in which the artist is a participant; art which gives evidence of that social irresponsibility which is akin to Freud's description of the feminine as lacking conscience and a higher moral sense. Nietzsche, as Eric Heller points out, sets the tone for this divorce of art from life : 'For a philosopher it is an abomination to say, "the Good and the Beautiful are one" : and if he dares to add, "also the True", then one ought to beat him. Truth is ugly. We have *Art* in order *not to perish of Truth*.'[18] Heller suggests that this is . . .

> the perfect definition of Rilke's poetic project. It also marks the summit reached by art and poetry in its steep ascent to the heights of absolute creativeness. At this point the separation between art and reality appears to be complete. Reality is the death of the spirit and art its salvation.
> . . . It is the redeeming achievement of Nietzsche and Rilke that they have raised . . . the abysmal contradictions of their age to a plane where doubt and confusion once more dissolve into the certainty of mystery.[19]

The oft repeated claim that Rilke is a 'feminine' poet loses some of its opaqueness in our present context. It is significant that the preface in which Gautier proclaimed his doctrine of art for art should be the one to *Mademoiselle de Maupin*.

Feminine, then, as a term of literary description would suggest an art of which the two distinguishing features are interiorization and the conscious creation of mystery either around or within the work of art. The long historical insistence on the otherness of woman, her core of feminine mystery, makes her the natural focus for an art which finds no fruitful material in what it considers the prose of ordinary life and which seeks to transcend the configurations of a known reality. We find a radical statement of this tendency in André Breton, the principal exponent of the Surrealists who could be said as a group to represent the apogee of mystification and interiorization in art. For Breton in *Nadja* and *Arcane 17*, woman is the other incarnate. Love of her leads to love of the other and hence its exploration. She is the prime mystery, the sphinx, the embodiment of the free spirit, a freedom based on amoral and anarchic elements. She is beauty and poetry and thus she is salvation for each individual man. But Nadja is not a mere woman. She is the distilled

[18] Friedrich Nietzsche, *Gesammelte Werke,* Musarioun Ausgabe, III (Munich, 1922–1929), p. 229.
[19] Erich Heller, *The Disinherited Mind* (Cleveland, Ohio, 1969), pp. 175–177.

essence of femininity. Breton unequivocally proclaims his desire for the feminization of art.

> The time has finally arrived to bring into relief the ideas of woman at the expense of those of men, for the bankruptcy of the latter these days is revealing itself in tumultous fashion. It is up to the artist in particular—if only as a protest against this scandalous state of affairs—to stress, to place a maximal emphasis on all that springs from the feminine system of the world, over and against the masculine system . . .[20]

It is interesting to note tangentially here that what appears to be in Breton's case a radical and revolutionary statement—and is at least apparently revolutionary as far as art is concerned—is essentially a reactionary proclamation within a political context. Breton turns to woman, that *'other prism of vision'* because of her irrationality, her lack of a social or moral sense. Indeed, his entire revolutionary thrust is based on the irrational, not on any critical confrontation with social issues. Thus he merely serves to prolong the superstition around woman's irrationality, which is precisely the heritage of the paternalist rationally-oriented world he is seeking to overthrow.

It seems almost unnecessary to add that the feminized art which Breton calls for, that art which is distinguished by what we have called mystification and interiorization, can in its most limited and hence least viable forms, lead to an exaltation of mystery for its own sake or to the submerging of aesthetic scruples in subjective and psychological distortions. As such, although it may dress itself in revolutionary garb, it does no more than protect the *status quo* by focusing attention away from what may be real and pressing issues. Just so, the long tradition of mystification around woman—the archetypal tableaux in which she appears as a sphinx-like deity, or a supernaturally immaculate virgin staring into the heavens, or a frenzied Medea devouring men—has served to shroud her historical condition.

But the greatest art leaves neither our perspectives of myth or reality unchanged. This is why in this study, I have chosen to deal with three writers who present, each in his own way, a total canvas, a fictional universe which encompasses the conflicts of its age and

[20] André Breton, *Arcane 17*, Editions 10/18 (Paris, 1970), pp. 62–64. My translation.

which can more profoundly illuminate the place of femininity in the creative imagination.

On the surface the works of James, Musil and Proust seem to bear little resemblance to one another and it may be questioned why they have been selected to illustrate the place of femininity and its link to literary creativity in this loosely defined historical period. The question is answered simply enough. James, Musil and Proust all write about the period which precedes the first World War and which marks the end of a historical era. More than almost any of the characters of other writers of this period, theirs crystallize and objectify the tendencies and contradictions of an age which has exhausted its historical dynamism and is about to be transformed by cataclysm into something radically different from itself. Meanwhile, however, in the works of these authors, there seems to be an appropriate moment of stasis in which cultural forces, myths and assumptions are reflected upon, analyzed and brought to self-consciousness through the act of writing.

All three are encyclopaedic writers whose oeuvres provide a vast canvas, a total world which is, especially in the case of Proust and Musil, almost a complete sociological model. James's world is that of triumphant Britannia and gilded American magnates, both gradually revealing their human insufficiency; Proust's the Third Republic, with its Dreyfus and Panama scandals. Musil, though he personally post-dates this period, finds his fictional world in the decay of the Austro-Hungarian Empire. If these three writers have been chosen to be dealt with here, it is not simply because, even at first glance, the feminine appears central in their work, but precisely because they are major writers whose works encapsulate and crystallize the contradictions of a declining age, as well as manifest a critical consciousness of it.

Furthermore James, Musil and Proust have as their central characters members of a leisure class. This means that their principal figures will have the fictional time, the freedom to embark on reflections which the total writer can manipulate in the direction of consciousness of their own dilemma as well as an awareness of the period. The major preoccupation of their characters is essentially this search for awareness in a world which is too complex to allow for immediate understanding: a world that does not readily divulge meaning. We have said that femininity as a generalized concept is at least partially a self-consciousness of feminine properties, a tendency towards introspection, meditation and the inward life; and precisely because the characters in the works of these three authors devote themselves to meditating upon their inner make-up and their relationship to the inwardness of those around them, they give us an insight into the nature of the feminine itself.

One could, of course, study woman in the works of Balzac and Sir Walter Scott, for example, but because Balzac and Scott's characters are intrinsically embroiled in the societies they fictionally inhabit, their primary preoccupation is not with the refined essence of what constitutes selfhood. Rather they are concerned with the tangible values of the external world, financial or political as the case may be. Leisure (where the desired end of consciousness and critique for the artist is not social revolution but rather the attainment of individual integrity or of breadth and depth of observation of a given situation, person or epoch) provides a vantage point of far-ranging lucidity and need not necessarily reproduce the ideological assumptions of the established power. In Thomas Mann's *The Magic Mountain*—to use a book which deals with the same epoch as those of the three writers here concerned—it is precisely the characters' leisurely retirement in a sanatorium which enables Mann to crystallize a conscious critique of their historical situation. Thus, even within the delimited sphere of femininity, one can suggest that James, Musil and Proust's focus on characters of leisure will allow them self-critically to illuminate the myth surrounding woman and yet, at the same time, consciously use the mystery, the suggestiveness of the feminine myth, in the creation of their fictions. (One should perhaps note parenthetically here that there seems to be a direct social link between woman and leisure in that the division of labour in this epoch makes of woman that being who is apparently not caught up in the modes of production and exchange; and hence—at least insofar as cultural myth is concerned— most prone to values based on luxury, such as aesthetic sensibility, inwardness, etc.)

The point here—since the femininity I wish to analyze is neither a biographical nor a social phenomenon but a purely literary one— is not to engage in an ideological attack on the way in which these writers may or may not mystify or distort woman. There is nothing to be gained from using or rather abusing literature as a sociological mine for the pillaging of half-truths which lead neither to an understanding of literature nor to the illumination of a social context which is inherently dynamic. The three studies in this book will centre around these basic issues :

What is it that James, Musil and Proust find in femininity which is fruitful to their art?

What can an analysis of the myth of femininity tell us about each individual artists' vision?

What does each one self-critically tell us about the myth of femininity which can be useful to an understanding of woman herself?

It should be noted that this is not to be a philosophical voyage. The picture of femininity we are searching for grows out of a close textual reading of James, Musil and Proust, almost as if it were a stylistic metaphor. By analysing femininity in these three authors, it becomes apparent that the feminine adapts itself to the peculiar idiosyncrasies that mark each of these authors and their particular preoccupations. In the case of James, we see not only femininity in many of its creative aspects, but also the particular light it casts on James's moral problem. With Musil, the artistic question takes on a primarily intellectual form in which the masculine and feminine are polarized. Finally, in the case of Proust, we come to grips with a psychological vision in which the feminine's relationship to creativity comes most clearly to the forefront.

I would hope that the kind of literary study embarked on here can contribute, in however small a way, to a wider exploratory form of cultural criticism by liberating the personality of contemporary woman from the unhealthier phases of the mystery obscuring her; yet, at the same time, trying to avoid the too fashionable sociological bias which refuses the creative insights available in tradition.

1 Henry James: Femininity and the Moral Sensibility

Henry James was born in 1843 in Washington Place, New York, into a family of more than usual intellectual prominence. His father, Henry James Sr, was a well-known Swedenborgian philosopher and his brother, William, is renowned as one of the founders of American pragmatism. He attended schools in America and Europe and in 1865 began to contribute reviews and short stories to American periodicals. His attachment to Europe brought him to settle in Paris in 1875 where he formed a friendship with Turgenev and frequented the Flaubert circle. The following year he moved to England where he spent the remainder of his days—apart from several visits to America and the Continent—first in London, then in Rye, Sussex. His life was divided between his passion for writing and his passion for dining-out, the latter providing him with the 'germs' of his fiction. He died in 1916, leaving behind him one of the largest oeuvres of any modern writer.

'FELT-LIFE' AND THE SELF

Looking at the spectrum of Henry James's characters, one is immediately struck by the number and importance of his female figures. From Daisy Miller and Catherine Sloper to Maggie Verver and Charlotte Stant, the central position in James's fictional canvas is given over to woman. This phenomenon is amply noted by James's critics. Philip Rahv, for example, has noted: 'Henry James is not fully represented in his novels by any one single character, but of his principal heroine it can be said that she makes the most of his vision and dominates his drama of transatlantic relations. This young woman is his favourite American type, appearing in his work time and again under various names and in various situations.'[1] There is no need, however, to limit James's focus on the feminine to his American heroines; his European women—Kate Croy, Miriam Rooth, the Princess Casamassima, Nanda Brookenham, Maisie and a score of others—have an equally important place in his work.

In fact, one could easily extend James's representation of the feminine to include certain aspects of his male figures, for James seems to have been fully aware of the idea that both masculine and feminine properties contribute to the make-up of the single individual. This is overtly stated in his description of Saint-Beuve : 'There is something feminine in his tact, his penetration, his subtlety and pliability, his rapidity of transition, his magical divinations, his sympathies and antipathies, his marvellous act of insinuation, of expressing himself by fine touches and of adding touch to touch.' But 'the faculties of the masculine stamp' which James emphasized in Saint-Beuve are those of 'completeness, the solid sense, the constant reason, the moderation, the copious knowledge, the passion for exactitude and for general considerations'.[2] Thus, without stepping out of James's own range of perceptions, we can say with Naomi Lebowitz that Strether's European experience is the gradual attainment of a feminine sensibility.[3] It can also be suggested that Hyacinth Robinson and Grey Fielder are cast in a feminine mould.

Although James's feminine bent has been widely acknowledged,[4] few critics have actually explored what James intends by it and how femininity takes its place in the totality of his artistic approach. Philip Rahv gives social reasons for James's stress on the feminine :

The advancement of this heroine takes on historical form against the period background of the American female's rise to a position of cultural prestige and authority. She it was who first reached out for the 'consummations and amenities' of life which her male

---

[1] Philip Rahv, 'The Heiress of all the Ages', *Image and Idea* (New York, 1957), p. 51.

[2] Henry James, 'Saint-Beuve', the *North American Review*, CXXX (January, 1880), p. 53.

[3] Naomi Lebowitz, *The Imagination of Loving* (Detroit, 1965), p. 66.

[4] See, for example, Bruce Lowery, *Marcel Proust et Henry James: Une Confrontation* (Paris, 1964), pp. 167–172. Leon Edel, *Henry James: The Untried Years* (London, 1953), p. 105.

relatives were still earnestly engaged in procuring its 'necessities and preparations.'

This social fact is balanced, according to Rahv, by James's own instinct, 'the most exquisite possible, for private relations and for their latent refinement of fact and taste. So estranged was he from typical masculine interests that he could not but fall back more and more on the subject of marriage, a subject dominated, in his treatment of it, by the "social note" and meeting the "finer female sense" on its own preferred ground.'[5] Naomi Lebowitz, following Rahv's thesis, studies this feminine sensibility from the point of view of James's primary concern with the problem of personal relationships. But it is necessary to take this question a little further if we are to understand what lies at the basis of James's focus on femininity.

James has old Mr. Touchett in *The Portrait of a Lady* say in a semi-joking tone, 'The ladies will save us . . . that is the best of them will—for I make a difference between them. Make up to a good one and marry her, and your life will become much more interesting.' (III, 11).In his review of Mathilde Serao, James echoes this statement in a more serious manner and gives us a possible clue to what lies at the core of his feminine orientation. 'It is the ladies, in a word,' he writes, 'who have lately done most to remind us of man's *relations with himself, that is with woman*'.[6] This statement seems almost to demand a Jungian division of male and female parts into animus and anima. The animus, that part of man concerned with external, social and public realities has already been sufficiently explored in works describing man's relationship to 'the pistol, the pirate, the police, the wild and tame beast',[7] or so James seems to be saying. But for an understanding of the anima, the inward, the not so easily recognisable 'feminine' part of the self, man must first begin to fathom his relations with woman.

We have already noted that James was perfectly aware of the masculine and feminine constituents of the individual. The masculine has a tendency to push outwards into the sphere of external activity, while the feminine suggests an interiorizing movement toward private sensibility. Significantly, in this review of the last phase of his career, James stresses the necessity of focusing literature on this latter movement: the movement toward self and the femin-

---

5 Rahv, 'The Heiress . . . ', p. 57.
6 Henry James, *Notes on Novelists* (London, 1914), p. 237. My italics.
7 Ibid.

ine with its property of introspective inwardness. In this role, the feminine, as will be seen more clearly later, becomes the cornerstone of James's ethics of consciousness.

There is a second aspect of James's art which is mentioned almost universally by his critics, yet again is never fully explained. This is James's reputed tendency toward the fairy-tale, especially noted in his early and late periods. Neither George Eliot nor Jane Austen, George Sand, Balzac or the Brothers Goncourt—all writers whom James admired—share this particular characteristic. It seems to derive from no external source, but to emerge from James's singular handling of the tools of his craft.

Perhaps this peculiarity is what places James—insofar as the English novel is concerned—at the head of the twentieth century. One could simplify the distinction between so-called 'modernism' in literature and what comes before by suggesting that the difference between the two lies in the step from a coherent explanation of a universe which is transpersonal to describing the loneliness of the individual who has to cope with existence in his own terms. The person in modern literature is no longer comfortably related to a unified society or taking part in a coherent cosmology, but is rather pitted against it. He is related only to himself; and the individual's problem then becomes how to achieve integrity of self. Although James's characters would seem, at first glance, to live in a highly structured and traditional world, with profounder analysis, one realises that—especially in James's later works—the test of character becomes precisely how to achieve integrity of self in a society from which one is isolated. James's unusual plot mechanism of thrusting his American hero or heroine into a foreign context in which he has no traditional social resources to fall back on perfectly mirrors the individual's dilemma in twentieth century fiction.

Given this initial description of the modern hero as an 'outsider', one can still distinguish two ways in which the writer or his principal character can react to the human condition. To proceed a little in advance of the argument, we can say that these two tendencies can be called masculine and feminine. The predominantly masculine writer has a tendency to see the importance of events in terms of the collective: he will externalise activity and judge it by collective, transpersonal, or mechanical standards. The predominantly feminine writer has a tendency to internalize activity, to find, like the James of the major phase, one centre of consciousness through which all events are sifted. His characters will adapt to their particular human condition in terms of guile or sagacity.

This first masculine category can be further defined as a tendency toward ritual, or to take things into a social sphere, ideology. It is not a distortion to say that Lawrence cajoled his lovers out of a merely existential plane to a ritualistic one; that the religious tone gives special forcefulness to the lovers' ultimate unity, be it ever so 'naturally sexual'. His supreme god, we must remember, is the male phallus. As Naomi Lebowitz points out, 'It is the masculine will that raises the status of relationship to a religious or romantic ritual'.[8] Precisely the male characteristic, as James himself noted, moves toward a wider sphere of reference than that which the self can contain. Lawrence's characters have no individual choice : they are personifications of forces, not fully human. They carry emotional events, sensations, to a transpersonal sphere, unlike James's more feminine characters who keep these emotions and sensations in the sphere of the self. One could, of course, list under this masculine strain of literature such naturalistic writers as Zola, who are seemingly opposed to the entire Lawrentian ethic. However, like Lawrence's characters, Zola's have no posibility of individual choice : they too, are the pawns of forces greater than themselves, in this case social forces.

When we enter James's fictional world, we come into a sphere which keeps itself peculiarly innocent of ritual, ideology, or any tendency toward a collective or transpersonal definition of the self. T . S. Eliot in saying that James 'had a mind so fine that no idea could violate it' is perfectly correct. This is what made James, for Eliot, the most intelligent man of his generation.[9] James seems to have been able to see around any one dominating fixed point.[10] His critical lucidity would not allow him to stop at any one definition of the absolute; one might almost say it prevented him from doing so. James's ethic is based exclusively on an intense personalism and a high intelligence : that is, on any *unfixed law* which allows the individual to develop his inner qualities to the furthest point of possibility. This development, James insists, must be taken note of con-

---

[8] Lebowitz, p. 66.

[9] T. S. Eliot, 'On Henry James', *The Question of Henry James*, ed. F. W. Dupee (London, 1947), pp. 125–126.

[10] James himself used the phrase to see around someone or something intellectually in his account of Flaubert.

sciously at its every step by the individual. In a statement which reflects upon his heroes as well as his art, James says:

> There is, I think, no more nutritive or suggestive truth in this connection than that of the dependence of the 'moral' sense of a work of art on *the amount of felt life* concerned in producing it. The question comes back thus, obviously to the kind and degree of the *artist's prime sensibility,* which is the soil out of which his subject springs. The quality and capacity of that soil, its ability to 'grow' with due freshness and straightness *any vision of life,* represents, strongly or weakly, the projected morality. That element is but another name for the more or less close connection of the subject with some mark made on the *intelligence,* with some *sincere experience.*[11]

To instil 'felt life' into a work is to render it moral and insofar as a character's experience within a work can be linked with a sensibility which permits growth and the expansion of felt life, he too can be judged moral.

It is telling that James's only 'external' ideology should be anarchism, as Lionel Trilling points out in his essay on *The Princess Casamassima*[12] and that even this anarchism should give way to the personal sensibility of the individual in question. Hyacinth's movement is away from any outward-looking system of values and towards a cult of the self—a self which is ever-changing and ever-developing. James does not allow him to die, a martyr to a cause, for this would lift him outside the level of personalism. If the tendency to move character toward an extra-personal or collective absolute does indeed arise in this book, and we shall see later that it does, then it is only to be denounced by James as something which goes against the grain of felt-life and the growth of sensibility.

In one of James's short stories, 'The Last of the Valerii', the hero, a count, reveals a masculine tendency to create a ritualistic and external form of worship and is made to fail in his venture. The pagan goddess, the mythical figure at whose altar he serves, is destroyed and the count is forced back into the realm of the 'ordinary' defined by his own person. As such he is made to return to his living wife,

---

[11] Henry James, *The Art of the Novel* (New York and London, 1934), p. 45. (My italics.)

[12] Lionel Trilling, 'The Princess Cassamassima', *The Liberal Imagination* (NY, 1961).

that is in reality, to himself. This is perhaps the clearest example of James's rejection of the ritualistic or transpersonal states of mind and being. His disapproval has its ground in the fact, as James sees it, that any transpersonal form of living, any systematized form of belief, be it godly or secular, imposes its own absolutes which can only be adhered to in a haze of superstition. James's insistence is on the fine intelligence, the critical self-scrutiny, which cannot permit a merely superstitious life. Perhaps one might point to the neutral life of the characters in the two short stories, 'The Altar of the Dead' or 'The Great Good Place' as immersed in a kind of superstitious aura. Yet the point here is surely that religion has been displaced from its usual external manifestation for the benefit of the person. Thought, subjective life, usurps the absolute in such tales and is oddly aware of the absence of an absolute. The cornerstone of James's femininity is in fact this refusal of ritual, systematized dogma, or any transpersonal way of life. Ethical worth is something opposed to rigid definition, to systems, to 'things everyone assumes.'

As Blake points out, the feminine principle is flux, change and the refusal of a fixed point of reference. James's partiality to water metaphors, the primal element of flux, supports this feminine orientation. It is the feminine sensibility that keeps relationships alive by disturbing ritual, by submitting it to the tests of change, as Naomi Lebowitz has suggested. James's art is built on this continual unwillingness to allow ossification of an inflexible centre.

This is the basis of his law of 'successive aspects' or the 'planned rotation of aspects' which prevents any one element from gaining absolute proportions, since any element, once it is seen from constantly shifting points of view, begins to lose its fixed and unchanging quality. Undoubtedly this leads to James's recognised 'ambiguity' and to the American critic, Yvor Winters' charge of obscurantism; for with James, ambiguity reaches the proportions of a moral cosmology. Although he seems to miss the point behind what he calls James's 'expressive form', Winters is correct in giving it this name. James's long containing sentences attempt to include the 'inextricable proliferating life, multiplied all over its surface' which is inherent to a vision seeking to examine an ever-changing reality from ever-changing points of view.

James leads us away from a masculine definition of the world in which the individual finds his essence in relation to transpersonal or social absolutes. Preoccupied with the personal and the changing, his art takes on a feminine orientation, and it finds a structure akin to itself in the fairy-tale or fable. It is in the fairy-tale that one finds the constant metamorphosis, the constant change of person externally materialised, as outcast children are transformed into princesses, frogs into princes, pumpkins into coaches. The only possible pivot for a world depicted as unstable must be responsibility incarnated by the integrity of person. It is the element of choice typical of the fairy-tale which provides mere life-felt flux with the possible residue of responsibility. For example, the characters of Aeschylus have no choice except to follow their fate, but Aesop's folk do seem to have both the possibility of choice as well as of criticism.

Jung points out that in fairy-tales, as in dreams, the psyche tells its own story.[13] Fairy-tales thus embody the relationship of the personal psyche to itself; and they reveal the single individual faced by a series of challenges which he must solve by ingenuity or perspicacity with no resource to a transpersonal force. In place of a god here, one finds the personalised fairy godmother or Rumplestiltskin, whose powers over the individual are much reduced. What this means in terms of literature is that the character functions as a 'free spirit' undirected by any particular didactic purpose of his creator.[14] It is important to note that the fairy-tale's animating spirit need never become explicit as an accepted core of doctrine. Hence, its essence can remain intangible, oblique, rather than direct. It is not a thoroughly crystallised form with specific designs on its audience.

The fairy-tale provides us with a significant counterpart for James's principal heroine in the Cinderella figure. Many of James's critics have noted that the Cinderella theme runs through his work and if we use it here, it is in order to investigate the particularly 'feminine' characteristics inherent in the figure of Cinderella. Freud

[13] C. G. Jung, 'The Phenomenology of the Spirit in Fairytales', *The Archetypes and the Collective Unconscious, Collected Works*, vol. 9, part 1 (London, 1959), pp. 207–254.

[14] One could make a basic distinction here between those writers who, like Thomas Hardy and D. H. Lawrence, turn to myth for their basic structure and those, like James, who turn to the fairy-tale. Edmund Leach tells us that the anthropologist's usual view is that 'myth is a sacred tale'; the myth is 'divinely true for those who believe, but fairy-tale for those who do not.' Furthermore, he points out that 'myth is not just a fairy-tale, it contains a message'. (Edmund Leach, *Lévi-Strauss* (London, 1970), p. 54 and 59). This would suggest that the 'mythic structure is more congenial for those writers whom we have termed 'masculine': while the non-sacred aspect of the fairy-tale, with its lack of ideological or religious orientation, is closer to James, whose bent will be seen to be distinctly feminine.

has pointed out how, archetypally, the figure of the third sister or youngest daughter is always the best and most desirable of women; she is at the same time apparently the simplest and most inscrutable feminine possibility.[15] To arrive at a fuller understanding of James's enigmatic heroine and to see how this particular figure of femininity provides a key to his vision, we can perhaps begin by examining the Cinderella story. One of the four hundred variants of the cycle of tales contains some elements which make it peculiarly relevant in the Jamesian context. Hence I am taking the liberty of quoting this tale, entitled 'The Invisible One,' in full.

There was once a large Indian village situated on the border of a lake. At the end of the place was a lodge, in which dwelt a being who was always invisible. He had a sister, who attended to his wants, and it was known that any girl who could see him might marry him. Therefore, there were few indeed who did not make the trial, but it was long ere one succeeded.

But it passed in this wise. Towards evening when the Invisible One was supposed to be returning home, his sister would walk with any girls who came down to the shore of the lake. She, indeed, could see her brother, since to her he was always visible, and beholding him she would say to her companions: 'Do you see my brother?' And then they would mostly answer 'Yes', though some said 'Nay'. And then the sister would say: 'Of what is his shoulder strap made?' But as some tell the tale, she would inquire other things, such as: 'What is his moose-runner's haul?' or 'With what does he draw his sled?' And they would reply: 'A strip of raw-hide', or 'A green withe', or something of the kind. And then she, knowing they had not told the truth, would reply quietly: 'Very well, let us return to the wigwam!'

And when they entered the place she would bid them not to take a certain seat, for it was his. And after they had helped to cook the supper they would wait with great curiosity to see him eat. Truly he gave proof that he was a real person, for as he took off his mocassins they became visible, and his sister hung them up; but beyond this they beheld nothing, not even when they remained all night, as many did.

There dwelt in the village an old man, a widower, with three daughters. The youngest of these was very small, weak and often

[15] Sigmund Freud, 'The Theme of the Three Caskets', *Complete Psychological Works*, vol. 12 (London, 1958), pp. 289–301.

ill, which did not prevent her sisters, especially the eldest, treating her with great cruelty. The second daughter was kinder, and sometimes took the part of the abused little girl, but the other would burn her hands and feet with hot coals; yes, her body was scarred with marks made by the tortue, so that people called her *Oochiqeaskw,* the rough-faced girl.

And when her father, coming home, asked what it meant that she was so disfigured, her sister would promptly say that it was the fault of the girl herself, for that having been forbidden to go near the fire she had disobeyed and fallen in.

Now it came to pass that it entered the heads of the two elder sisters of this poor girl that they would go and try their fortune at seeing the Invisible One. So they clad themselves in their finest and strove to look their fairest; and finding his sister at home, they went with her to take the wonted walk down to the water. Then when He came, being asked if they saw him, they said, 'Certainly': and also replied to the question of the shoulder strap or sled cord: 'A piece of raw hide'. In saying this they lied like the rest, for they had seen nothing, and got nothing for their pains.

When their father returned home the next evening he brought with him many of the pretty little shells from which wampum was made, and they were soon engaged in stringing them.

That day poor little Oochiqeaskw, the burnt-faced girl, who had always run barefoot, got a pair of her father's old moccasins, and put them into water that they might become flexible to wear. And begging her sisters for a few wampum shells, the eldest did but call her a 'lying little beast', but the other gave her a few. And having no clothes beyond a few paltry rags, the poor creature went forth and got herself from the woods a few sheets of birch bark of which to make a dress, putting some figures on the bark. And this dress she shaped like those worn of old. So she made a petticoat and a loose gown, a cap, leggings and handkerchief; and having put on her father's great old moccasins, which came nearly up to her knees, she went forth to try her luck. For even that little thing would see the Invisible One in the great wigwam at the end of the village.

Truly her luck had a most inauspicious beginning, for there was one long storm of ridicule and hisses, calls and hoots from her own door to that she went to seek. Her sisters tried to shame her and bade her stay at home, but she would not obey; and all the idlers seeing this strange little creature in her odd array, cried 'Shame!' But she went on, for she was greatly resolved; it may be that some spirit had inspired her.

Now this poor little wretch in her mad attire, with her hair singed off, and her little face as full of burns and scars as there are holes in a sieve, was for all this most kindly received by the sister of the Invisible One : for this noble girl knew more than the mere outside of things as the world knows them. And as the brown of the evening sky became black, she took her down to the lake. And erelong the girls knew He had come. Then the sister said 'Do you see him?' And the other replied with awe, 'Truly I do—and he is wonderful'. 'And what is his sled-string?' 'It is', she replied, 'the Rainbow.' And great fear was on her. 'But my sister', said the other, 'what is his bow-string?' 'His bow string is Ketaksoowowcht, the Spirit's Road (the milky way).'

'Thou hast seen him,' said the sister. And taking the girl home she bathed her, and as she washed all the scars disappeared from face and body. Her hair grew again; it was very long and like a blackbird's wing. Her eyes were like stars. In all the world there was no such beauty. Then from her treasures she gave her a wedding garment, and adorned her. Under her comb, as she combed, her hair grew. It was a marvel to behold.

Then having done this, she bade her take the wife's seat in the wigwam—that by which her brother sat, the seat next to the door. And when he entered, terrible and beautiful, he smiled and said 'Wajookoos! So we are found out!' 'Allajulaa Yes', was her reply. So she became his wife.[16]

This Cinderella variant contains all the aspects of the rich-little-poor-girl story, the outcast child with burnt face or 'cinders' who because of and through her sufferings seems to merit some kind of magical reward which will mean her transformation. Cinderella, like the major Jamesian heroines, is an outsider and she is essentially free to choose a course of action which will consolidate her integrity of person. Like Maggie Verver—James's most fully worked out Cinedrella prototype—the Indian Cinderella chooses to exercise her ingenuity (symbolized in her efforts at concocting a proper costume)

---

[16] Quoted by MacLeod Yearsley, in *The Folk-Lore of the Fairy-Tale* (London, 1924), pp. 113–116.

and to meet the challenge of winning over the 'Invisible One', her particular Prince Amerigo.

What is clearly emphasized and concretized in this Cinderella variant is that domination of the inner world which is the distinguishing property of the Cinderella figure; and we have already seen how inwardness is a prime feminine property. The Indian Cinderella conquers because she is the only one to hold the keys to the invisible kingdom—that further dimension of reality which is the seat of all moral and spiritual qualities. Her inner struggle and her particular form of femininity allow her to behold the invisible and having beheld it, she is transformed into the princess who was locked inside her previously. Attuned to spheres of being, different from those of surface reality, she can fathom the 'spirit's road'. This, in a Jamesian context, suggests that she holds the keys to an attainment of full consciousness.

The burnt-faced girl's transformation is based on her recognition, on finding out. This is what makes this particular Cinderella variant so akin to James, for it stresses the crucial action of 'seeing'—an action central to James with his high estimation of the fine intelligence. James, as he suggests in the third chapter of his autobiography, made almost a religion of consciousness. It is only by being fully conscious, by fully seeing, that James's characters can fully be. But to fully see means that life must be led according to the principle of successive aspects. Only the individual who is capable of flexibility, of an open-ended existence devoid of absolute values, can experience the fullness of felt-life and exemplify the Jamesian ethic. To reach the heights of being and consciousness, one must see into the depths. Only the feminine, with her 'inwardness' is capable of this.

Feminine inwardness is linked in the Cinderella tales to the element of fire. Burnt-faced girls, Cinder-ellas, all have a kinship to this prime transformative element and all are either transformed in themselves or exert a transformative influence on others by turning them inwards to the core of self. Fire is also related to the capacity for musing, for reverie[17] which is implicit in all the Cinderella figures. This too is a central characteristic of James's heroines from Catherine to Isabel and finally, Maggie. If the life of the latter is lived out in a fairy-tale atmosphere, it only echoes the inner make-up of her predecessors.

[17] Gaston Bachelard, *La Psychanalyse du Feu* (Paris, 1949), pp. 31–40.

The innocence of the Cinderella figure, the youngest child, is similarly important to James's vision. It is an innocence, a freshness and a childlike imaginative freedom, which she never loses even in the attainment of maturity. It is this which allows her to embark on adventures which a more worldly being would not undertake in her place and it gives her that pliability which is necessary for the attainment of fullness in life.

A final aspect in the Indian Cinderella tale which helps to illuminate James's approach lies in its inexplicitness. As in most fairy-tales, there is no direct revelation here as to who the Invisible One really is. It is enough that his presence is an animating one, which throws a light upon character and action. Yet he need never become tangible or explicit. His influence may be other worldly, but it does not result in a static definition of his essence, nor in a determination of what exactly his external reference may be. The spirit which animates the fairy-tale is the spirit which casts its glow over the intangible, inexplicit quality of 'The Altar of the Dead' and 'The Great Good Place'. It is a spirit 'feminine' in essence which shies away from any definition of an absolute while exploring realms which are usually prone to such definition and systematization.

James's feminine orientation and his use of the fairy-tale seem thus to bear some relationship to each other. But how is one to account for the sophistication of his craft which, one would assume, would take him away precisely from the primitive structure of the fairy-tale? And what is the total configuration femininity takes on in his work? By examining certain representative works from James's early, middle and late periods, a fuller understanding of these problems can be arrived at.

There are two related patterns to be traced in James's work as it is seen here. By following his artistic and technical development, it becomes apparent that the early work is characterized by an unconscious use of romantic and fairy-tale elements; the middle period is the sphere of the fully conscious realist manipulating the tools of his craft in the direction he desires—that is, an artist totally removed from the unconscious and primitive sphere of the fairy-tale; while the final and major phase is marked by a return to the fairy-tale, but here a fairy world which contains within itself all the elaborations and sophistications of the consummate craftsman. Simultaneously, by tracing what can be called the 'life-line' or the line of feminine sensibility in James's work, we note a parallel development. Whereas the earliest Jamesian heroines are marked by a private and inward sensibility, the principal heroine in the middle period can be temporarily described as the woman of outward vision or of the public, social order. Finally, in the major phase, this public vision is subsumed in the private sensibility, as the importance of the integrity of the self comes into the foreground.

THE EARLY PHASE

In *Roderick Hudson,* which following James's example we can call his first major work, the two poles of Jamesian femininity are brought into play. The figures of Mary Garland and Christine Light are, according to James, 'antithetic' and they present the twin directions which his central female figures will take. Mary Garland bears the seeds of the Cinderella figure which will flower in Isabel Archer and finally Maggie Verver, while her antithesis, Christine Light, points in the direction of James's outward-looking women who find their fruition in the figures of Kate Croy and Charlotte Stant.

Mary Garland, who both Philip Rahv and Oscar Cargill agree looks back to Hawthorne's allegorical figures in *The Blithedale Romance* and *The Marble Faun,* is James's initial venture into the world of the fairy-tale princess. Although, as Rahv points out, in her 'the ferment of experience is yet more potential than actual',[1] Mary Garland contains all the budding qualities of the Cinderella. A puritan innocence, associated with the youth of America, is central to her make-up together with a pronounced tendency for the inward life, a predilection for the world of revery and imagination. Rowland's first major impression of her emphasises these characteristics and suggests that what she has of beauty is only visible to those who see with an inward eye.

> Mary Garland . . . had not the countenance to inspire a sculptor . . . She was not pretty as the eye of habit judges prettiness, but he noted that when he had made the observation he had somehow failed to set it down against her, for he had already passed from measuring contours to tracing meanings. In Mary Garland's face there were many possible ones, and they might give him the more to think about . . . (p. 53)

[1] Rahv, p. 61.

Mary Garland's appearance is expressive of an inward life and a strength of character. She is not a being who can be summed up in one fixed definition, in a sculpting, for she suggests a range of changing possibilities which demand more than a superficial understanding. Rowland who is an appreciative judge of unostentatious beauty is immediately drawn to her.

Perceptive to a high degree, as are all James's Cinderella figures, Mary Garland immediately recognises Rowland's role as a fairy godfather. James did not name his central figure to suggest the chivalresque knight of yore to no purpose.

> Miss Garland objected after a pause. 'It's this that's so much like a fairy tale.'
> 'It's what, pray?'
> 'Why, you're coming here all unannounced, unknown, so rich and so polite, and carrying off my cousin in a golden cloud.' (p. 65)

The fairy-tale atmosphere of the novel is emphasised by Roderick's singing of: 'The splendour falls on castle walls/And snowy summits old in story'. Finally Mary is snatched up into the action of the tale, as she too makes her way into the twilight glow of the old world through the magical effects of Rowland's wizard-wand.

It is through the experience of Europe, which for the American Cinderella is the sphere of fairy-tale, that the 'felt-life' of James's heiress figures reaches its maximum intensity. And Mary Garland, although she is only the heiress in embryo, responds to the old world with no deficiency in sensibility.

> She was restless and excited; she moved about her room and went often to the window; she took everything in; she watched the Italian servants as they came and went . . . She might have been an exceptionally fine specimen-islander of an unclassed group, brought home by a great navigator and treatable mainly by beads and comfits. Rowland was sure she observed to good purpose, that she only needed opportunity, and that she would gather impressions in clusters as thick as the purple branches of a vintage.

The depth of Mary's inwardness and her powers of reflection are noted by James as he shows her being transformed by the magic of Europe, the only soil on which his Cinderella women truly undergo inner change. Mary says in a climactic scene:

> At home . . . things don't speak to us of enjoyment as they do

here. Here it's such a mixture; one doesn't know what to believe. Beauty stands here—beauty such as this night and this place and all this strange sad summer have been so full of—and it penetrates one's soul and lodges there and keeps saying that man wasn't made, as we think at home, to struggle so much and to miss so much, but to ask of life as a matter of course some beauty and some charm. This place has destroyed any scrap of consistency that I ever possessed, but even if I must say something sinful, I love it. (p. 456-457)

Mary is capable of giving up her Puritan ethic and replacing it by nothing more than the value of change, esteemed even though it destroys consistency. For Mary, and this is a recurrent pattern in James's vision of life as viewed through his feminine sensibilities, Europe may act as a catalyst to perception and transformation, but any true recognition and growth of consciousness must come from the personality itself. Mary's essential being is what allows her to respond to the life around her and the same situations do not effect any development in less sensitive instruments. Character and life are magical for James, though Europe may have influential effects. And his central figures are those, as he says time and again in his notebooks and prefaces, who contain a life of their own and chart their own development.

The depths of Mary's sensitivity and the accuracy of her intuitions which mark her as one of the chosen ones who can see the invisible —the essence of things—is gauged by her initial response to the Cavaliere. She immediately states, upon seeing him, 'I like the wise little old gentleman'. The only one to comment upon the much neglected Cavaliere in this way, Mary proves her nearness to psychic forces, for as Jung points out, the wise old man habitually recurs as an image of the spirit 'when the hero [in this case the heroine] is in a hopeless and desperate situation from which only profound reflection or a lucky idea . . . can extricate him'.[2] Mary here has suddenly become fully aware of the depth of Roderick's attachment to Christine and her spiritual resources are manifested in her recognition of the place of the Cavaliere.

Yet Mary's intuitions have not reached the point of conscious recognition, that recognition which would allow her truly to see and hence, fully be. She bears the seeds but not the fruit of the Cinderella figure and this is certainly due to the early stage of James's career

[2] C. G. Jung, 'The Phenomenology of the Spirit in Fairytales', pp. 217–218.

in which she appears. As Philip Rahv notes, 'At this stage James is already sure of his heroine's integrity and liveliness of imagination, knowing that in this fine flower of a provincial culture he had gotten hold of a historical prodigy admirably suited to his purpose as a novelist. He is still doubtful, however, of her future, uncertain as to the exact conditions of her entry in the "great world" and of the mutual effect thus created.'[3] Hence Mary Garland is made to return to America unfulfilled. Even at this embryonic stage of his career, however, James implies that his Cinderella's double heritage of the old world and the successful marriage will never be fulfilled by the American male. With Roderick Hudson, the American flower of sexual potency and artistic creativity is forced into suicide, and at the end of the novel Roland is subsumed in a haze of stultifying inertia.

Christine Light, Mary's antithesis, points the way to the second phase of James's exploration of woman. A more vibrant and more fully achieved figure than Mary, she is yet within the framework of what can be called James's moral cosmology, a lesser being, for while Christine projects outward toward a definition of an absolute, Mary moves inward towards the ultimate possible limits of seeing and being, limits which are ever in a state of flux. This is not to deny Christine's essential interest as a character. Apart from Count Gloriani and Madame Grandoni she is the only figure whom James felt it necessary to reintroduce in a later work. Yet, with all the fascination which she exudes, Christine Light is essentially a more static and fixed character than Mary. What attracted James most in character was the possibility, given the character's initial freedom, of the figure developing as in life and reacting to the ever-proliferating nuances of existence. In this latter aspect, Mary, even though her portrayal is incomplete, ranks higher than Christine, for her sensibility is more open to the inwardness of existence. She is in this sense more 'feminine' than Christine, closer to what we have defined as fairy, for looking inwards rather than outwards, she turns man back to himself rather than out to the external aspects of life. Christine, with all her capriciousness, is a static figure moving within predictable limits and incapable of suffering a true inward change. As she says of herself, revealing the fixity of her being and seeing, together with her lack of innocence, 'I was an old woman at the age of ten'.

[3] Philip Rahv, p. 61.

The tension within Christine, which draws her to tell Rowland time and again that she is capable of performing the good, the sincere and inward action, heightens her interest as a character. Yet we are warned by the Cavaliere, the wise old man of the tale, that Christine, for all her good intentions, will always do the outward thing, that which is expected of her by the world at large. She is tied by her very nature to those values which are external and which form the absolutes by which society tunes its functions. This is brought into focus by the Cavaliere's talk with Roderick, who insists on the flexibility and inner freedom of Christine. The Cavaliere tells Roderick :

'She'll never listen to you—she can't.'

'She can't?' demanded Roderick. 'She's not that sort of person —she's the very last—of whom you may say that. She can if she will. She does as she chooses.'

'Up to a certain point. Beyond it—*niente*!' And the Cavaliere's two forefingers made a wonderful airy sign. 'It would take too long to explain; I only beg you to believe that if you think you can pretend to Miss Light you prepare yourself *de mauvais draps*. Have you a princely title? Have you a princely fortune? No? Then you're not her affair.' (p. 204)

And again :

'I too have admired her. She *is* a brave ragazza; she has never said an unkind word to me; the blessed Virgin be thanked! But she must have a great position and a brilliant destiny; they've been marked out for her and she'll submit. You had better believe me; it may save you some rash expense.' (p. 206)

The stress on the fact that Christine is only free up to a point and that she will inevitably submit to her fate suggests that her limits and external values are not only the result of circumstantial necessity. Illegitimate daughter of the Cavaliere or not, she would certainly have pleased Roderick. James seems to have worked out the ploy of forcing Christine to leave Roderick because of the threatened revelation of her illegitimacy merely in order to make Christine fit the definition given of her earlier in the book. It is essentially an unnecessary piece of mechanical plotting, since Christine's true lines are sufficiently traced to reveal that she would in any case, in the final outcome, turn to some Prince, be it Casamassima or another. The Cavaliere points out the romantic and imaginative side

of Christine's nature when he admits that she would be quite capable of taking even a serious interest in a young genius like Roderick.
She is James's original 'remarkable' woman, the magical Circe who
Yet once again he stresses her limits by saying that at the end she
would go back to the more brilliant 'parti'. (p. 242-3)

The essential difference between Mary and Christine lies in the
latter's tendency to be circumscribed by extra-personal limits. Christine is the epitome of the *male* concept of the eternal feminine, *la
donna mobile*—beautiful, capricious, mysterious, capable of fantastical imaginings and grand self-deception, yet ultimately predictable.
turns all men grovelling at her feet to swine. Madame Grandoni
gives an apt portrayal of her magnificent outwardness and her limits
—a portrayal which is at once prophetic of James's later excursion
into this genre in the figure of Miriam Rooth.

> She likes drama, likes theatricals—what do you call them? histri-
> onics for their own sweet sake. She's certain to do every now and
> then something disinterested and sincere, something for somebody
> else than herself. She needs to think well of herself; she knows a
> fine character when she meets one; she hates to suffer by com-
> parison, even though the comparison is made by herself alone;
> and when the figure she makes, to her imagination, ceases to
> please or to amuse her she has to do something to smarten it up
> and give it a more striking turn. But of course she must always
> do that at somebody's expense—not one of her friends but must
> sooner or later pay, and the best of them doubtless, the oftenest.
> Her attitudes and pretences may sometimes worry one, but I
> think we have most to pray to be guarded from her sincerities.
> (p. 369)

Christine judges and forms herself by standards outside herself,
and she shines by means of refracted light. This is perhaps the relevance of her name which James puns upon when he has Roderick
imagine Christine in all her glory shining down upon the Jesuit
fathers' little school boys. 'Fancy the poor little devils looking up
from their Latin declensions and seeing Miss Light shine down
upon them!' (p. 238) There is an ironic reversal here, for the holy
little children of the Jesuit fathers rather than looking up to Christ
are imagined to be looking up to Christine, whose rather sectarian
light could easily turn them away from godliness. Yet Roderick's
fantasy is revealing, for to him Christine's feminine is no less than

a godly light, and she has taken on for him the form of an absolute. She is the living myth of womanhood. Circe in the world of men. As Madame Grandoni puts it, 'There's the veritable sorceress! The sorceress with her necromantic poodle!' (p. 373-374)

With all her magnificence, Christine Light presents the loosing strain in James's vision. Her femininity is the creation of a male imagination and like all masculine creations she tends toward an absolute and turns man outwards, away from himself, rather than inwards where the core of being and potential consciousness lie. Christine limits the free ranging of possibility. Her influence is the destructive one leading towards fixity, while the less ostentatious influence of Mary tends toward the more beneficial end of constant reformation.

We shall not pause here to examine *The American,* the second major novel of James's early period, in detail. Since this is perhaps the only important book of James's career to concentrate on a fully 'masculine' hero, it offers us little ground for our exploration of the feminine. Christopher Newman, James's American male par excellence, seems to emerge from his experience of Europe and the feminine unscathed. His beloved, Madame de Cintré, because we are never allowed to enter into her own sensibility, appears as little more than an idealized object which Newman wishes to possess. The only feminine who appears in this work and recurs throughout James's opus is Mrs. Tristram, the confidante. Like Mrs. Tristram these confidantes all possess funds of sensibility and intelligence, but since they are only secondary characters, these are never brought to total fruition. It is worth noting, however, that James chooses the female to act as confidante, rather than the male; for it is a feminine characteristic, from James's viewpoint, to seek to discover the inner make-up of character and action. This indeed is the function of the confidante, who serves as a half-way house between the mystified reader and subtleties of James's principle figures.

Catherine Sloper of *Washington Square*[4] presents a second Jamesian variation of the Cinderella figure. The 'plain, dull' simple child, with 'no histrionic' outward talents, no worldly cleverness or glitter, Catherine is victimized by all those around her : her father, who recognises her potential as a victim, her ruthless fiancé, and even her Aunt Penniman. Catherine, however, with her fund of un-

---

[4] Henry James, 'Washington Square', *The American Novels and Stories of Henry James,* ed. F. O. Matthiessen (New York, 1956).

acknowledged sensitivity—her liking for music in a land devoid of
that particular sensibility, her thoughts of Morris Townsend as 'a
young knight in a poem', and her high esteem for a good conscience
—is never touched by the magic wand. Her fairy godmother, Aunt
Penniman, with her 'buckles, bugles and pins', and her limpid
romanticism, is totally ineffectual; and her Prince Charming dis-
solves in the sterility of the American bourgeoisie, turning into a fat
and bald old man. In a world dominated by masculine factuality,
the inflexibility of 'geometric propositions' and solidly defined public
values, the innocent 'childlike' Cinderella, continually sitting before
the fires of reverie is a fruit rotten before it is ripe. In Catherine
we see the beginnings of James's middle period of realism, where
the fairy-tale world dies before the hard world of fact. There is to
be only one more excursion into the partial fairy realm before the
outward-looking women of the middle period take over. But the
portrait of Isabel Archer provides us with the fullest figure we have
yet met, a figure who reveals the very movement of James's art from
his early explorations of the inward fairy realm toward the second
stage of his career devoted to the realism of public morality.

TRANSITION

The Portrait of a Lady is in many ways a transitional novel. It reveals James moving from a stage in which his not as yet fully con-
trolled art explores the inner sensibility attached to the fairy-tale
realm to a phase where he is complete master of his craft and involved with the repercussions the outward social and political world
have on the private sensibility. The break, however, is by no means
a clean one and *The Portrait* illuminates precisely the tensions
between these two modes of feeling and being. James himself realised
the importance of this book in his development and wrote to his
mother that it would be, in comparison to his earlier works, as 'wine
is to water'. His claims for the novel's 'seriousness' and 'bigness'
seem to suggest that he was well aware, even before he had begun
the writing of it, that *The Portrait* would be a book which included
all his former tendencies as well as pointing the way to new ground.
Indeed, the book reveals the main trends in the development of
James's vision up to this point and directs his feminine orientation to
the realistic and eventually masculine world of the middle period.

Philip Rahv calls Isabel the 'American Cinderella', but in Isabel the Cinderella character is not brought to its ultimate development. Isabel does not see the invisible; she does not in James's terminology, achieve 'consciousness'. In this she is the perfect receptacle of James's art and vision at this period of his career. Leon Edel, James's biographer, notes that *The Portrait* is 'pure fairy-tale: a rich uncle, a poor niece, an ugly sick cousin who worships her from a distance, three suitors, a fairy godfather who converts the niece into an heiress, and finally her betrayal by a couple of cosmopolitan compatriots into a marriage as sinister as the backdrop of a Bronte novel.'[1] Yet a close examination of Isabel's unfolding character would seem to lead the novel further from the intensely inward world of the fairy-tale than any major work of James thus far. In *The Portrait* James seems to be relocating his forces and directing the reader's eyes toward the fixity of those external powers which will not permit the magic of the fairy world to function for the full flowering of the Cinderella figure.

Isabel, of course, begins with all the necessary qualifications of the Cinderella heroine. She is an innocent, virtually an orphan whose full imaginative life leads her to see everything as being 'just like a novel'. Although James claims her to be a 'frail vessel', he seems quite willing to satirize her innocence and her delusions. In fact, all the characters in the book, except Isabel herself, seem to be aware of her naiveté and illusions, for our Cinderella has been, in many ways, lifted out of the fairy sphere into the cold eye of a critical reality. Fairy godmother Touchett has taken on a critical air and states, 'It occurred to me that it would be a kindness to take her about and introduce her to the world. She thinks she knows a great deal of it—like most American girls; but like most American girls she's ridiculously mistaken.' James, with superb irony echoes this criticism of the unsuspecting Isabel, while in the same breath lauding her fineness.

> Altogether, with her meagre knowledge, her inflated ideals, her confidence at once innocent and dogmatic, her temper at once exacting and indulgent, her mixture of curiosity and fastidiousness, of vivacity and indifference, her desire to look very well and to be if possible even better, her determination to see, to try, to

[1] Leon Edel, 'Preface', *The Portrait of a Lady* (Cambridge, Mass., 1956), p. ix.

know, her combination of the delicate, desultory flame-like spirit
and the eager and personal creature of conditions: she would be
an easy victim of scientific criticism if she were not intended to
awaken on the reader's part an impulse more tender and more
purely expectant. (III, 69)

Isabel, with her romantic illusions, her penchant for grand definitions and her innocent belief in an ideal of happiness, certainly
provides an easy victim for the factual and conventional society in
which she finds herself. 'I'm very fond of my liberty', she says, in
the strain of all James's Cinderella heroines, yet the world she is
thrown into is not the fairy-tale realm where this independence can
result in successful fulfillment. The old world for James is the realistic sphere of corruption and frustration, which forces innocent and
presumptuous idealists to succumb to its decadent framework. It is
a static and defined sphere, old in its worldly wisdom, a climate
unfavourable to the retention of innocence. The Palazzo Roccanera,
home of Osmond's[2] perversity, stands solid and dungeon-like, firmly
fixed in the still centre of this old world. Yet it is Isabel's own lack
of awareness, her inability truly to see, as well as the inclement atmosphere, which is responsible for her victimisation. James seems
to give her freedom precisely to see how far innocence can be
stretched before it breaks down in the face of a public order which
beckons the individual to gaze outward at the standards of the
external world rather than inward to the heart of full being.

Isabel contains a tension within her own nature which makes her
kin both to the Cinderella heroine, like Mary Garland, and to the
more defined and predictable Christine Light. It is her similarity
to this latter figure which leads her to her downfall. The picture
which Madame Grandoni draws of Christine has many points in
common with James's early depiction of Isabel, although, of course,
Isabel has none of Christine's worldly lucidity. 'She had an un-
quenchable desire to think well of herself . . . Her life should always
be in harmony with the most pleasing impression she should produce (III, 68-69). And later, 'Isabel's chief dread in life at this period
of her development was that she should appear narrow-minded;
what she feared next afterwards was that she should really be so'
(III, 83). Isabel's high regard for appearances, her willingness to

---

[2] It is surely not merely coincidental that this name suggests the bones
of the world, the dry, sterile remains of a society based on convention.

play at the great lady, are similar to Christine's taste for histrionics and her willingness to do only those things which will contribute to her grandeur. Although Isabel's values are in many ways different from Christine's, the respect for appearances which lies dormant in her character at the start, but which gradually expands, is precisely what leads her so willingly to Osmond's altar and to a betrayal of her great desire for inner and external freedom. This aspect of her character is what allows her to be so greatly drawn to Madame Merle, who is in many ways an older Christine and hence an older and wiser Isabel. We remember that Madame Merle in her youth similarly had grandiose ambitions and illusions.

Madame Merle is totally a being of appearances, a perfect picture. Isabel's fallacy lies in admiring these qualities which make up the static, the fixed, and hence prevent eternal fluidity and flexibility of the being who is to experience the 'felt life'. Madame Merle is indeed a perfect picture, a totally outward-looking woman, circumscribed by a social frame.

> Her nature had been too much overlaid by custom and her angles too much rubbed away. She had become . . . too final. She was in a word too perfectly the social animal that man and woman are supposed to have been intended to be; and she had rid herself of every remnant of that tonic wildness . . . Isabel found it difficult to think of her in any detachment or privacy, she existed only in her relations, direct or indirect, with her fellow mortals. One might wonder what commerce she could possibly hold with her own spirit. (IV, 5)

Yet Isabel excuses these elements in Madame Merle, thereby prophesying her own ultimate turn to this external world of appearances. She reacts against Madame Merle's pronouncement, 'We're each of us made up of some cluster of appurtenances . . . I know a large part of myself is in the clothes I choose to wear. I've a great respect for *things*. One's self—for other people—is one's expression of one's self; and one's house, one's furniture, one's garments, the books one reads, the company one keeps—these things are all expressive'. However, she ends by marrying these 'things'. This is the expression of the doctrine of an arch materialist, with no respect for the spirit, the inner side of man. Isabel proceeds to marry Osmond precisely because his taste is expressed so exactly by his *things*.

The tension within Isabel between the Cinderella qualities of imagination and her respect for outwardness and absolute values, is resolved in the direction of the latter. She is less of a victim than Catherine, for her fate is in many ways the direct outcome of her inner make-up. Although she has sensitivity enough to recognise the fixing and stultifying elements of Osmond's house and hence of himself, she is attracted to it none the less. 'There was something brave and strong in the place; it looked somehow as if, once you were in, you would need an act of energy to get out.' Osmond's inertia, his affirmed indifference, his studied and wilful renunciation, his admission to these qualities and to the fact that he is 'convention itself' before his marriage to Isabel does nothing to deter her. Isabel feels she has a mission to perform. She wishes to be self-less in her marriage, to give not only to Osmond but also to his daughter Pansy. Her ideals fully distort any critical powers she may have and she wilfully gives up that openness of spirit which comprises the basis of Jamesian femininity in order to serve in a small way. 'The desire for unlimited expansion had been succeeded in her soul by the sense that life was vacant without some private duty that might gather one's energies to a point' (IV, 82). Moreover, the idea of totally filling the role of being 'the most important woman of the world' for someone, strongly appeals to Isabel, since she measures her own value in the eyes of others. Slightly frightened, but more than a little enticed by Osmond's pronouncements, she blindly marries herself to 'convention'—a convention based on empty forms, on exquisite taste and external values. She is prepared to pay homage, to do her duty—a word she holds in high esteem—to the sterility of convention; to take a 'pose' which is lived exclusively for the world.

If Isabel's attraction to Osmond can be explained away before her marriage by the fact of her innocence, this innocence does not justify her final action in the book. As we see in her reverie by the fire, she is now fully aware of Osmond's sterility and egotism. However, her recognition does not penetrate far enough into herself to allow her to see what lies at the core of the 'felt life'. Isabel sets limits of propriety for herself; she is afraid to bring the full brunt of her sensibility into the open and thus she cannot fully *be* in the Jamesian sense. Unlike Maggie in *The Golden Bowl*, she never attains self-consciousness, precisely because of the tendency in her own nature to overvalue appearances. Her faulty vision always sees further outwards than inwards. She recognises that both she and Osmond have been deceived in their marriage, yet ultimately she once again turns toward a form, a fixity which Osmond calls 'magnificent' and which she herself views as 'something transcendent and absolute like the sign of the cross or the flag of one's own country'. (IV, 356)

Isabel leaves the feminine orientation of the inward-looking Cinderella behind her; she mistakes professional connoisseurship for true artistic imaginitiveness. She accepts the superficial as profound. Thus she does not transgress the grounds of her own portrait of a *lady* to become a full-fledged feminine principle with the possibility of a creative or transformative effect. She emerges at the end of the book merely as a 'lady'—a finished social product in which imagination and freedom have given way to the rigidity of forms. James has the child of her marriage to Osmond die, thereby suggesting the barrenness of the life she has chosen.

By succumbing to the bounds of her portrait and returning to the ritual and form of marriage with Osmond, there is a suggestion that Isabel suffers the fate of one of Osmond's earlier victims, Madame Merle, who says to Osmond:

> You've not only dried up my tears; you've dried up my soul . . .
> I don't believe at all that it's an immortal principle. I believe it
> can perfectly be destroyed. That's what has happened to mine,
> which was a very good one to start with; and it's you I have to
> thank for it. You're very bad. (IV, 337)

This, in the 'cool' Jamesian world is tantamount to damnation and the paradise lost imagery of this part of the book seems quite in keeping with the idea of Osmond, the serpent, as a destroyer of souls. It seems quite unlikely that Isabel at the end of her tale is returning to Osmond in order to create a fresh version of an inward paradise. She *has* succumbed to definition, to the inflexibility and static quality of an absolute, a portrait.

Her final scene with Caspar Goodwood testifies to this as she is fixed into the mould of Diana—the female archer, whose sign is the sterility and purity of the moon. Isabel's fear of passion, of that which will disturb her to the core of her being and thus force her to see herself fully, is suggested throughout her portrait. Her putting off of Warburton is based on this fear, and it is once again illustrated in this description James gives us. 'Deep in her soul—it was the deepest thing there—lay the belief that if a certain light should dawn she would give herself completely; but this image on the whole was too bookish to be attractive.' Cargill is certainly right in saying:

> Bookish and without passional experience she had married Os-
> mond out of illusion, but even though she had given him a child,
> he had never really touched the core of her nature—it needed
> Goodwood's kiss to do that, and Matthiessen is right in testifying
> to its effectiveness in revealing the virginal nature of the heroine.[3]

Isabel runs away from Goodwood and in doing so she renders her
portrait complete. She emerges as the slightly ascetic Diana who
lives, as she herself puts it, in the mind of Osmond, the moon (IV,
194). She has become another masculine emanation, a static figure,
whose outlines are complete, defined, and whose possibility for expanding the circuit of 'felt life' and attaining consciousness is closed.

There is nothing to say that James approved of Isabel's actions.
Indeed his ironic approach to her should make us wary of idealising
her as the consummate Jamesian heroine. If we rid ourselves of this
assumption, we see that Isabel emerges as the first Jamesian venture
into the realistic world of his middle period, when he holds the tools
of his craft well under control and explores the various dead ends of
static and outward definition of character. James's orientation in
this period may be 'feminine' as it has been before, yet what he is
essentially examining is the defeminized world which tends towards
absolutes, toward extra-personal definitions of the self rather than to
the flexibility and openness of personalism and the fairy-tale.

THE MIDDLE YEARS

In Olive Chancellor of *The Bostonians,* James creates his first major
heroine in which the feminine principle of inwardness and flexibility has totally given way to the systematized hardening of ideas. Of
the same mould as the 'gubernatorial' and masculine Mrs. Touchett, Olive is the self-styled victim and symbol of a society governed
by external values and fixed absolutes. Having set out to describe
'the decline in the sentiment of sex', James, in fact, depicts the
decline in the sentiment of life, for Olive together with her male
counterpart, Basil Ranson, epitomizes that death urge which tends
toward static absolutes and goes against the grain. Olive is a
being totally devoid of that freedom and openness which permits
the flexibility of relationship and growth. A perverse soul, with eyes

[3] Oscar Cargill, *The Novels of Henry James* (New York, 1961), p. 105.

like 'green ice' and incapable of laughter, Olive is completely chained to her neurosis. Whether we term it lesbianism or not, this sickness which is the essence of her being, cuts her off from life, and binds her personality to an immovable centre.

As Irving Howe says, Olive is a creature deeply entangled with ideology who hates and fears the 'personal' element in life. 'When Olive and Verena listen to Beethoven, "Symphonies and fugues only stimulated their convictions, excited their revolutionary passion . . ." the very music becomes a medium of ideology. Everything is touched by it, from politics to sex, from music to love.'[1] The tendency toward ideology, toward any fixed definition or systematization of life, is for James, with his feminine orientation, a movement away from life; for ideology restricts the possibility of 'seeing' and hence of truly being. And with a few deft touches, James depicts the death of femininity and hence of life in Olive and its corruption in her victim, Verena. He shows Olive's entire personality to be based on a series of masochistic tendencies which culminate in fantasies of martyrdom. 'She was constantly exposing herself to offence and laceration',[2] delighting in 'contention' although it caused her intense pain. 'The most secret, the most sacred hope of her nature was that she might some day have such a chance, that she might be a martyr and die for something.' (p. 430) Olive is more interested in dying for something than in living for it. Her self-immolatory quality is brought out by James in his reference to Olive as an Antigone and especially in her final confrontation with the Boston mob.

. . . With a sudden inspiration, she rushed to the approach to the platform. If he [Basil] had observed her, it might have seemed to him that she hoped to find the fierce expiation she sought for in exposure to the thousands she had disappointed and deceived, in offering herself to be trampled to death and torn to pieces. She might have suggested to him some feminine firebrand of Paris revolutions, erect on a barricade, or even the sacrificial figure of Hypatia, whirled through the furious mob of Alexandria. (p. 745)

With all her instincts geared to death rather than life, Olive is a

[1] Irving Howe, 'Introduction' *The Bostonians* (New York, 1956), p. xxvii.
[2] Henry James, 'The Bostonians', *The American Novels and Stories of Henry James*, ed. F. O. Matthiessen (New York, 1947), p. 442. All references to this edition will be placed after the quotation.

figure far removed from the feminine Strether and Milly whose focus, like James's own, lies in living life to its fullest. It is noteworthy that Olive's favourite quotation from Goethe is, 'Thou shalt renounce, refrain, abstain!' Her renunciation of experience, unlike Strether's, is a negative one based on fear of life rather than on an instinct for retaining the freedom of personality.

If Olive epitomizes the death-like sterility of a fixed quantity, then Verena Tarrant and Basil Ransom offer no alternatives to the decline of sex and life in an outward-looking society. Verena, with all her original innocence and intuition oscillates from one immovable centre to another and she finally yields to the poisonous influence of Basil, who sees in woman a captive or agreeable 'toy' whose role it is to make 'fools of men'. Throughout Verena remains essentially the hypnotized being incapable of the remotest forms of conscious awareness. The only remaining 'frail vessel' with an aptitude for life in this society, Verena fails on the ground of 'seeing', and binds herself to the image of masculine convention. James, in his last sentence, warns us that the union is to be far from happy. Master of his now realistic craft, he succeeds admirably in exploring one of the dead ends of a society which makes a farce of living and dies by the inflexibility of a false ideology.

With *The Princess Casamassima,* James makes his second excursion into the world of realism where femininity gives way before the transpersonal and collective values of the masculine world. Christine Light returns as the Princess of the 'great house' and has now become the 'most remarkable woman in Europe'. Her Circe characteristics, however, have not been altered, but rather intensified, and we see her making victims partially of the Captain and totally of Hyacinth. Christine's movement outward, toward convention and the great house of her marriage, is further solidified as she identifies herself with the ideology of revolution. Fixed within a form which renders development, except within well-defined limits, impossible, she is immobilised in all those tendencies which move counter to the 'felt life'. Lionel Trilling aptly defines this masculine principle which has worked itself out in her nature.

> She is the very embodiment of the modern will which masks itself in virtue making itself appear harmless, the will that hates itself and finds its manifestations guilty and is able to exist only if it operates in the name of virtue that despises *the variety and modu-*

lations of the human story and longs for an *absolute humanity,* which is but another way of saying a nothingness.[3]

Although she is a more attractive figure, Christine in her nervous energy and self-hatred, her attraction to immolation for a revolutionary ideal, is greatly akin to Olive Chancellor.

We have already noted that James was aware of the fact that masculine and feminine characteristics are inherent in any single individual. Thus in our attempt to distil those properties which form the feminine aspect of being, we can now turn to Hyacinth Robinson, who in the world of *The Princess Casamassima* is the prime receptacle of the feminine sensibility. In him we find the conflict between the masculine society which forces the individual to look outward toward ideals and forms and the personalistic feminine sensibility which seeks self-consciousness and intensity of being. Surrounding Hyacinth is the Cinderella mood of transformative possibility—a mood which is prevalent in all tales of young men from the provinces or the working classes who seek a magical change of fortune in the great world of politics, society, or art. James proves Hyacinth's superiority of inwardness by centering the greater part of the novel in his consciousness. Furthermore, Hyacinth is the only character in the book to undergo development, perhaps because he is the only one to enter it with sufficient intelligence and sensitivity. As Mr. Vetch says in his charateristically ironic tone :

> He's a thick-skinned, morbid, mooning, introspective little beggar, with a good deal of imagination and not much perseverance, who'll expect a good deal more of life than he'll find in it . . . One sees that he has a mind and even a soul, and in that respect he's —I won't say unique, but peculiar. (V, 32)

A superior sensitive vehicle, with a capacity for introspection, Hyacinth can search for awareness and the full life. However, in the society in which he is placed, this search can only end in deception and doom. Hyacinth's suicide is symbolically necessary, for he cannot resolve the tensions between his inwardness and society's outwardness. He dies, a sacrificial victim to Christine, the socio-political Circe, and his potential for seeing in a fully conscious way is cut short in the world James here describes.

[3] Lionel Trilling, 'The Princess Casamassima', *The Liberal Imagination* (New York, 1961), p. 91. (My italics).

In Hyacinth Robinson and Christine, James reveals the dead end of ideology as it is related to 'felt life'. The absolutism of ideology, can only limit and fix the possibility of the free development of character. Hyacinth, for all his feminine sensibility can do nothing else but suicide in a society with stultifies the personalism of relationships and impedes development toward full recognition. It is the only act which can consolidate his self-integrity. By focusing on the omniverous social order, James is deliberately delineating the fate of those who move toward the masculine definition of ideology and the destiny of the sensitive vehicles who lie in their wake. The master's orientation, however, remains a feminine one, for he points out the doom inherent in this outward path.

Compared to *The Princess Casamassima, The Tragic Muse,* James's final work to lie totally within the framework of his middle period, seems rather tame. The reason for this would seem to lie primarily in the fact that the only inner sensibilities which are portrayed, those of Nick Dormer and Peter Sherringham, are so much less vibrant in the openness to 'felt life' than that of Hyacinth. Indeed, *The Tragic Muse,* is totally a novel of public life. Even Nick Dormer, the artist, with whose portrait James himself was dissatisfied, presents little more than the outward accoutrements of the painter's life, for the inward 'felt life' of the artist seems to lie in the realms of a theoretical proposition, and his choice of one over the other yields no visible development in his character. James had reached the end of the possibilities of realistic portrayal and his feminine orientation, which desired fluidity and openness of character was soon to lead him into other grounds.

In Miriam Rooth, James sums up all the characteristics of the outward-looking female. By making her a public figure—an actress who is the object of the multitude's worship—he sums up in one figure both Christine Light's histrionic and Olive Chancellor's feminist ideology. A creature of the same vital energies as her predecessors, Miriam Rooth is likewise lacking in that form of sensibility which leads to inner recognition. Her life is based on an outwardly orientated fiction—the stage—and her entire being is focused on the playing of the various roles which she makes her own. An extension of Christine, who possessed the same mesmeric and attractive qualities, Miriam is the sum effects of her external personality. She is *complete,* and we are never tempted to look beneath her exterior to find another, more personal, being, for she exists solely in outwardness—her various roles. As Peter Sherringham puts it to Miriam herself:

> What's rare in you is that you have—as I suspect at least—no nature of your own . . . You are always playing something; there are no intervals. It's the absence of intervals, of a *fond*, a background, that I don't comprehend. You're an embroidery without a canvas . . . Your feigning may be honest, in the sense that your only feeling is your feigned one. (VII, 210)

James himself had foreseen in his *Notebooks* the fact that his *nature d'actrice* required no inner and fine sensibility, since she was totally to exist by her qualities as an actress.

> The girl I see to be very crude, etc. The thing is a confirmation of Mrs. Kemble's theory that the dramatic gift is a thing by itself —implying of necessity no *general* superiority of mind. The strong nature, the personal quality, vanity etc., of the girl: the artistic being, so vivid, yet so purely instinctive. Ignorant, illiterate. Rachel.[4]

Hence Miriam Rooth's portrait is based on the completeness of the archetypal histrionic nature. There is no necessity for James to show us any of her inner being to achieve that 'manageable vividness' that he seeks. As Blackmur puts it, 'Miriam Rooth is the veritable tragic muse herself, all objective and nobody intimate or inside her, but seen by everybody, the actress who captures us all, and the central figure for the length of the novel—the standard or touchstone—by her presence, in the lives of Peter Sherringham and Nick Dormer.'[5] She is what Julia Dallow seeks to be, the apotheosis of the public figure.

The Tragic Muse marks the end of James's experimentation with the realistic, outwardly focused novel and to complete this phase James turned to the most public of all the literary arts—the drama. His unsuccessful ventures in this medium are the object of our interest only insofar as they influenced his consequent return to the novel of inwardness—that final phase of James's career where art becomes more and more the conscious manipulation of the tone of the fairytale. It is in this last phase that James's art is most visibly oriented toward femininity and the exploration of the inner sensibility.

What experimentation in the dramatic medium seems to have

---

4 Henry James, *The Notebooks* (New York, 1961), pp. 63–64.
5 R. P. Blackmur, 'Introduction', *The Tragic Muse* (New York, 1961), p. 11.

taught James is not only the central importance of that dialogue which moves inward toward self-awareness, with which his last books abound. The principal feature of conventional drama lies in its focus on report and recognition, so that the brutal aspects of existence are not actually shown on the stage, but surround the visible action with a cloud of invisible events. These latter are seen only insofar as they are filtered through the minds of the players, so that what becomes central to the audience is precisely the process by which the characters recognise the existence of these unseen events and their effect on the characters. As James moves towards his major phase, we are aware of a similar process at work. No longer are we directly shown scenes of suicide or public confrontation. Rather, such major events as Milly's death and her last interview with Densher, or a principal feature such as the exact nature of Madame de Vionnet's relationship with Chad, are brought to the reader's attention only through the report or recognition of the central intelligence in question. Hence what emerges as central in the books of James's last period is precisely the workings of a character's mind as he seeks to understand in a realm of semi-grasped facts. We are presented with a cinematic screen on which only one face is carefully delineated, while a myriad of events is kept in the background, out of focus. Only as these events or figures move toward the central position on the screen and into direct contact with the individual viewed in a constant close-up, do their outlines gain concrete and fully apprehensible form. Thus James's art becomes more and more the art of representing inner processes of seeing and being. And this process of interiorization is closely linked to what James himself named as the function of the feminine—describing 'man's relationship with himself'.

Yvor Winters writes that in this last stage, 'James's art becomes more and more an art not of inclusion, but of representative and essential selection—that is the art of the allegorist, or the symbolic poet.'[6] Moving toward this art of selection, James moved away from the realistic sphere of factual portrayal and into the suggestive and inner world of the fairy-tale. The gap between a given rational motive and the resulting state of mind, between tragic action and its effect, which Yvor Winters sees as one of the major causes of James's obscurantism, is a gap which is similarly not explained away in concrete terms in the realm of the fairy-tale.

6 Yvor Winters, *In Defence of Reason* (New York, 1938), p. 312.

THE MAJOR PHASE: BEGINNINGS

The seeing intelligences of James's last period are once again little 'burnt-faced' girls whose femininity is their distinguishing characteristic. This femininity, it is increasingly apparent, lies in their inwardness, their intuition, flexibility and openness to the 'felt life'. Those qualities of tact, penetration, subtlety, rapidity of transition, and a capacity for magical divination, which James named as 'feminine' in Saint-Beuve, all coalesce in these final figures of femininity. What these abstract qualities in fact suggest must now be investigated.

Echoing his experiment with Isabel Archer, James, in his portrayal of the first central intelligence of this final period, says: 'The free spirit, always much tormented, and by no means always triumphant, is heroic, ironic, pathetic, or whatever, and as exemplified in the record of Fleda Vetch, for instance, "successful", only through having remained free.'[1] In his return to the inner world of the fine intelligence—removed from the realistic sphere which confines being within convenitonal limits—James allows Fleda Vetch, heroine of *The Spoils of Poynton,* to remain free of the outward and sterile forms which constitute Isabel's prison. This freedom is in fact an openness to continual change, a feminine pliability, and it will become the central characteristic of James's final figures of femininity. Released even from the material presence of fairy godmothers or godfathers, these late sensibilities incorporate the magical powers, which produce transformation, into their own being. Unlike his earlier Cinderellas, they ultimately triumph over the outwardly oriented and initially more powerful, 'remarkable woman'.

Fleda Vetch, the first of these ultimate 'frail vessels', incorporates many of those qualities which simultaneously reveal and are the consequence of James's feminine orientation. Not beautiful to the general eye, she shines only by the light of her fine sensibility. And like the little 'burnt-faced' girl, she possesses that intuition which allows her truly to see connections that 'in their inner mystery were a blank to everybody else'. That instinctive good taste which James appreciates as a finer instrument of seeing—insofar as it does not limit being, evidently the case with Osmond and Mrs. Gereth—is also hers. 'Almost as much as Mrs. Gereth's, her taste was her life,

---

[1] Henry James, 'The Spoils of Poynton', *The Art of the Novel* (New York, 1934), p. 130.

but her life was somehow the larger for it.' She appreciates Poynton, the emblem of Mrs. Gereth's life: 'What had her whole life been but an effort toward completeness and perfection?' but this totality, this 'completeness' somehow runs counter to her own taste.

Fleda's sensibility attracts her most fully not to spoils, things, but to life with its manifold possibilities of relationships and change. 'She thought of him [Owen] perpetually, and her eyes had come to rejoice in his manly magnificence even more than they rejoiced in the royal cabinets of the red saloon.' The taste for completeness, that is, the static quality of the dead end, is not totally natural to this free spirit whose quality of reverie and roving imagination is pronounced, and who, in her subtlety, is like James, capable of seeing from many points of view. Time and again Fleda 'dodged and dreamed and romanced away the time . . . she gave herself, in her sentient solitude, up to a mere fairy tale. This imagination of Fleda's was a faculty that easily embraced all the heights and depths and extremities of things; that made a single mouthful, in particular, of any tragic or desperate necessity.' Fleda, with her penchant for reverie, prefers those things which are open and allow her all-encompassing imagination to inject them with a touch of her own inwardness. Thus her attraction to the much less grand and more personal quality of Ricks, is more fully akin to her native sensibility than her taste for the statuesque, total environment, of Poynton. 'The house [Ricks] was crowded with objects of which the aggregation somehow made a thinness and the futility a grace.' Finally, Ricks rather than Poynton becomes the symbol of Fleda herself. The voice of Ricks was 'a voice so gentle, so human, so feminine— a faint far-away voice with the little quaver of a heartbreak . . . the impression, somehow, of something dreamed and missed, something reduced, relinquished, resigned; the poetry, as it were, of something sensibly *gone*.'

The personal, feminine voice of the maiden-aunt's Ricks which speaks of something dreamed and missed, of resignation, is the voice of Fleda, as she recognises that the possibility of a relationship with Owen is something of the past. (One could almost say that it is the voice of James, himself, in the last phase of his career.) Yet how are we to reconcile Fleda's openness to the fullness of 'felt life' with this final resignation, after her failure to relate to Owen? The critics, notably Yvor Winters, have pointed out that Fleda's actions vis à vis Owen are confusing and that the minute moral point which results in her loss of him is out of all proportion to the issue in question. James, however, has pointed out in his 'Preface' that the sole triumph of the free spirit is to remain free; and Fleda's attitude toward Owen is essentially a manifestation of this freedom which is intrinsic to her nature. Her actions are confusing because they are based on no external and recognisable moral code, but rather on Fleda's own inward perceptions, all of which are directed at leaving personality personality and thus decide and act for him. However, to turn Owen and her failure and fear are not that of Isabel with Casper Good-wood. What Fleda essentially does in her final interview with Owen when she stresses his duty to Mona rather than to herself, is to give Owen his freedom to act according to the dictates of his own per-sonality. She does not wish to press him by the force of her own personality and thus decide and act for him. However, to turn Owen free, to turn him inward to himself, is in effect to give him up to his true self which is more clearly mirrored in the externally-oriented Mona than in the intensely inward Fleda.

Owen, as James presents him, is essentially a blank entity who oscillates between the three women in the tale. He appreciates Fleda's perceptive intuition and recognises it as a higher form of being. But given total freedom by Fleda, he can only turn to what is most naturally his own—Mona—especially since Mona is not unwilling to exert her influence. Fleda, for whom the greatest sin lies in chaining or victimising personality (and in this she is akin to James) realises only too late her failure in the principle of mani-pulation. She does not incorporate into her own being the compo-sitional and social characteristics of Mrs. Gereth, and she is incapable of achieving the miracle of transformation. To transform Owen, to allow him to 'see' as she does, is beyond her range. This is a power which the Cinderella figure will only acquire in the person of Maggie Verver. Fleda, with the recognition of her failure, can only remain a free spirit, whose openness to the 'felt life' has merely led her further inward to the personalism of the poetry of 'something sensibly gone'.

To say that James is super-subtle in his moral nuances as they are figured in Fleda's announcement to Owen that he must do his 'duty' is to misunderstand the nature of his art and vision. What James is showing us in Fleda is essentially that morality is measured only by standards of inner sensibility—a sensibility which allows the individual to experience life to its fullest without diminishing the freedom of other people's sensibility. Fleda's responses to life are not measured by any external moral standard, and like Little Bilham in *The Ambassadors* we can see her saying that the relationship of Chad to Madame de Vionnet is essentially a 'virtuous attachment', although illicit by society's code, precisely because it increases the individual's possibility of living fully. The dictates of James's morality are not based on convention, but rather on the flexibility of the profound inner sensibility and the fine intelligence which allows life and consciousness to develop freely. Fleda is not given the chance to keep a memento of Poynton (whose burning marks the last instance of the grandiose effects of James's middle period) precisely because its spoils manifest that outward fixity and completion which is dangerous to the free spirit. With the burning of Poynton, the material world disintegrates, and Fleda, purified by the transformative element, is fully given over to the realm of spirit—a spirit essentially free from the limits of *things*. In *What Maisie Knew*, his next major work, James shows us the corruption of a society which attempts to fix the innocent's development within superficial bounds and once again the triumph of the free sensibility which sees beyond these external and fixed values.

With Maisie Farange, James recommences the definition of his Cinderella figure and moulds her in the garments of his final period. Maisie will become Nanda Brookenham and finally Milly and Maggie, just as Mrs. Beale will grow into Mrs. Brook, Kate Croy and finally Charlotte Stant. Depicting the child's world of growing awareness, James enters fully into that fairy-tale mood which is the property of the young. To Maisie the world is full of strange and incomprehensible beings, whose essential grotesquerie or sensibility is stressed by the innocent eye she focuses on them. She is the perfect receptacle for James's feminine vision of expansion and developing consciousness along the line of life, for, open to all the manifold possibilities of experience, Maisie has no preconceptions as to the form things will take. Hence she is much more than an adult, completely free from any static and defined social or moral code.

To live with all intensity and perplexity and felicity in its terribly mixed little world would thus be the part of my interesting small mortal; bringing people together who would be at least more correctly seperate; keeping people separate who would be at least more correctly together; flourishing to a degree, at the cost of many conventions and proprieties, even decencies, really keeping the torch of virtue alive in an air tending infinitely to smother it, really in short making confusion worse confounded by drawing some stray fragrance of an ideal across the scent of selfishness, by sowing on barren strands, through the mere fact of presence, the seed of moral life.[2]

It is here that we see what exactly morality would seem to mean to James. Not an instance of proprieties and conventions, it is rather that intrinsically personal sense which allows the individual to flourish along his or her own particular lines to the fullest point of sensibility and consciousness. It is not because Mrs. Wix has instilled her with a sense of propriety or conventional virtue that Maisie goes with her at the end of her story, for Maisie has, for a long time, seen round the rather comical Mrs. Wix. Her preference would be to go off alone with Sir Claude, whom she loves, and to whom she repeatedly offers herself as a woman. Yet as she recognises the compulsive depth of Sir Claude's attachment to Mrs. Beale, Maisie's sensitivity tells her that to stay within the precincts of this ritual and limited relationship would be to tie herself to the superficialities of the existence which has surrounded her from her first moments. By leaving with Mrs. Wix, Maisie chooses to leave behind her those relationships which would chain her to being an implement, a jealous tool of adult corruption. She selects the path of openness and freedom. As Sir Claude has pointed out, Maisie is 'free'.

As James states in his 'Preface' Maisie wanders to 'the death of her childhood'. Like all the Cinderella heroines, she begins with a fund of innocence which allows for the openness of her sensibility as a 'register of impressions'. But Maisie brings us one step further into what we have defined as James's 'fairy-tale' world—a sphere where intensity of experience and the striving for consciousness, which will permit transformation, form the cornerstone of an ethic. Like her older and more fully developed counterpart, Maggie, 'instead of simply submitting to the inherited tie and the imposed complication of suffering from them, our little wonderworking agent would create, without design, quite fresh elements of this order— contribute, that is, to the formation of a fresh tie, from which it would then (and for all the world as if through a small demonic foresight) proceed to derive great profit.'[3]

2 Henry James, 'What Maisie Knew', *The Art of the Novel*, p. 143.
3 Henry James, 'What Maisie Knew', *The Art of the Novel*, p. 142.

Maisie shows us the progressive line of James's feminine orientation as she takes into herself the 'wonder-working' compositional
and transformative aspects of the fairy godmother. Wandering to
the death of her childhood, she looses her innocence, but her recognition of depravity and empty forms is still the partial and instinctive one of the child. Maisie retains that essential 'freshness' undes-
troyed in the face of appearances in themselves vulgar and empty,
which is necessary to the flexibility of the true feminine.

Nanda Brookenham leads us one step further toward that point
where the inwardness of the fairy-tale realm subsumes the masculine fixity of public morality. Essentially a Maisie who is now fully
aware of the corruption of the outward life as personified in the
figure of her mother and the salon society, Nanda has reached the
point of adult 'muddlement'—a state which James saw as being one
of 'the very sharpest of realities'. Nanda's confusion arises from
her peculiar position vis à vis society. She has understood the corruption of the 'great world' but she is still expected to play the role
of the innocent. True to her inner nature, Nanda is incapable of
pretending she does not know, yet like Maisie her recognition of
'evil' has not tainted her being, for she shows herself still open to
change. At the end of the book, Nanda goes into a stage of self-
communion. James implies that after this period of self-scrutiny, his
principal heroine will emerge in a form which will permit her to
develop in a positive fashion.

THE MAJOR PHASE: CULMINATION

In *The Ambassadors,* the least difficult of James's three completed
final works, James once again reveals his full awareness of the masculine and feminine principles. One of these can predominate in an
individual, regardless of his sex. In Strether we find a sensibility,
feminine by the terms James has defined, inhabiting a male body;
while Mrs. Newsome, present throughout the book even in her
physical absence, embodies the masculine characteristics of a forceful
will and a moral fixity dependent on social norms.

Transported to Paris, which his New England compatriots with
their fixed puritanical values have warned him is a den of iniquity
and corruption, Strether, with the sensitivity of all James's 'seeing
registers', remains open to the full possibilities of experience. His
judgment of people and situations is free from preconceived stan-

dards of conduct and is based only on his own perceptions of what constitutes the authentic human gesture. Willing to believe that Chad had changed for the better in his new milieu, Strether is equally willing to agree to terming Chad's illicit love affair with Madame de Vionnet a 'virtuous attachment' once he has discovered the intensity of 'felt life' which is involved on Madame de Vionnet's part. His morality is an inward one, based on an intelligence which turns him toward the depths of personality rather than to the superficial appearances created by society.

Like James's other vehicles of 'fine intelligence' Strether begins in an innocence which leads him to perceive only what is best in others and particularly to idealize women. Even when that phase of recognition which leads to fuller consciousness has set in and Strether sees the reality beneath his idealisation, he does not recoil from Madame de Vionnet, does not give her up. Rather, he attempts to make Chad realise the depth of her attachment. Seeing and being are interrelated for James, and Strether's earlier pronouncement of 'Live, live all you can', is played out by the later intensity of his vision. His femininity lies in his flexibility, his willingness to remain open to insight and experience, and even after the period of recognition has begun, to continue to 'see'.

Strether realises that 'Women were thus endlessly absorbent, and to deal with them was to walk on water'. This perception, in fact, is a recognition of his own inner state. His entire Paris existence has been constantly linked with this feminine and fluid element, and he emerges from it a free spirit. Like Fleda Vetch's, his oft-noted renunciation is a positive one in that he does not wish to attach himself to any particular form of possibility. He chooses to remain 'free' and open to the constant proliferation of experience. Like Leopold Bloom, who fulfills this role on primitive and unconscious grounds rather that in the domain of ethical action, Strether is the prototype of the 'new womanly man'. As Leslie Fiedler remarks in *Love and Death in the American Novel* in a somewhat simplified analysis of James's women, Strether 'is the most maidenly of all James's men'.

With *The Wings of the Dove* and *The Golden Bowl*, we arrive at that final point in James' development where what we have called the 'life line' returns to its point of origin in the private and inward feminine sensibility, having in its course subsumed public and external morality. Simultaneously, James's art in this last phase has

reached the point where the fairy-tale mood is integrated in a work
conceived in full artisitc consciousness.

The Wings of the Dove is a 'tale of enchantment' a 'fairy tale'
which explores that inner sensibility and that growth to full consciousness which lies in the domain of the feminine principle. The
fairy-tale, however, is now consciously exploited by a self-critical
craftsman, who has delineated that realistic world of public life,
in order to present the tension between the two realms. James's use
of the fairy-tale mood is no longer accidental and as F. O. Matthiessen points out, he now keeps the 'tale of enchantment from being
a tale of escape'; rather he manipulates it for the sake of evoking
his own particular version of universal truth.[1] This truth, which
Matthiessen names without defining, is perhaps what we have described as the Jamesian ethic. It is based precisely on the intensity
with which the life experience is felt and the degree of fully-integrat-
ing consciousness which it brings to the individual.

The Wings of the Dove embodies a tension between the worlds
and forces manifested in the figures of Kate Croy and Milly Theale
—a tension which is partially resolved in Merton Densher and more
fully in the reader, himself, who can grasp the totality of the book.
All vital and highly sensitive instruments, James allows his characters to mark out their places in the fullness of his vision by participating equally in the viewpoints of all three.

Kate Croy, who opens and closes the book, is one of those Jamesian women whose character combines masculine energy of will
propelled by and directed toward the morality of public life and a
feminine intuitive intelligence, which sees to the core of all situations. Kate's 'talent for life' which Densher so often mentions lies
in her manipulative 'will' and in her magnificent social presence.
Akin to her aunt Mrs. Lowder, Mrs. Brook and Christine Light,
Kate has the intuitive cleverness which James always attributes to
his 'remarkable women'. As Merton Densher recognises early in the
book, 'Women had . . . so much more imagination'.[3] And as Kate
herself says, 'There are refinements . . . I mean of consciousness, of
sensation, of appreciation, . . . no . . . men *don't* know. They know
in such matters almost nothing but what women show them.' (XIX,
98) Kate's perceptions about life and relationships are acute. However, she uses these qualities only within the framework which her
corrupt society has given her. Aware of its depraved code, she con-

[1] F. O. Matthiessen, *The Major Phase* (New York, 1944), p. 59.

tinues to function within it as had Mrs. Brook. Her lesson to Milly concerning this social canon, reveals her awareness of it as well as suggesting that she fully accepts it.

> Everyone who had anything to give—it was true they were the fewest—made the sharpest possible bargain for it, got at least its value in return. The strangest thing, furthermore, was that this might be in cases, a happy understanding. The worker in one connection was the worked in another; it was as broad as it was long—with the wheels of the system as might be seen, wonderfully oiled. People could quite like each other in the midst of it . . . (XIX, 179)

The casualness of this last sentence suggests that in the Jamesian ethic, Kate's hierarchy of values, such as it may be, is standing on its head.

This vampire system of the user and the used, the strong 'eating' the weak and so on down the line is, as we know, the most hateful aspect of society to James. The recurrence of this theme in his work proves his obsessive involvement with it. The very title, *The Wings of the Dove,* has implicit in its source an attempt to escape from this code which tends to destroy the 'free spirit' and the sensitive vehicle by its invidiousness. In a world of user and used, deceit, the breakdown of faith between man and man, of the possibility of communication, and of true relationship, is inevitable.

> And I said, Oh that I had wings like a dove! for then would I fly away and be at rest./ Lo, then would I wander far off, and remain in the wilderness . . . for I have seen violence and strife in the city . . ./ Wickedness is in the midst thereof: deceit and guile depart not from her streets./ For it was not an enemy that reproached me; then I could have borne it: neither was it he that hated me that did magnify himself against me; then I would have hid myself from him:/ But it was thou, a man, mine equal, my guide and mine acquaintance./ We took sweet counsel together . . . He hath put forth his hands against such as be at peace with him: he hath broken his covenant./ The words of his mouth were smoother than butter, but war was in his heart: his words were softer than oil, yet they were drawn swords. (Psalm 55)

Milly is deceived by her friends in precisely this way and her death is hastened by her discovery of this deceit. Yet it is her companion, Kate, who tells her of society's ruinous code and in her approval of it ('This might in cases be a happy understanding'), she reveals her own place within the social framework of morality. Kate, however, is not the archetypally evil heroine. Rather her tragic flaw—for she is the only fully tragic figure of the book—lies in her choice of conforming to social canons and attempting to rise by them within a public order. She does not have the ability of abstracting her actions and seeing them within a heirarchy above that of social norms and rooted purely in the integrity of the self.

Kate's perceptions are acute. As James himself says, she is formed for 'seeing and being'. Yet she chooses not to see everything and to be actively and deeply involved in the external world. Her seeing powers fail once she concretely chooses to base her actions on standards set by the world and aimed at achieving a place within this world rather than acting according to inner forces of integrity aimed at attaining full consciousness of self.

Kate's choice—and we remember that all tragedy is grounded in choice— lies in deciding between the fullness of a personal relationship which Densher offers her from the beginning; or in taking on the role of the remarkable and powerful social creature by using for her own benefit both what Mrs. Lowder and Milly Theale leave open to her. That she is originally motivated by her impecunious family position to give Densher up, as Mrs. Lowder wishes, is excusable, and in itself would certainly have no tragic repercussions, but it shows us Kate's social bent.

Her second choice, after once again putting Densher off—to manipulate Milly's emotions to her own advantage—is what brings tragedy down on her. Fully enmeshed in the game of user and used, Kate attempts to entangle as well a being who is essentially removed from this system. In doing this she hides any pangs of conscience which might deflect her from her course and she sacrifices the possibility of full self-consciousness and personal integrity for material gains. Like Mrs. Lowder's, Kate's will—a quality we have noted to be masculine—predominates over anything else in her and she believes that what she wills must be. It is part of Kate's blindness that she recognises this will only in Mrs. Lowder, the symbol of the society in which she lives—Britannia in the Market Place, the eagle with the gilded beak : 'There's every appearance for her . . . that what she has made up her mind to as possible is possible; that what she had thought more likely than not to happen is happening. The very essence of her . . . is that, when she adopts a view, she . . . really brings the thing about, fairly terrorizes with her view, any other, the opposite view, and those with who represent it' (XX, 188). This has echoes of the indomitable Mrs. Newsome and is far-removed from the sphere of the 'free spirit'.

Kate sacrifices certain aspects of her fine sensibility in order to attain eminence in the social world. As she grows further and further into the image of this society of user and used, Kate gradually —as we see through Densher's growing apprehension—begins to 'simplify', 'to lose no minute in the perception of incongruities' in which half of Densher's person is wasted and misled. And as Kate's vision narrows, she loses the possibility of being aware of the multitude of impressions which is the distinguishing characteristic of all those Jamesian figures with a potential for attaining full consciousness, that is with a potential for fully being. Kate's tragedy lies in that she has in all good faith drawn around her limits of seeing, feeling and being and ends enclosed in the cage of her own actions. She has done violence to the integrity of her own feelings for a material end. Kate ends by being one of those female figures who have turned outward for fulfillment, and thus she represents something essentially non-feminine, in the Jamesian context.

If Kate's is the tragedy of the feminine sensibility which has succumbed to the two-dimensional society—a systematized order and hence what we have termed masculine—then Milly Theale's tale is the fable of pathos—the poor little rich girl faced by death. But the total effect of Milly's life is a transformative and therefore a triumphant one. A fairy-tale princess who enters the book through the influence of a 'fairy godmother' and the wave of a neat little wand, Milly is isolated from the world by that very fact. Since all her court attendants either pay her homage or use her, her greatest need, that of truly relating, is denied her. It is in her desire for personal relationships rather than social glory and esteem, that Milly presents the apex of femininity, for truly relating is based on the ability to turn inward to the self, that ability which James noted as 'reminine' in his review of Mathilde Serao.

Milly contains all those qualities of the feminine sensibility which will ultimately triumph over the social and public realm with its limited awareness. Her perceptions, which unlike Kate's, are originally founded on innocence, are acute and she looks inward to the core of being. She recognises Kate as 'brutal' and rightly sees Mrs.

Lowder as a person of whom the mind might in two or three days roughly make the circuit', whereas Kate, with her action potential, 'would indulge in incalculable movements that might interfere with one's tour'. Echoing Strether's pronouncement of 'Live, live', Milly wishes to take 'full in the face the whole assault of life', and what this means to her is not a guided tour through museums and picturesque scenery, but human contact. The focus on relational values rather than on political or social ambitions is again the property of James's true feminine intelligences.

Not as naive as many of her critics would like to believe, Milly's initial bewilderment in the grasping social world develops into an awareness of her position in that world and her distance from it. Very early she sees that these social people are 'familiar with everything, but conscious of nothing'. They lack 'imagination'. Termed a 'dove' by Kate and Mrs. Lowder, Milly realises that she cannot be fixed into a conceptual definition, and seeing that this is what the others wish her to be, she decides to function—at least as far as the external eye can see—according to this definition.

> It was moreover, for the girl like an inspiration : she found herself accepting as the right one, while she caught her breath with relief, the name so given her. She met it on the instant as she would have met the revealed truth; it lighted up the strange dusk in which she had lately walked. *That* was what was the matter with her. She was a dove. Oh, wasn't she? (XIX, 238)

Taking this in, Milly in the next instant decides to use the dove-like quality attributed to her to her own advantage with all those who cannot see her as a being who has her own inwardness. She lies to Mrs. Lowder and she registers her effect with, 'It gave her straightway the measure of success she could have as a dove'.

Milly's deepest feeling is directed toward Densher (and in a different way Sir Luke) perhaps because he is the only one in her entourage who has the possibility of relating to her as a subject rather than an object—of seeing her as a human being rather than a dove or a princess. Yet Densher, too, originally only sees Milly as the 'little American girl'. And Milly is fully aware of the role he is asking her to play. As Dorothea Krook notes :

> She is the American girl grown conscious of herself as acting out the character of the American girl; and it is this capacity at once

for 'being' and 'seeing', for at once suffering intensely and being intensely conscious of suffering, that defines the kind and quality of her tragedy.[2]

Densher's view of Milly only changes when, at the party in Venice, he begins to see her essence rather than her exterior. He recognises that her dove-like quality is a property of soul rather than a mere mildness of exterior. Milly, with her passion for relationship, sees this even in the face of her knowledge of his secret tie with Kate. Thus she leaves him and only him, feeling 'forgiven, dedicated, blessed'.

Milly's path to consciousness is gradual and reaches its culmination only when she finally turns her face to the wall, for she is incapable of suffering the full weight of her awareness. She dies in the precincts of her isolated palace existence in the midst of her Maeterlinck fairy-tale. But in Milly we see that perception of the depths of existence—a perception feminine in essence—which is necessary for the individual who is to attain full powers of 'seeing', the ideal position in the Jamesian ethic. The religious aura which surrounds Milly's existence and the last part of the book, intensifies the cult of consciousness and the 'felt life' which James concretizes in Milly. To understand the effects of Milly's 'being' and her dying it is necessary to look more closely at the figure of Densher, who like Strether is the beneficiary of the feminine sensibility. Through woman, he too is turned inward to himself and hence he attains to full powers of seeing.

Densher, like his American predecessor, is the only character to enter the book not completely formed. That is, the outlines his figure will take are left open, and they remain open, but changed at the conclusion of the novel. 'He suggested above all, however, that wondrous state of youth in which the elements, the metals more or less precious, are so in fusion and fermentation that the question of the final stamp, the pressure that fixes the value, must wait for comparative coolness.' Caught in a world of petticoats where he is a passive register, Densher is the one incomplete item. Fully and passionately involved with Kate—whose ideal side, her 'talent for life' he is initially aware of—he allows himself to be manipulated by her without totally recognising the direction she is taking. 'There

² Dorothea Krook, *The Ordeal of Consciousness in Henry James* (Cambridge, England, 1962), p. 210.

glowed for him in fact a kind of rage for what he was not having; an exasperation, a resentment, begotten truly by the very impatience of desire, in respect to his postponed and relegated, his so extremely manipulated state. It was beautifully done of her, but what was the real meaning of it unless that he was perpetually bent to her will.' In retrospect, Densher sees himself as a young man, 'Far off, in a relation inconceivable . . . hushed, passive, staying his breath, but half understanding yet dimly conscious of something immense and holding himself, not to lose it, painfully together.'

Densher's total awareness is not to come until after his final meeting with Milly, yet his perceptive and feminine sensibility is apparent from the first. As soon as Milly comes fully into the picture, he begins to contrast her and Kate, and to move away from the latter. Where he had first taken her pronouncements as fully correct, he now commences to divide 'the things she might have been conscious of from those she might have missed'. Recognising that he and Milly are victims, he grows more and more surely toward the possession of a full consciousness of his own position in relation to the world.

James's identification with him, rather than with any other character in the book is evident in the slip where in describing Densher's reactions, he writes 'I' rather than 'he'.[3] Indeed Densher's sensibility is acute and along with Maggie—another character who reaches to the full extent of 'seeing'— he looks at the society he has always been critical of, as a caging force, holding people like 'fish in a crystal pool'. His deepening feeling for Milly who is finally to replace Kate in his imagination, leads him to see her in her true light. His description of Milly in the Palazzo Leporelli reminds us of Fleda's description of Ricks. The same personal tone is there.

> This spectacle had for him an eloquence, an authority, a felicity—
> he scarce knew by what strange name to call it—for which he
> said to himself that he had not consciously bargained. Her welcome, her frankness, sweetness, sadness, brightness, her disconcerting poetry as he made shift at moments to call it, helped as
> it was by the beauty of the whole setting and by the perception,
> at the same time, on the observer's part, that this element gained
> from her, in a manner, for effect and harmony, as much as it
> gave—her whole attitude had to his imagination, meanings that

[3] This slip has been rectified in the New York Edition (cf. 226) but exists in earlier editions, as well as the Dell edition.

hung upon it, waiting upon her, hovering, dropping and quavering forth again, like vague faint snatches, mere ghosts of sound, of old fashioned melancholy music. (XX, 184-5)

Milly's disconcerting poetry is intensely personal yet at the same time, one could say, that what Densher senses here is the distilled essence of all poetry.[4] Milly is for him a sparkling bitter sweet substance, no sooner beheld that it is gone, yet radiating an aura much more suggestive that its mere material presence. Milly's poetry yields meaning only for those who are capable of seeing it. Densher must make an exertion akin to the little burnt-faced girl's in order to see the invisible. He too is caught up in the fairy-tale mood. And James notes Densher's ability to 'see' when he has his hero realise at Milly's last party that Kate is somehow 'lacking in lustre' in comparison to Milly—and this especially after the 'remarkable' girl has given him the full details of her plan.

Yet it is only after Milly's death, after Densher has been 'forgiven, dedicated, blessed', that we are given the full effect that the world of personal relationship and feminine sensibility has on the developing consciousness. It is by this effect that we recognise Milly as the full representative of 'femininity'. It has already been noted that Sartre saw in the feminine a call to being. And Milly is *being*—intense and brief. Being attracts being and Milly's last summons to Densher is a summons for him to *be* with full integrity and inwardness. He is veritably transformed by this feminine influence after the interview. His feeling for Kate is transferred to a passion for Milly, through whose death he has been given back to himself. Kate sees the result of her actions as 'quite ideal' and Densher is in turn struck by her shallowness and glibness. Densher has turned to

---

[4] Milly as a symbol for 'poetry' takes on an intenser light if we compare her function in the novel to what Nietzsche saw as the role of art as a whole. Nietzsche said that: 'We have Art in order *not to perish of Truth*'. For him the essential function of art was to create perfection and the fullness of life, to affirm, bless and deify existence. This latter function is almost identical to that of Milly in her forgiving, dedicating and blessing of Densher's existence. Furthermore the reference to art as an instrument for creating perfection and the fullness of life is surprisingly close to what we have described as James's ethic. It would seem that within *The Wings of the Dove*, Milly fully takes on the role of art, or in this case, fiction. She is the beautiful illusion, while Kate Croy, whose existence is solidly grounded in reality, is Nietzsche's 'ugly truth'. This parallel seems to provide further evidence for the hypothesis that James's central feminine figures, his Cinderellas, are closely allied to his creative imagination.

Milly and Milly has, in the full force of her very absence, redirected him to himself.

In this final phase of James's vision, the feminine, in all the power of its inwardness, triumphs over the external world of limited existence, by bringing man to the depths of inner awareness—to the full possibility of seeing and being. Densher is transformed and redeemed once he sees that the only authentic, harmonious and intelligent gesture in the action of the book has been Milly's. As R. P. Blackmur writes, the book thus becomes for Densher a 'testing of Kate—not of good or bad, but of what she is: of the truth in her. Milly stands or floats, above all she dies, behind him; a test of what she stands for when she is not there.'[5]

The Golden Bowl presents the apotheosis of James's feminine orientation in the figure of Maggie Verver, whose feminine inwardness triumphs actively in life by creating a harmony in the social sphere of everyday existence. In this final work of the major phase, James reveals the full force of his vision and crystallizes the inherent limitations of the social fallacy vis à vis the moral totality of personalism and inner recognition. The fairy-tale once again absorbs the two-dimensionality of the social sphere and provides a viable realm for self-discovery, a self-discovery which provides the essence of a moral cosmology. Through Charlotte and Maggie, the master delimits the boundaries of the surface existence, where action stems from no fund of inner awareness, and at the other pole, the fullness and triumph of those manipulations which are the result of true recognition and which thus have magical powers of transformation.

Charlotte Stant is essentially a development of the Kate Croy figure, the powerful social personality, endowed with those visible superiorities which are the property of all James's outward-looking women. Her role, once she becomes Mrs. Verver, is precisely to shine in all social and public situations. Conscious of her power in this line, Charlotte is not devoid of those sensibilities which constitute good taste, and Mr. Verver, with his collector's instinct for the great object, is fully aware of her qualities—both as an appreciator of the beautiful and as a being herself endowed with personal magnificence. Charlotte is, furthermore, in possession of an integrity which allows her to offer the revealing telegram from the Prince to Mr. Verver on the occasion of their betrothal. She is also capable of

    [5] R. P. Blackmur, 'Introduction', *The Wings of the Dove* (New York, 1957), Dell Paperback edition, p. 146.

great passion, as we see in her relationship with the Prince. Truly a remarkable figure, Charlotte is yet condemned by James to be shipped off like some animal in a cage to the American wasteland and, at the end, to be termed 'stupid' by her lover.

It is thus excusable that some of James's critics (F. R. Leavis, Jean Kimball and R. P. Blackmur, for example) should see Charlotte as the true heroine of the book, misunderstood and defeated; or, judging James to approve of her defeat, say with F. R. Leavis:

> Actually if our sympathies are anywhere, they are with Charlotte and (a little) the Prince, who represent what, against the general moral background of the book, can only strike us as decent passion; in a stale, sickly and oppressive atmosphere they represent life.[6]

Yet to read *The Golden Bowl* in this way and to accuse Adam and Maggie of merely buying their mates as they would any other beautiful objects for their museum, is to misunderstand James's intention and vision.

One can grant that the passion of Charlotte and the Prince is profound and decent; we know from the 'virtuous attachment' of Chad and Madame de Vionnet that James was not one to disapprove wholly of illicit relationships. On the other hand, James did not believe in the isolation of sensual passion—and Charlotte's relation with the Prince is nothing if not sensually passionate—if it acted in such a way as to shut out the 'rest of life'. This we see in his criticism of d'Annunzio where he reveals his view of the place of sexual passion within the novel and hence within life.

> The sexual passion from which he extracts with admirable detached pictures insists on remaining for him *only* the act of a moment, beginning and ending in itself and disowning any representative character. From the moment it depends on itself alone for its beauty it endangers extremely its distinction, so precarious at the best. For what it represents, precisely, is poetically interesting; it finds its extension and consummation only in the rest of life. Shut out from the rest of life, shut out from all fruition and assimilation, it has no more dignity than—to use a homely image —the boots and shoes that we see, in the corridors of promiscuous hotels, standing, often in double pairs, at the doors of rooms.

6 F. R. Leavis, 'Henry James', *The Great Tradition* (London, 1962).

Detached and unassociated these clusters of objects present, however obtruded, no importance.[7]

What James is actually objecting to here is what has often been
defined as decadence; taking the part for the whole, seriously believing that sexual passion constitutes a total human relationship.
The sexual passion of Charlotte and the Prince is such that, by its
very secrecy, it would seek to ignore or annihilate their roles in the
'rest of life', that is, their respective positions as wife and husband.
Totally based on sensuality (note the Prince's initial description of
Charlotte), their relationship is an enclosing and limiting one which
does not effect any growth within their own characters. Rather, it
lessens the possibility of their becoming aware of the proliferating
nuances and full complexity of existence. Hence, it cuts them off
from a full appraisal of 'felt life'. In contra-distinction to this limiting passion, James places the equally sensual, yet fuller love of
Maggie for the Prince, which is conducive to growth and change,
and forces the Prince to grasp the fullness of life in all its aspects.
For James, only by experiencing the fullness of life can the individual attain a harmonious existence. Charlotte, like Kate before her,
stands lower in the hierarchy of James's vision than do Milly and
Maggie, whose loves stem from a fuller awareness. These latter force
their lovers to question themselves, while at the same time leaving
them the freedom to encompass the 'rest of life'.

The second reason why Charlotte fails while Maggie and Milly
triumph lies again in one of her likenesses to Kate Croy. The Prince,
when he calls Charlotte 'stupid' at the end of the book in comparison
to Maggie, is essentially correct within James's idea of what constitutes intelligence. Charlotte, like Kate, acts out of self-delusion.
She rationalises away any pangs of conscience she may have in order
to facilitate her actions. This is implicit in the scene where she comes
for the first time to see the Prince alone and together they seal their
vow of being solely responsible for taking care of Maggie and Adam,
whom they both believe to be 'beatifically happy'.

> Well then, there is is. I can't put myself into Maggie's skin—I
> can't, as I say. It's not my fit—I shouldn't be able as I see it, to
> breathe in it. But I can feel that I'd do anything to shield it from
> a bruise. Tender as I am for her too . . . I think that I'm still more
> so for my husband. He's in truth of a sweet simplicity.

[7] Henry James, 'Gabriele d'Annunzio', *Notes on Novelists*, p. 26.

Acting, as she believes, to protect the happiness of Adam and Maggie, Charlotte brings herself into closer contact with the Prince, and she achieves a renewal of their passionate entanglement. We must not too quickly discredit her solicitude for her husband and step-daughter, yet we must not over-rate it. It would seem quite obvious that Charlotte's true—and perhaps unconscious—motivation in originally approaching the Prince is not merely to testify to a protective feeling for father and daughter. Rather, Charlotte seeks to bring things to a head with her one-time love. She is successful in this as the kiss which closes the chapter proves—a kiss which for James is equal to a multitude of bedroom scenes. Yet through this scene, James reveals what is essentially Charlotte's limitation and what will result in her eventually being termed stupid.

Charlotte's flaw, and for James this is a highly serious one, is a narrowness of vision. Like Kate, she is incapable of seeing a situation from another's viewpoint. Hence she fails to understand Maggie, to put herself into 'Maggie's skin', and she feels that both Maggie and her father are simple innocents. This inability to understand Maggie reveals Charlotte's own lack of awareness. It is brought to the fore in her two final encounters with her step-daughter, where Maggie permits Charlotte to believe that the latter has the upper hand. It is pointless to speculate that if we were permitted to see more from Charlotte's standpoint, we would find a being whose field of vision was less limited, in the Jamesian sense. By placing his 'seeing' intelligence first in the Prince and ultimately in Maggie, James seems to be stressing that Maggie is the more fitting receptacle for his vision. If, in the post-Freudian age, we prefer Charlotte's 'directness' to Maggie's 'niceness', we would, nevertheless, be falsifying James's ethics if we interpreted the book from Charlotte's perspective.

Maggie, unlike Charlotte, is capable of projecting herself into her step-mother's position. She has 'imagination'. It is because of this that she feels sympathy for Charlotte and ultimately triumphs with the Prince. Similar in this to Milly, she is capable of seeing round Charlotte intellectually, and her profundity and elasticity of vision arise precisely from her intense self-consciousness. In the Jamesian context, self recognition permits one truly to 'see' all others and thus to use one's compositional and transformative powers on them. Our next task lies in dscovering the essence of Maggie's recognition and what use she makes of her self-consciousness. Having done this we will arrive at a precise knowledge of what constitutes Jamesian 'femininity' and how it is the corner-stone of his artistic approach and his moral cosmology.

Maggie is the culminating point of the Cinderella figure, the heiress of all the ages who takes into her own being the metamorphic power of the fairy godmother. The innocent little 'burnt-faced' girl, diminutive in comparison to Charlotte at the start of her tale, turns herself into a true princess without the help of an external magic wand. Like the Indian Cinderella, she is transformed by her ability to see what to everyone else is invisible; and having seen, she turns her bridegroom back to himself. The fullest feminine in James's fictional canvas, Maggie is at once wife, daughter and mother. Her creative superiority is noted by the fact that she and only she gives birth within the limits of her tale. In this latter she is only comparable to Isabel, whose child notably dies. Through Maggie we discover the meaning of femininity not only by its effect on others : we can also trace the feminine through all the stages of its development, so that we become aware of its constituent factors.

Maggie's development takes place within a realm which is fairy in mood, and the density of images in her part of the book intensifies the dream-like quality. Yet, as is evident when she comes into contact with the other characters of the book—notably the Assinghams, Charlotte and the Prince—what she has learned in her personal world can be used actively to affect life around her. Maggie's relationship with her father, so central to the book, is intrinsically part of her fairy world—that is, it is closest to her process of discovering the invisible. Notably all her conversations with Adam in her half of the book are efforts to arrive at self-knowledge and at an awareness of his own particular knowledge. As Jung points out : 'a positive father-complex in women induces the liveliest spiritual aspirations and interests. In dreams, it is always the father-figure from whom the decisive convictions, prohibitions, and wise counsels emanate.'[8] And Adam's counsels and warnings are indeed wise. He is not the complete innocent that so many critics have named him, a feature which would be incompatible with the shrewdness of his money-making background. Adam tells Maggie :

'We want each other', he had further explained; 'only wanting it each time, for each other. That's what I call the happy spell;

[8] C. G. Jung, *The Phenomenology of the Spirit in Fairytales*, pp. 214–215.

but it's also, a little, possibly the immorality.'

' "The immorality"?' she had pleasantly echoed.

'Well, we're tremendously moral for ourselves—that is *for* each other; and I won't pretend that I know at whose particular expense you and I, for instance, are happy.' (XXIV, 91-92)

After quoting this passage, Cargill correctly states, 'Adam Verver is not talking about their selfish exclusion of people generally, but of their exclusion of their mates in their "opium den" obliviousness and mutual security. He is trying to hint that duty to those mates, to husband and wife, has primacy over affection for daughter and father—one of the most urgent themes of the novel.'[9]

This kind of hint is one Maggie frequently receives from her father, and to use Jung's terms, her positive father complex testifies to her possibility for grasping spiritual and inward matters. Psychically, her son the Principino plays much the same role, for Jung tells us that in fairy-tales the young boy, for a woman 'corresponds to the so-called "positive" animus who indicates the possibility of a conscious spiritual effort'.[10] This conscious spiritual effort, as we shall see in a moment, is precisely what Maggie's development and transformation consists of. To round off the fullness of the psyche figures which are an aid to Maggie's growth, however, we must first look to the figure of the wise old man who is responsible for Maggie's acquisition of the golden bowl and with it one segment of her knowledge.

The shopkeeper's accidental appearance and his importance in the book is in keeping with its fairy-tale tone. It is noteworthy that the bowl finally into Maggie's possession rather than Charlotte's or the Prince's, for the bowl, aside from its symbolic value as an image for the flawed relationships within the book has psychic importance in itself. Essentially it symbolizes Maggie's potential for growth in her knowledge of the invisible.

The wise old man of our tale describes the bowl as a product of a 'lost art' and of a 'lost time'. A lost time is a time out of mind and a time out of mind suggests the timeless sphere of psychic existence wherein all true recognition takes place. The fact that the bowl is both golden and flawed intimates that it is, first of all, the image of a very high, ideal psyche, of a paradisical or total selfhood; and furthermore, that this selfhood, this total integration of personality

9 Oscar Cargill, p. 408.
10 C. G. Jung, *The Phenomenology of the Spirit in Fairytales*, p. 215.

has been flawed and exists no longer. Hence, the bowl becomes an image for Maggie's state of being before she has attained the fulfill-ment which comes after her reunion with the Prince. It suggests the ultimate integration not only of the two beings, but of Maggie as a complete being whose powers of vision are acute. This analysis of the bowl's significance is not extreme if it is remembered that we are dealing with a fairy-tale world which must be open to wide interpretation before its truths can be deciphered.

Maggie's development, if traced from the opening pages of her part of the book, fulfills the bowl's prophecy of ultimate integration of self and world. We see Maggie at the end of her tale emerging as the most fully defined feminine of James's art—a being trans-formed into the princess, the highest position open to James's women and symbolizing a spiritual awareness and a full consciousness. Maggie's section of the book opens with the elaborate image of the pagoda existing at the centre of the garden of her life. This image conveys her exact state of being at this particular point of her devel-opment.

> The great decorated surface had remained consistently impene-trable and inscrutable. At present, however, to her considering mind, it was as if she had ceased merely to circle and to scan the elevation, ceased so vaguely, so quite helplessly to stare and won-der; she had caught herself distinctly in the act of pausing, then in that of stepping unprecedentedly near. The thing might have been by the distance at which it kept her, a Mahometan mosque, with which no base heretic could take a liberty; there so hung about it the vision of putting off one's shoes to enter, and even, verily, of one's paying with one's life if found there as an inter-loper. She had knocked in short— . . . Something had happened; it was as if a sound at her touch, after a little, had come back to her from within; a sound sufficiently suggesting that her approach had been noted. (XXIV, 4)

On a simple level, the mosque in question here exists as an image of the secret relationship between the Prince and Charlotte, which Maggie is slowly growing to realise. However, the complexity of James's image will not allow us to rest here. Maggie's recognition is markedly more profound and she is beginning her initiation into the realm of the invisible which ultimately becomes visible. We see Maggie grasping for a knowledge of that which has always been for her 'impenetrable and inscrutable' and coming remarkably close to a full discovery. Her instinctive powers, like those of all the Cinderella figures are strong. This 'indescribale' thing, this awful Mahometan mosque becomes for her and for the reader, precisely that hidden intuitive aspect of life which defies verbalization, but which, once it has been fathomed, lets one see things as they really are. Finally it reveals the 'road of the Spirit' and the 'beauty of the Rainbow'.

One must put off one's shoes to enter, one must take off the garbs of unseeing civilisation, and one must pay with one's life once one has finally entered, for a grasping of this knowledge of the invisible necessitates the re-organisation of our life as we have previously known it and lived it, since it causes our relationship to ourselves and to our environment to suffer a telling change. This is Maggie's initial intuition of the transforming and metamorphic powers which come with full consciousness. It is telling that for James this full consciousness comes only once the individual has been hurled into the depths of selfhood, for it is only by a steady inward gaze that consciousness can be achieved. This is what lies at the basis of James's intense personalism and his feminine orientation: as we have seen it is through confrontation with the feminine principle that man is turned inward. James finds, at the secret depths of being, not ritualistic habits and patterns, not chaotic and destructive forces, but the seeds of what can develop into full consciousness.

From the moment that Maggie has her first intuitive perception of what constitutes being, in the mind's eye, one begins to see her walking across her own inner landscape and the objects and those people she encounters start to assume a dream-like and fairy-tale dimension. It is from this dimension that Maggie's power will come. Maggie's moment of full recognition, not only of the adulterous relationship between her husband and Charlotte, but of this profounder insight into being, comes with her discovery of the golden bowl and with the appearance of the wise old man who helps her to her psychic knowledge. This moment is the summation of many previous intimations and does not come upon her *ex nihilo,* in a state of total unawareness. It is an important aspect of James's art that, as in life, his characters only come gradually to recognition of the real state of being.

As Maggie is confronted with the bowl, she gains an insight into the totality of life, into its three dimensionality. She sees beyond the screen of surface reality. When the bowl is smashed to the ground

by Fanny Assingham, Maggie does in a sense pay with her life, or
at least life as she has known it up to the moment. The mobility of
the bowl as a symbol is well brought out by James in this scene. As
the bowl lies in pieces on the ground and as the prince enters, it
becomes one with Maggie's dissociation : the shattered state of being
which follows upon epiphany. Intuition becomes knowledge, for
Maggie here, but knowledge momentarily brings with it a shattering
of selfhood as it has previously been organised. Maggie's composure,
however, is quickly regained after this disintegrating flash of awareness. As she picks up the three pieces of the bowl and holds them
in her hands so that the whole appears totally unbroken, the bowl
becomes a joint symbol for the way in which she will, from now
on, not only hold herself together, but also manipulate the three
pieces—the Prince, Charlotte and Adam—so that no superficial sign
of rupture is apparent. Finally Maggie's holding together of the
bowl prophesies her reintegrated selfhood once her manipulations
are successful.

Maggie's recognition of the invisible in her moment of total insight consists of a dawning awareness that before this epiphany she
existed as a being who was essentially unconscious : things existed
in her and around her without her being aware of them. This is
the full force of unconsciousness for James and it is as damning a
characteristic as any within his vision. James's entire stress on the
fine intelligence and on the importance of 'seeing' for being fully
and integrally oneself, shows us the value he places on consciousness;
for without consciousness, man is incapable of acting to the full
degree of his potential and of experiencing life to its utmost. He is
preventing himself from taking in all the proliferations and complexities of existence.

This is Maggie's state before her recognition and this recognition
lies precisely in the discovery that hitherto she has been unconscious,
hence incapable of truly experiencing love or understanding—incapable of engaging in a profound relationship. One of the descriptions
of Maggie which James places into Adam's mouth implies this by
linking Maggie with the essential deadness and fixity of a statue. She
had for Adam :

> the appearance of some slight, slim, draped antique of Vatican or
> Capitoline halls, late and refined, rare as a note and immortal as
> a link, set in motion by the miraculous infusion of a modern

impulse and yet, for all the sudden freedom of folds and footsteps, forsaken after centuries of their pedestal, keeping still the quality, the perfect felicity of the statue : the blurred, absent eyes, the smooth elegant, nameless head, the impersonal flit of a creature lost in an alien age and passing as in an image in worn relief round and round a precious vase. (XXIII, 187)

This description testifies to the fine quality which is Maggie's. Yet intrinsic to its meaning is her unconsciousness, her limitation of vision as she travels round and round in never-expanding circles. This static quality and limitedness, in spite of all the movement and freedom of draperies and footsteps, is also the unconsciousness of all James's characters if they have not been granted a moment of recognition. Only when Maggie is given insight, when she becomes aware that her previous existence of the surface was unconscious, can she exist in all the flexibility and openness which is the property of those who have attained full consciousness. It is now that she has seen the invisible, that she is transformed and capable of empathizing, of adopting various points of view and hence of using her metamorphic powers on others. Maggie has now, in the Jamesian context, reached the fullness of femininity.

What does the Jamesian moment of recognition—of full consciousness—consist of? What is it exactly that Maggie's development gives her an insight into? Adam Verver in his role as psychic counsellor illuminates this when he tells Maggie, 'Everything is remarkably pleasant isn't it?—but where, for it, after all, are we? up in a balloon and whirling through space, or down in the depths of the earth in the glimmering passages of a gold mine?' (XXIV, 73) Man's duality and the dichotomies of literary experience are evident here. On the one hand we have the balloon man : consciousness leaving earth and all literature which deals with the mystical side of being. It suggests the spiritual vertigo of an expanded consciousness, the ascension of the ego and the refined feeling of being unearthly. On the other hand, we have the earthly gold-mine, the original source of the mineral man as he appears in the Book of Daniel. These excavations beneath the earth represent the exhumation of man's inner being and are suggestive of all the literature which probes the depths rather than the heights of man's psyche. The conflict between these two—between the balloon man and the mineral man—and its resolution, is, in a few words, the summation of James's vision, for the way up and the way down are the constituents of Maggie's whole spiritual recognition. The path of her inner landscape has brought her down to the depths of being, to a seeing of the invisible and by the act of this 'seeing' she attains full consciousness and total selfhood. In her acquired awareness of the 'twin world' she can function in the middle world of daily experience with a new found power.

Since Maggie's moment of recognition shows her that she has up to this time been living in a truly unconscious way, it is followed by a sense of awakening from a deep sleep into a world which seems unreal, dreamlike, because the things around her still exist in their two dimensional state. 'It was as if she had come out—that was her most general consciousness; out of a dark tunnel, a dense wood, or even simply a smoky room.' (XXIV, 207). Here James couples two rebirth or reawakening motifs, the 'dark tunnel', and the 'dense wood', with all their Dante-Spenser spiritual overtones, with the 'smoky room' which brings the reader from the depths of dream experience into reality. Maggie's fullness of vision, upon emerging from the 'dark tunnel' results in a sensation that the world around her is a world of fantasy, a fictional universe. This accounts for the many images in which she sees herself as some kind of performer in a totally unreal situation and for her observer-like role as she gazes at the other characters as if they were a party of 'panting gold-fish in a tank'.

Maggie's transformation once she has seen the invisible allows her to begin to use her metaphoric power on others. Having recognised that she is existing in what is essentially a fictional universe, she also grasps the fact that the lines of convergence in the perfect pattern of relationships between Charlotte and the Prince, the Prince and herself, herself and her father, and Adam and Charlotte, are in themselves imaginary and are fulfilled in an abstract geometrical quality. These relationships are only superficial, that is they are not true relational ties based on full self-knowledge. Once Maggie has seen the abstractness and hence unreality of these lines of convergence, then she also realizes that they are capable of being manipulated in any fashion that she, the seeing intelligence, wishes.

Maggie realises that the unconsciousness which she suffered from, those around her must also suffer. They are totally unaware of these simplified, abstract and two-dimensional lines of communication, for they lack the third dimension—consciousness. Hence, Maggie can rearrange the apparent yet imaginary lines of convergence without seemingly destroying the balance in the pattern. 'The equilibrium, the precious condition lasted in spite of rearrangement; there had been a fresh distribution of the different weights, but the balance persisted and triumphed.'

Maggie's new compositional and metamorphic powers over the other characters are further illuminated as she stands watching her companions from the terrace at Fawns.

> They might have been figures rehearsing some play of which she herself was the author; they might even, for the happy appearance they continued to present, have been figures as would, by the strong note of character in each, fill any author with the certitude of success, especially of their own histrionic. They might in short have represented any mystery they would; the point being that the key to the mystery, the key that would wind and unwind it without a snap of the spring, was there in her pocket. (XXIV, 235-236)

To Maggie, the rest of the characters are fully manageable because they exist only in their outward and two-dimensional quality as actors. Only she herself, as author, can provide that third dimension —that inner reality— which will force them to act according to her own demands. Maggie, here, becomes the feminine as artist. Fully conscious herself, she infuses the flat two-dimensional figures around her with the inwardness of 'felt life'.

With her newly acquired powers of action and control, Maggie does not force the issue in such a way as Kate or, for example, Mrs. Gereth would have done. She has none of the, for James, odious characteristics of the vampire figure who functions within a system of user and used. Her manipulation is more subtle and consists in turning both the Prince and Charlotte inward so that each, confronted by their own inner being, is led to see wherein the authentic gesture, the conscious gesture, lies. Making no recriminations to either of the adulterous pair, Maggie allows Charlotte to believe that she has the upper hand in both their final interviews. Her influence is felt, especially by the Prince, precisely because of her superiority of being and seeing.

The lines of convergence between the characters are reorganised in such a way that a new and truer harmony is attained without the side effects of violence and damage. Charlotte in the final scene of the book is no longer the caged animal shipped off to the American wasteland, but a woman 'great' in her new found mission of bringing the arts, that is civilisation, to the primitives. The Prince, forced to introspection like all those affected by the 'feminine', penetrates the white Poe-like mist of unconsciousness and hazy values defined by social norms, which surrounded him in the first part of the book. He recognises the value of inwardness and the power of consciousness. Maggie, he sees, is a person far above Charlotte in her possibilities of 'seeing and being'. He attains that moral sense which he initially lacked: that moral sense which for James is so intrinsically allied with the feminine principle and which allows man to exist free from the system of user and used, to make the authentic inward gesture which can only lead to harmony.

James sees both the masculine and the feminine ways of life: man's relationship to ideology, to the absolutes, to external phenomena as well as his relationship to himself. The stress of his art, however, is on the latter and this he himself has defined as a quality of the feminine. This femininity supplies James with the tone of his greatest achievements, the tone of introspection and constant examination of the self in relation to itself and to others. It also forms the basis of his ethical vision.

Femininity is a call to being for James in that it is a call to inwardness and introspection, the prerequisite of all true relationship and action. When one is fully conscious of self, then and only then, one *is*. And being for James means being open to the whole assault of life—delimiting experience in no way—while intelligently grasping the significance of this assault. Thus the feminine, with its quality of an open and flexible sensibility, and its insistence on both interiorization of events and personalism in relationships, introduces into the Jamesian world the possibility of full consciousness.

2 Robert Musil: Femininity and Completeness

Robert Musil, an Austrian of partly Czech descent, was born in Klagenfurt in 1880. His father was a professor of engineering remembered for his improvements of the steam turbine, and his mother, a gifted pianist. He was educated at the military academy at Eisenstadt and then at Weisskirchen, the school Rilke attended and which finds its fictional equivalent in The Confusions of Young Torless. Shortly before entering upon a planned military career, Musil made one of his several professional about-turns and decided to take up engineering in which he received a diploma in 1901. After completing his military service and working as an engineer for a year, he immersed himself in the study of philosophy and experimental psychology—a long-standing interest. He took a degree in philosophy at the University of Berlin and wrote his dissertation on Mach's epistemology. During this period, he invented a chromatometer which is still known by his name and wrote his first novel, The Confusions of Young Torless (1906). The recognition which this first book received made him decide to live as a writer rather than take up a post as an academic philosopher. He was married in 1910, served as an officer with the Austrian army from 1914 to 1918 and after the war worked as a press liaison officer for the Foreign Ministry and then as a scientific adviser to the War Ministry. From 1922 onwards he supported himself as a freelance writer, contributing to various literary journals, and participated in the rich Viennese café and literary life of the post-war years. It was in these years too that he began work on The Man Without Qualities which was to occupy him for the rest of his life, and to remain unfinished—

*though two volumes appeared in his lifetime—at his death. When
Hitler came to power in 1933 Musil, then in Berlin, moved back
to Vienna and in 1933 to Switzerland where he died suddenly four
years later while doing his morning gymnastics—a discipline which
reflected the greater discipline of his multi-faceted life.*

AN INTELLECTUAL APPROACH

In Robert Musil's highly intellectual and masculine universe it is
almost surprising to find such a large number of female characters
of central importance. Why, one asks oneself, should a profoundly
self-critical writer, with a scientific and philosophical background,
who sets out lucidly to appraise the conditions leading to a world
war and to offer a solution to the modern dilemma of man's 'not-at-
homeness' in the world, immerse himself so deeply in the study of
the feminine? It would seem that in such a hard-minded world,
woman, with what has become known as her social frivolity and
intellectual vagueness, would be out of place and the effort made to
understand her would be minimal. Yet, it is clearly the case that
Musil, in *The Man Without Qualities* through his major hero,
Ulrich, does make a pronounced effort to include the feminine in
the decidedly male world of theory and intellect. In fact, one might
say that the impingement of the feminine into Ulrich's or Musil's
lucid world of scientific strictness and exactitudes could be charted
from the very opening of *The Man Without Qualities* when the
first woman, Leona, enters this encyclopedic universe.

Leona, with her basic bluntness and stupidity, could be treated in
a hedonistic and trifling manner, purely as the object of coitus in a
world dominated by the male principle, and this is predominantly
the way in which Ulrich deals with her. However, even in this first
simple confrontation with woman, there is something which Ulrich
is intrigued by because it cannot be fathomed by his intellect. Leona,
for all her bluntness, is ultimately closed to Ulrich and he can only
try to explain her effect by calling her 'Junonian', or again by feeling that her beauty of bygone days exerts the uncanny fascination
of a *'tableau vivant'*. It is in her opaqueness that Leona's femininity
lies and as Ulrich moves up the hierarchy of women in this book,
this opaqueness increases: all the women he comes into contact
with become more and more difficult to apprehend.

From Bonadea's mixture of morality and nymphomania, he moves to the bewildering idealism of Diotima, the incipient madness of Clarisse and finally to the ordinariness yet complete extraordinariness of his sister Agathe, whom Ulrich feels he must fathom if he is to understand himself. Hence, just by glancing at territory yet to be explored, it becomes evident that Musil's emphasis on the feminine arises from an attempt to comprehend even those spheres which cannot be grasped intellectually and from a wish, perhaps, somehow to harness the energies found in these realms in order to find a total solution for the human condition. Musil, in his scientific exactitude and his completeness must explore those areas which are paradoxically closed to scientific investigation. He must demystify the 'other'; and this otherness for the moment can, without further explication, be called 'femininity'.

Yet, for all his lucidity and hard-mindedness, there is something in Musil which inclines him precisely toward this sphere of the 'feminine', because Musil is essentially the philosopher of possibility or of manifold potentiality, of that which cannot as yet be logically defined. When Ulrich embraces the concept of 'Essayism' as that most beneficial for understanding the world and himself, he is, in a masculine context, selecting the approach of most integrity for trying to capture the multitudinous possibilities reality offers to the mind. Essayism for Ulrich is that form of exploration which sees everything from many points of view without ever comprehending it fully 'for a thing wholly comprehended instantly loses its bulk and melts down into a concept'. Essayists are the masters of the floating life within and their domain lies between religion and knowledge, between example and doctrine, between *amor intellectualis* and poetry.

This inclination toward Essayism can be taken as Musil's own from the many indications to this effect in his notebooks, and what it reveals is precisely a thinker who would like to see the ultimate union of 'precision and soul' or rather 'exactitude and spirit', what many of Musil's critics call *Ratio und Mystik*. Ulrich's definition of Essayism permits not only that kind of exactitude which insists on a thing being seen from all sides and in all of its relationships, but also on the potentiality involved in the unfixed world of spirit and poetry. The first half of this union is definitely the male's for Ulrich is the man of precision *par excellence,* the man of empirical reality continually tempted by possibility. It is necessary to remember, however, that even though Musil depicts Ulrich in the first

pages of *The Man Without Qualities* as a man of possibilities and
attributes to him a conscious Utopianism and a total lack of the sense
of reality, the author's irony is directed at his hero. Musil himself
points out the inconsistencies of his hero's viewpoint, for Ulrich can
theorize about possibility but cannot necessarily live by it. He is
firmly grounded in an intellectual reality and only tempted by *Möglichkeiten* (possibilities). This is the situation of the arch male in the
Musilian universe.

The second half of the conjuncton between precision and soul
lies in the region of the feminine, as is made clear by Ulrich's attempted union with the most important female in the books hierarchy, Agathe. Well-versed in depth psychology, Musil was fully
aware of the masculine and feminine components that go to make
up the total being. His reading included the works of Freud, Jung,
Adler, Weininger,[1] as well as Ellis and Bachofen. The marriage of
masculine and feminine, together with their essential separateness;
man and woman's relationship to the self; these questions appear
time and again in Musil's notebooks as well as in his final work. But
it is too glib an explanation of Musil's work to make the masculine
equivalent to the world of science and exactitude and the feminine
to spirit and poetry, for Musil's world must always stand up to the
test of existence and no man or woman was ever purely one thing
or the other. What becomes evident, however, and provides a working formula, is that in the relativistic and highly realistic world of
Musil's works, if the masculine represents that reality which is continually tempted by possibility, the feminine is then that possibility
which must always be tested by reality.

Musil's desire for completeness—for a synthesis between the dialectical opposites of mysticism and reason—is evident in his choice
of the myth of Isis and Osiris as a symbolic substructure for his central work and as the subject of his only poem. This myth represents
the integration of the self, for Isis and Osiris, female and male, are
tied together in all possible ways through their incestuous relationship. Brother and sister, husband and wife, and finally mother and
son, they provide the fullest mythical marriage of opposites. What

---

[1] Although there is no direct reference to Weininger in Frisé's edition of
Musil's notebooks, it is more than likely that Musil knew the work of this near-
notorious Viennese figure. In any case a reading of the two men immediately
reveals their closeness in so basic a question as the polarization of the sexes into
masculine-intellectual, feminine-all that is removed from intellect. cf. also, Musil's
and Weininger's similar interest in the question of genius.

is important for our present study is the totality of the Isis figure
who reveals the feminine in a good many of her possible manifestations and who takes the male into herself first as wife, and then
more explicitly as mother, thereby attaining the peak of feminine
selfhood. In his encyclopedic scope, Musil systematically investigates
the various manifestations of the Isis figure and their significance.

If in the mythical substructure of Musil's work there is a union
attained between male and female as such and between their respective elements within the human entity, as Kaiser and Wilkins,
Musil's principal English translators and critics would like to believe,
this union is never fully resistant to the daylight world of dry wit
and irony where Musil would like to place it. Musil's daylight and
masculine world has an intellectual anguish at its very foundation
which ultimately will not allow it to accept fully any total solution,
any completeness. The exact pursuit of various points of view, which
is basic to Ulrich's Essayism, can never totally relinquish its aversion to forming anything which is a concept and hence complete.
Nor can it ever fully give in to the feminine 'spirit' qualities, to
unlimited and nameless possibilities not controllable by intellect
alone—except under the light of the moon, the night-time world of
dream. Musil seeks for a *taghelle,* a daylight mysticism.

The basis of his intellectual anguish lies in the fact that although
in many ways he would like to dissolve those limits of what the
mind can grasp as reality, limits which lie in the twilight of the
post-Kantian dilemma, he intellectually agrees with Kant's definition of the existence of these limits. Since he accepts what Kant
defines as the 'necessary conditions of knowledge' and, further, that
the 'transcendental' as such must remain doubtful, he realises at the
same time that if these limits were to be by-passed, he would then,
ipso facto, have achieved the impossible. This achievement, however, is for Musil the essential feat of fiction—the possibility of
integration offered by and through fiction's flexibility. In fiction the
unio mystico can take place : that synthesis of masculine and feminine, of intellect and soul can exist. But if fiction is to encompass the
entire sphere of 'real' relations to self and society, then this synthesis
can only be momentary. It cannot have duration as a total solution.

For Musil the self—like any other object in the orbit of the sensible world—exists as an object, something seen from the outside
looking in. Thus the inner world and the outer cannot fully unite.
Much as Musil seems to desire this solution or synthesis, he cannot

—perhaps because of his intellectual integrity and strictness—allow Ulrich to live it, except in certain isolated moments of mystical ecstasy. Ulrich, the male dominated by intelligence, must remain that form of reality which is eternally tempted by possibility but can never arrive at a fixed solution of any problem.

Ulrich's inability to arrive at any absolute is paralleled by the book itself, *The Man Without Qualities,* which similarly can find no real 'end' since the dialectical oppositions which it initiates between being and possibility, male and female, reason and mysticism, are not capable of synthesis in the kind of world Musil insists on describing as totally relativistic. As Elizabeth Albertsen, who has made a careful study of Musil's literary remains, points out :

> The essence of dialectics is that it is unending; and Musil's dialectic is still more agile than those we presently know, because in this dialectic, not only one synthesis emerges from the opposition of thesis and antithesis, but rather a number of mediations : possibilities. Only in this way—by using an open-ended system—can Musil's novel end; for each end, each mighty reconciliation which offers itself as an *ultima ratio* is only blackmail, an easy cliché solution which Musil's demand for precision opposes. Therefore, one must always say—'It could just as easily be otherwise'.[4]

One notes in passing an analogy here to Nietzsche's dislike of synthesis because it is degenerate or all-too-early.

Thus, no universal solution, no total human lucidity linked with completeness, can ever be realized in a sphere of endlessly fluctuating but never uniting, 'collateral campaigns'.[5] And Ulrich's attempt to establish a marriage with Agathe, much like the integrating motif of Isis and Osiris, must be made outside the limits of a society of 'collateral campaigns'. This marriage, however, is shaken by precisely what it hopes to exclude. Musil in his major work knows no bounds of reflection. Hamlet, placed into a relativistic world, can only go on eternally exploring inner and outer possibilities without ever initiating any action or solution.

---

4 Elizabeth Albertson, *Ratio und 'Mystik' im Werk Robert Musils* (München, 1968), pp. 126–127, my translation.

5 I use the *Parallelaktion* or collateral campaign in its wider symbolic sense as it emerges from the actual facts of the book. It suggests parallel yet never uniting attempts to arrive at a solution, just as the ever-opposed splinter groups of the actual collateral campaign never succeeded in anything but further splintering.

It is left to the feminine to attempt to reach that form of selfhood, of completeness, which is within her grasp precisely because her conditions of knowledge are vaguer than the male's. The embodiment of possibility, the woman, is the only figure within the Musilian universe who is capable of attaining crystallization within the limits of her own being. This, then, is the second aspect of Musil's completeness in his exploration of femininity. Horizontally, one could say, Musil presents a vast canvas of womanhood covering all of the feminine's traditional psychological roles; woman as mother, daughter, wife, prostitute, widow and sister. These manifestations are studied as if, in a sense, each one were an essay in the search for a total view of femininity. Vertically, on the other hand, Musil investigates the feminine in depth, in an attempt to reveal the core and the components of that which is essentially feminine. In other words, he sets out to demystify what we have called the 'myth of femininity'. The stress in this latter investigation lies on femininity in search of itself, on woman treading the difficult upward path from her mythological, primitive roots to a consciousness of her own femininity. It is on this vertical line that this study will concentrate, for in analyzing woman in search of her own femininity, one can reach a fuller understanding of Musil as a philosopher of possibility.

UNIONS

The two stories included in the collection entitled *Vereinigungen* (Unions) provide a suitable starting point for an investigation of the feminine in Musil. In these stories the two opposite poles of feminine possibility in the Musilian universe are described. On the one hand there is Claudine, a wife figure, who represents the ambivalence of femininity trying to grasp that which constitutes her femininity, a consciousness of self in a world defined by strong masculine limits. On the other hand, there is the dark world of Veronica, both virgin and widow, who is plunged into unconscious depths and a sphere of limitless illusion from which the masculine strength which could define a saving test of reality is missing. Around these two women, one could form clusters of all the female characters whom Musil explores in depth. It is easy to see that Claudine, who for lack of a better term can be called the higher feminine, is in embryo a Regine and Agathe figure, while Veronica, the lower feminine, is the initial form of the Clarisse figure. The title of the collection,

Unions, brings to mind the all-pervading theme of Musil's work. It implies both the coming together of the masculine and the feminine in marriage and the union of these principles in the individual.

In the latter part of his career, Musil said of himself that if anything, he was a *Liebesdichter* (a poet of love) and the first story of this collection is suitably entitled *The Perfecting of a Love.* The plot of the story is almost transparent. It simply describes a woman who must take a trip without her beloved husband in order to visit a daughter begotten in a past affair. Although her husband is indispensable to her, the woman, in their separation, commits adultery. Yet to strip the story in this way is to do Musil a gross injustice, for within this simple framework, what unfolds is a profound insight into the psychology of any single woman merging back into the essential nature of her femininity, her roots. Musil at the time of the writing of *Unions* and during most of his life was greatly preoccupied with the problems of fidelity, man's relationship to woman, and jealousy, by which he means not only sexual jealousy, but 'one's uncertainty about the value, or even the real nature, of one's self and of the person nearest to oneself'. Claudine's story is the tale of a woman coming to know her own real nature and how this affects her relationship with the man closest to her, her husband.

In Claudine's story Musil utilizes an intensely lyrical style in order to follow closely the complex and vague thinking as well as feeling processes of the woman. Yet, his close following of Claudine is in no way a stream-of-consciousness technique : that is to say, he does not actually adapt himself to what one feels must be, in Claudine's case, a far less grand and exact mind. One is distinctly aware that Claudine is ordinary and yet the elaborate, almost expressionistic imagery Musil uses to depict her emotional states works as if to place these simple states into a vaster landscape of total femininity or the myth of womanhood. Musil's technique, with all its acute observations, performs the transfiguration of one simple state into a larger context by the trick of giving interior, almost invisible features of emotions, an exterior hue—literally transferring a feeling by describing it as one might describe a landscape or an object.

Also important is the fact that Claudine's adventure takes place in a mythic and vague time of feminine duration which is more a sense of some unconscious time, than an exact definition of a personal past, present or future. The opening scene which introduces husband and wife is set in a kind of timeless present which only

gains actual presence because of the convergence of husband and
wife, whose love is the starting point for a 'crystallisation' as yet
not defined, a crystallization which is the beginning of consciousness.

It would seem from the opening pages of this story that the only
fixed, the only defined thing in Claudine's life is the love which ties
her to her husband. This becomes evident from the opening description of the teapot which Claudine is holding, where mingled reflections form a pool of colours running together, in contrast to which
Claudine's gaze at her husband forms an angle with the line of her
arm, a rigid pattern in the air. Yet this relationship which is the one
defined thing, the beginning of a crystallization in a world of unknown third persons, who threaten to dissolve unity, is yet a burden,
a stability which holds the woman captive in her own being.

The first few pages of this story, before Claudine begins her
journey, introduce the motifs and themes which will prevail throughout in changing relationships to each other. What is here at first
a bewildering complexity becomes, as the story progresses, a hand-
ful of oft-repeated images which form a pattern, in the same way
that Claudine's mind moves toward a pattern. The repetition and
recurrence of these motifs gives a musical overtone to the tale.
Among the first of the themes introduced is the important idea of
the world of third persons which surrounds the security of this union
between male and female. Everything outside this union is vague
and dreamlike to Claudine. She has

> an obscure feeling of the world around them, which made them
> draw together; it was a dreamlike sense of the cold all around
> them except on that one side where they leaned against each
> other, screened each other, unburdening themselves like two won-
> derfully well-fitted halves. (PD 164–165)

It is this world of third persons, this form of reality, that Claudine
must come to grips with before the total crystallization, the germ of
which lies in her union with her husband, can be realised.

A further theme which makes its appearance in this first section
is that of the essential separateness of the male and female even
within this form of mysterious union. Claudine remembers the time
when she and her husband were making love when suddenly she
was deeply distracted from it, and in her eyes they were no longer

essentially together. Distressed by this, she has reached an intimation of what she will learn more distinctly later on in her search : that separation is an essential experience in the perfecting of a love and on the road to a consciousness of her own femininity. The first section of the tale ends with the hint of this as the lovers, in the security of their union, have the feeling that an opening out, a separation, is imminent which will perhaps give them the vaster unity of the four corners of the sky.

The talk about the mentally sick man 'G' which occupies most of the first section is somehow related to this intimation of the need for separation and furthermore to Claudine's own being. Claudine feels an affinity with this sexual deviant whose actions are judged socially evil. She thinks that he must believe his actions to be good, and her reason for this would seem to lie in the fact that G goes about stirring up his victim's erotic urge in such a way that it can never again find a single aim or a point of rest. He is an elemental and unconscious force, like Moosbrugger, and he opens up that realm of possibility for Claudine which is loosely connected to her past as a semi-nymphomaniac. He fascinates her because of the anarchic and asocial depths which she feels within herself. A man may do what is judged socially evil and still remain a good man, so Ulrich and Agathe, Clarisse as well as Regine in *Die Schwärmer* intimate time and again, for these 'evil' actions open up a realm of *Möglichkeiten,* a series of possibilities which have not as yet taken on the stultifying reality of concepts and values. Furthermore G causes Claudine to think of the essential solitariness of the mind which once again throws her back upon herself, away from her husband.

Hence what is presented in this first section of the story is the picture of a woman whom Musil later identifies as 'unhappy, ordinary and promiscuous', and who is essentially just any figure of femininity. Beneath the unity and rigidity of a pattern which is the love which she feels for her husband, lie vast unconscious depths of which she as yet only has a half-vague, half-aware intimation. Before she can come to a realisation of her own femininity and a perfection of love, these will have to be explored. Only then can the crystal of consciousness attain it full proportions and give Claudine that self-hood which comprises inner unity.

Erich Neumann in his book on Psyche and Eros, the basic myth of love, provides a revealing parallel to Claudine's situation in what he calls Psyche's feminine individuation. 'Love', Neumann writes, 'as an expression of feminine wholeness is not possible in the dark, as a merely unconscious process; an authentic encounter with another involves consciousness, hence also the aspect of suffering and separation.'[1]

On the train which will bring her to her daughter, Claudine thinks of her constancy and love for her husband. She notes, however, her frequent fearful rebellion against this state of togetherness which is an unceasing movement forward, a running hand in hand. In this mood of rebellion, Claudine realises that she is often faced with the temptation to stand still, completely alone, and to look around. At such times her passion for her husband is something compulsive and tyrannical which threatens to sweep her fragment of selfhood away, this as yet unformed self which provides a lure to further searching. Musil describes this lure in terms of a March sunlight aching with Spring, and hence suggests the possibility of Claudine's being reborn into a fuller self with the blossoming of summer and the pain which is implicit in any growth. It must be remembered that it is Claudine's husband who has planted the kernel of consciousness in her and has put some shape into her formless being. However, the rest of her development must be fulfilled in separation.

Claudine's relationship with her husband and her dawning self-realisation which will permit a unity between her inner and outer worlds, are still in a mere embryo stage when she leaves him. Her thoughts on the train, nevertheless, show the beginning of that reflection which will lead to selfhood. Here Claudine feels the whole accidental nature of her union with her husband and senses that another part of her exists which has somehow been lost yet which yearns for fulfilment in a different kind of existence, and which leads to a dark tunnel in her dreams. And she has the feeling that she is to suffer some unimaginable pain in love. As Neumann points out, this suffering and separation are what will lead to the possibility of perfecting her love with her husband and will allow her to attain a consciousness of her own femininity.

From the moment when Claudine boards the train, she embarks on a journey which leads her not only into her own past, that is into that stage of her existence where she acted separately from her husband, but also into the mythological and primeval depths of femin-

[1] Erich Neumann, *Amor and Psyche* (London, 1956), p. 85.

inity. Her journey is ultimately a search which takes place on two separate planes. On the lower one she regresses into the unconsiousness which forms her past existence and the deep memory of all women. In this state, alienation between the being which she feels within herself and the actions which she performs on an external plane is acute. On the higher plane, this journey into memory which is past as well as present and future, is a slow unfolding and growth of that kernel of consciousness which will lead to self-realisation.

> There was something remarkable in all her actions and experiences at that time . . . She performed and endured acts of a passion so strong as to amount to humiliation, but somehow never lost the awareness that whatever she did, basically did not touch her and essentially had nothing to do with her. (PD 166)

As Claudine begins to think of the unconsciousness of her past actions, her alienation from the world, she yet sees herself thinking and sitting quietly on the bank of the stream of life always running along at one remove from her. She is aware of some intimate integrity deep within her which has never as yet been clearly defined, but which is always present. It is this core of self which her journey will allow her to understand as everything within her is brought to consciousness.

It is interesting to note that as soon as Claudine leaves her husband, that is, as soon as she is free from that force which gave shape to her being—the formative love of the masculine consciousness—she moves step by step into her chaotic past and unconscious depths. The first beneficial aspect of this freedom is that she has once more embarked, totally alone, upon that path of possibility which is the proper realm of the feminine. She opens herself up to another form of experience and with her glimmering light of growing awareness, sees her existence with her husband as just another of the traps in which reality ensnares the passive being. It occurs to her that she is just like everyone around her, like those people whom she scorned in the row of identical houses when she was with her husband. Furthermore she realises that she has spent her life 'bound to one place and to one very small sense of herself'.

Stability provides a predicament if it is something that happens to one from the outside. Before Claudine can enter such a situation actively, thereby no longer feeling herself trapped in it, she must relive her experience as a woman and be reborn into a fuller being.

Her alienation from the world of external realities, which is visible in her entire experience, is much the same as that of Musil's other 'higher' women, who can find no home in the world. But Claudine performs the essential step in her journey to self-knowledge as she gives up all her protestation and struggle against this inability to belong to the masculine world of external and social realities. She allows herself to slip into the state of final passive strength which lies at the brink of the abyss and which comprises the anonymous root of femininity.

But what is it that lies at the core of the feminine experience of itself? Claudine intimates one aspect of this when she gives in to passivity, for 'that subtlest, ultimate passive strength of weakness' is what lies at the basis of the feminine principle, for Musil. This passivity is most obvious in the sexual make-up of the feminine : the woman's role lies precisely in living in the environment of being continuously desired by every male and in succumbing to his sexual embrace with that passivity and total sensual abandon which has always been hers. The feminine's 'natural' state—that is, her primal state—is this unconsciousness which fulfils itself in the darkness of love-making.

As Claudine continues on her journey through memory into primal stages of civilization, while continually remaining in the present and intimating the future, the root of the feminine principle becomes clearer. The sensuality of the imagery which Musil uses to describe this journey—the pan-like beard used to identify the sexual qualities of the stranger, the light in Claudine's hotel room casting five pale swaying circles like five sentries, which represent her easily-stimulated senses—sets the tone for Claudine's experience and realisation. Claudine feels herself travelling towards the roots of the feminine being and there is only the little light of consciousness which she has lit to allow her to know herself in this past.

And very slowly she began to feel as if she were actually not here at all, as if a small part of herself had wandered and wandered through space and years, and were only now waking up, far from herself and lost among the precipices, and she herself still stood in reality alongside that old absorbing feeling of dream. . . . The following morning, a queer atmosphere of the past pervaded everything. (PD 180–1)

What she encounters in this journey into the mythic past is the feeling that she has already been unfaithful since she has left her husband, without ever performing any act of adultery. This is due to the fact that the very nature of Claudine's inner environment, mirrored in the snow-bound town, puts her back into the primeval and unconscious stage of the feminine psyche—that stage where every woman is a hetaera. Bachofen calls this first era of human development the 'swamp stage'. In it each woman is a whore involved in anonymous lust and dark, unconscious embrace. It is a primal stage where the fertility of the species governs human action.

As Claudine correctly points out, by merely having a body, she is unfaithful to her husband. This is an intimation on Claudine's part of the hetaeric core of femininity and also a realisation that the basic physiological make-up of woman is somehow intimately linked to her psychological framework. This link is perhaps dangerous within society's restrictive set-up. However, it is also the reason why esoteric doctrine, notably Paracelsus, sees woman as a higher form of life than man. Closer to her body and her instincts than man, woman is also closer to knowing what both reality and possibility are about since she is constituted for suffering through the very fact that she gives birth. In the act of giving birth, she is firmly rooted in reality, but she also engenders possibility in the creation of a new being.

Claudine recognises her closeness to the physical, hetaeric core of femininity, which has dominated her past life filled with nameless lovers, when she meets her daughters' schoolmasters. In Claudine's eyes these schoolmasters are themselves creatures of a barbaric and mythic past.

And looking upon these masculine creatures whom at one point she calls 'ludicrously Olympian', Claudine thinks of the women who could take such men seriously. Then, suddenly, she is overcome by something which she cannot quite fathom—her own sexual instinct, whose shadow, like a shaggy animal, gives off an overpowering smell. She wants to whip this strange feeling into submission, but she receives a flash of illumination which shows her the depth of the feminine character. 'People like us might even be able to live with men like these', she thinks secretly. In this phrase she reveals her awareness of the basic hetaerism of femininity. The thought fascinates her and in trying to picture her husband, she can now only see him abstractly, as someone slightly faded. He too has suddenly sunk into that anonymous mass of masculinity which feeds the hetaera's lust and which comprises Claudine's mythic as well as actual past.

It is noteworthy that the men who present Claudine with this illumination are her daughter's schoolmasters, for the daughter in this way becomes symbolic of Claudine's own younger state. Her daughter's masters are those same early men to whom she consistently submitted. Here again Musil uses an exterior device to illustrate Claudine's interior thinking and feeling processes.

With this insight into the feminine's basic hetaerism, Claudine has come one step closer to a consciousness of her own femininity. As Erich Neumann says of Psyche, once she has brought light into the cave of sensuality where she and Eros live in a dark embrace, a rebellion is set in motion against the mythological and collective principle of sensual drunkenness. This is a rejection of the transpersonal love which has hitherto governed all life, and individuation is introduced into a world fascinated by the attraction and the fertility of the species.

Claudine's knowledge of her own passive and sensual core becomes more and more exact from this moment on. Suddenly her past falls into place and she sees her many submissions to anonymous love as part of her being. This is the aspect of her make-up which is far removed from consciousness. Yet it is more truly herself than any of the acts which she performs consciously.

> And suddenly, in a flash of illumination, she saw her whole life dominated by that inexplicable, unceasing betrayal with which—while remaining the same for everyone else—one cuts loose from oneself at every instant without knowing why, yet sensing in this that ultimate, inexhaustible tenderness, far removed from consciousness, by which one is more deeply linked to oneself than by any of one's actions. (PD 185)

This promiscuous element of her being, as she consciously realises its significance, loses its 'sick' qualities and Claudine takes note of the duality within herself. If it is as much part of herself to give in to any man as it is to single out one man, how is she to choose?

The two planes of Claudine's journey have now reached their mid-point. She has travelled into the nether realms of the feminine principle, the dark, chaotic, asocial world of hetaerism, and she has consciously recognised that part of her properly belongs in this sphere. The last part of her journey must now be completed. The feminine's possibility of attaining an equilibrium between herself and the outer world, together with a total consciousness of the core of her own femininity has not yet reached its full measure. Neither has full abandonment to the mythic and personal past, for Claudine has not yet performed her act of infidelity which is the final step in the lower plane of this psychological journey.

As Claudine remembers that the stranger desires her and prepares herself for her submission to him, the final part of her experience moves swiftly to its close. The term 'sodomy' which she uses to describe this submission is an ambiguous one. It could simply denote Claudine's perversity in succumbing to this 'Tier'. However, when Claudine follows this exclamation with an address to her husband in which she states, 'So that in the realm of reality you must feel it is I . . . I . . . here under this beast! The unimaginable', the implications of the term widen. It would seem by this statement that Claudine wishes her husband to recognise her infidelity by transferring himself into her and seeing *himself* as the object of the stranger's animalistic embrace. What Claudine seems to be asking for is a realisation by her husband of the manifold possibilities contained within the feminine and only given fixed form in that reality which, for Musil's women, always belongs to other people. Her husband, through her, must be released into this realm of possibility where he can come into relationship with the sick man, G. It is noteworthy that one of the last ways in which Claudine thinks of her husband is described in similar terms as the earlier depiction of this mentally sick man.

Thus Claudine proves her existence in that realm of possibility by committing an adultery which springs from the chaotic and annihilatory element, amoral and asocial, which is so deeply part of her. She does the unimaginable, just as the sick man G did within the sphere of fiction. Thus she once again establishes her contact with him. It is interesting that Musil time and again connects sickness with the road to consciousness as if implicit in each thing there is also its opposite. Sickness in *The Perfecting of a Love* would seem to signify the pain connected with the attainment of self-realisation and also the danger of imbalance which thwarts the individual dedicated to the search for selfhood. Claudine's pain in the struggle for consciousness is symbolized by an image which suggests a crown pressing into her brow, a diadem of dream glass like Christ's crown of thorns. Through suffering, she gradually comes to the end of her journey toward consciousness: she enters the 'swamp stage' and simultaneously realises the impersonality of the sexual encounter of the hetaera.

> It was as if something were there surrounding her and staring at her. She felt the man's excitement like something ablaze in a distant expanse of futility, something dark, pulsing, surging, in solitude. And little by little it began to seem to her that what this man desired of her—this act apparently so important—was something totally impersonal; it was nothing more than being stared at like this, with a gaze full of stupor and obtuseness, just as points distant in space which some incomprehensible thing has joined into a haphazard image, look at one another. (PD 188)

Claudine's consciousness of her own intrinsic being goes one step further as she is tested by the reality which this stranger, this 'third person' brings with him. He is in a sense that reality, that orderliness, which Claudine initially tried to shield herself from. He says of himself that he is 'merely human', but a whole man—that is, the representative of all masculinity. What Claudine realises in this encounter with reality is that her body, her senses, hold a powerful sway over her—a sway which makes her soul sick and which her unconscious depths must yet give into. But to become aware of this and to be freed of the guilt which is usually attached to such a recognition is to become fully conscious of femininity. As Neumann points out, woman must maintain that strength of and closeness to unconsciousness which is the essentially feminine element in her make-up.

Claudine, as she loses herself in sensual abandon on the rug in her hotel room, that rug which contains the smells and footprints of all humanity, experiences a sensual communion with the whole of reality. She embraces the physical and unconscious part of humanity. And once her body, in spite of everything, fills with 'voluptuousness' at the advances of the stranger, Claudine's initial guilt disappears and she feels a total all-salving equilibrium. She is innocent in spite of her adultery, and Musil, suggesting her newly found purity, rightly finishes the story with the mention of children talking of God.

Claudine has come to consciousness of her own femininity and

has succeeded in solving the duality of the choice between all men
and one. Her journey completes itself with a feeling of spring and
rebirth : a coming back into the innocence of the child while possessing the consciousness of the adult male—the god of love. She
achieves a total equilibrium of self. Following her inclinations, she
travels into the realm of possibility and she survives the test of
reality. Claudine's separation and suffering has resulted in an awareness of self. She has succeeded in taking that small crystal of consciousness, which is the male's gift to the feminine through love,
and expanding it to its full powers so that whole in herself and in
her separateness, she is now capable of the perfecting of a love. In
Claudine, Musil gives us the first example of the possibility of
attaining a synthesis between masculine and feminine principles
both within the self and within marriage.

The Temptation of Silent Veronika provides a parallel to Claudine's story and at the same time reveals the self-annihilatory characteristics which endanger the feminine quest for self-awareness.
Veronika is the dark side of the Claudine figure, for she travels further and further into the depths of her own being without succeed-
ing in exteriorizing, in bringing into the light of day, the chaos
which she finds there. Claudine's journey into the core of the feminine character is always guided by that strong male consciousness
which her husband represents and this saves her from totally abandoning herself to the dark, primitive forces which she discovers in
herself. She exteriorizes this inner turmoil and its powerful sensuality
by succumbing to the stranger and the concrete reality which he defines. Hence her flight into possibility, the unknown, is rewarded
with that consciousness of herself which allows her to harmonize
the dark and light aspects of her being.

Veronika, on the other hand, has no powerful enough male force
to stop her flow inwards, to awaken her with the power of reality
into the 'Klare' and 'Tagfeste' (the clear and that which is tied to
daylight order). Her tale becomes that 'wheeling and revolving of
things' which moves eternally within the grips of a never-advancing
centre. This, in essence, is the structure which Musil uses for Veronika's story : it contains no past or future, only a revolving round an
eternal present haunted by the ghosts of both. The characters in the
tale are themselves 'scattered fragments' like the voices of the diary
which Musil depicts in the opening paragraph. The coming together
of these scattered fragments would mean the attainment of whole-

ness for Veronika herself—a wholeness which is, in effect, a sound-ness and harmony of mind and body.

It is rather puzzling that Musil begins this story by stating that it is composed of two voices, for one could as well interpret its entire sequence as taking place wholly within Veronika or as the interplay of three voices, those of Johannes, Demeter and Veronika. Yet the fact that Musil does make this cryptic statement leads one to believe that Johannes and Demeter are really the fragments of one male being, which in its duality represents elements within Veronika her-self. It is noteworthy that all three are members of one family. For purposes of coming to grips with this difficult and haunting work, it is perhaps necessary to define what these elements actually are.

Johannes, whose voice begins the tale, speaks of some fearful crisis which has involved and suspended him between imagination and the reality of the daylight world. He tries to grasp that incom-prehensible other thing which exists in his imaginative world and pull it into the realm of reality, but his fear and his exhaustion will not allow him to do this. And in these moments, he gives this in-comprehensible other thing the name of God. He wishes to give this God actual existence so that he will draw him into his own strength. Johannes, here, represents the male world trying to define itself in a more rigidly metaphysical context, and parallel to this, he represents the male who wishes to merge with that superior form of conscious-ness which he can only call God—although the word only makes the feeling at its base lose its meaning. He suffers from the pain, the difficulty involved in trying to attain this consciousness. A vague *angst* accompanies his groping growth to knowledge and Musil describes his struggle in terms reminiscent of Claudine's crown of thorns pressing into her head. (We notice that this higher conscious-ness is, for Johannes, still vague and faceless.)

> And yet it happened—as if to draw a strength out of his weakness, a strength which he sensed and which lured him on as nothing else had ever enticed him except sometimes in his youth: the mighty, still faceless head of some great, but as yet obscure power. And one felt that one could grow up into it from below with one's shoulders and set it up as one's own head and merge one's own face with it. (PD 201)

Notably for Claudine, a woman, consciousness comes pressing down on her from above, from the realm of the male. For Johannes, on the other hand, consciousness is something one must painfully grow into from below, just as a child crosses the difficult path from youth into maturity. Yet, this something which Johannes must grow into and which he calls God has no firm substance in him as yet, only direction; it is still gliding beyond the present limit of his seeing powers and he can only intimate that it is a premonition of some wholeness that it is as yet too soon to comprehend. Hence, Johannes represents a consciousness which is not yet fulfilled and is certainly too weak to guide Veronika into awareness and equilibrium.

Mythologically one could say that Johannes is a St. John the Baptist figure intimating the coming of a full union between body and spirit in Christ, yet not himself the possessor of the kind of consciousness which allows this wholeness. He is a transition, a fragment of a possibility which can merely promise totality without achieving it. In relation to him, Veronika takes on something of the Salome figure.

Demeter's entrance into the tale comes at a point which reveals the position he holds in Veronika's mind. After Johannes has related to Veronika his premonition of this 'other thing' which can introduce wholeness into existence, he springs up and flings out his arms in a movement of almost physical desire.

It is the physicality and desire of this movement which brings Demeter into Veronika's thoughts, for Demeter is the embodiment of that pure animality which lies at the extreme pole of Johannes' straining grasp at consciousness and spirituality. Throughout, Veronika associates him with the pure sexuality of the rooster and with the two dogs with whom the peasant woman indulges in bestiality. Finally, when she sees him merely as a beard, he recalls the sexuality of Claudine's stranger. Demeter points out his role to Veronika in words which testify to his sensuality. He tells her that it is Johannes who inhabits the purely male domain of words, theories and hence, intellect, while he is the animal who attempts to draw out that core of sheer sensuality which is growing sick in Veronika.

It is telling that Musil gives this personification of brute sensuality the name of the goddess of fertility, for in this sense he clearly comes to represent that part of Veronika which is common to all women, the hetaeric quality of femininity. Within the terminology thus far used, Demeter is a messenger from the swamp stage of human development, the primal world of lust and impersonal, animalistic sexuality. And within this sexual realm, Veronika thinks of him as a stranger who can swallow her like a drinking animal. Like Claudine, she feels that all men who involve her in sexuality are indiscriminate, all are strangers. Yet, like Claudine, she also yearns for that union between action and being, a wholeness which Johannes calls 'God'.

Veronika cannot attain this totality unless the tension between Johannes and Demeter, one pulling her towards consciousness, the other towards the unconsciousness of hetaerism, is resolved within her. She is stretched out tautly between that which presents her with an intimation of a fully conscious and spiritual realm (Johannes) and that which draws her back into the primitive roots of a dark and sensual faith (Demeter). The resolution between the two must come from her, yet that force which draws her to consciousness and which would allow her to see the Demeter-powers in their proper perspective is not strong enough to guide her. She cannot go back to the hetaeric world of Demeter but, on the other hand, Johannes' 'faith' is not sufficiently defined to bring her all the way into consciousness. It is not complete enough to include her.

Johannes' weakness is clearly shown in that he backs down from Demeter's attack and his lack of 'seeing' power is evident in his inability to understand Veronika when she speaks about Demeter. Hence the story revolves endlessly around the poles symbolized by the two men, while Veronika moves further and further into an inwardness of illusion, an insanity. This sickness of illusion is well defined in Johannes' thought and his recognition of it makes it clear that he is the one dim light of consciousness in the tale: 'as if the two of them, standing there were a phantasy in an illness'.

This 'phantasy in an illness' haunts the entire timeless present of the tale in the figure of the old Aunt and in the image of the house, which in the earlier version of the story was called 'enchanted'. The old aunt and the house are the symbols which dominate the story and together they represent the entirety of Veronika's being, past, present and future. Claudine travelled toward her daughter, her youth and at the end of her journey, as at its beginning, stood the figure of her husband, the strong male consciousness. For Veronika, however, there is only the figure of the old Aunt, both virgin and widow, immolated in the enchanted house.

Once Demeter has told Veronika that neither he nor Johannes will marry her and has warned her that she will stay on in this house growing old like her Aunt, Veronika is continually haunted by this future which is already present. Her Aunt represents for her that non-being which is neither man nor woman, and which seems to be eternal. The Aunt is that undistinguishable force which Veronika fears she will become and already is. Like Veronika, the Aunt is neither masculine nor feminine because she is the 'eternal virgin' who has never succumbed to the depths of her own sexuality and has never quite attained that height of consciousness which is the domain of the male principle. Furthermore, she has that impersonal quality which Veronika sees in everything around her and is somehow associated with the house in which all four live. This house, like Claudine's hotel room, is an image of Veronika herself: it too is always in a twilight state between consciousness and unconsciousness, neither masculine nor feminine. Filled with creaking stairs and whimpering windows, gloomy nooks and crannies, like some dark labyrinth, Veronika's description of it clearly evokes the chaotic, fearful nature of an anarchic unconscious state. The small trickle of light coming from a 'high' window, is the glimmer of a waking consciousness which Veronika fears and which she ultimately rejects just as she rejects the man with a lantern in her willingness to see Johannes dead.

Thus, this house, together with Veronika's Aunt, becomes identified with Veronika's body: that which encloses her and that to which Johannes eternally returns, like a 'returning memory', like the 'wheeling and revolving' of things. However, he is never able to marry Veronika and to make his glimmering of consciousness her own. She sees him in the image of a Christ-figure walking through the wilderness of her life to which he gives some pattern. Yet Veronika will not permit Johannes, this precurser of redemption, to save her from her own wilderness. She gradually turns further and further inwards until she feels abhorrence for all that is not herself. Like Salomé, she prefers to kill the prophet rather than to emerge into the light of day where her virginity, her infrangible isolation, would naturally be shattered. It is only in Johannes' imagined death that Veronika can unite with him, for to be married to death, to be raped by it, is still to remain within a narcisstic and inviolable world of illusion. Veronika's sensuality here takes on the destructive quality of the raging Maenads. She symbolically kills Johannes in order to return to her destiny, which she feels is solitude and nothing else.

When she comes home after having seen Johannes off to his supposed death, she feels that she has shut a solid door behind her. Musil purposely gives the impression that this killing of Johannes and Veronika's subsequent return to a world of total illusion and subterranean madness—linked with the enchanted house of her own body into which she locks herself (PD 220)—is something which recurs eternally within Veronika's own memory. Like everything else, this too is part of the illusion of a deranged being.

Yet by killing Johannes, Veronika becomes a widow without ever having had to be a wife. She has made the perfect imaginative leap : she has become the Isis who takes her lover, husband and brother totally back into herself and achieves a perfect unity in giving birth to him in the form of a son. The wholeness which she feels, however, the unity between herself and her surroundings—the mystical ecstasy of being everything and nothing at one and the same time—is clothed in madness for it cannot come into the light of day. It can only remain within this enchanted house from which Veronika, at the end of the tale, like her Aunt, can never emerge. She can only stand at the door in her nightgown, experiencing imaginary rapes, waiting for Johannes' return—a Johannes who still stands tensely in conflict with the sensuality of Demeter. The temptation of a Veronika pulled between two extremes never reaches beyond temptation and she remains locked in the silence of her own madness.

In her moments of insane insight, which parallel those of Clarisse, Veronika sees why, symbolically, she has killed Johannes, or forced that departure which is like death. She thinks to herself :

> Children and dead people have no souls; but the soul living people have is what prevents them from loving no matter how much they may want to. That thing which in all love cannot give itself away fully is that very thing which gives all feelings a direction . . . But children and dead people, they are 'not yet' or they are 'no more'. Thus they allow one to think that they may yet become everything or have already been it. They are the hollowed-out reality of empty vessels which lend their form to dreams. (PD 220)

Veronika is faced by an insoluble dilemma. That very element which distinguishes one being from another and which motivates him in life is precisely that element which forces the separation and solitariness of each being. The soul, that kind of superior consciousness which has not as yet formed itself within Johannes, but which he nevertheless represents for Veronika, is that very thing which prevents people from unity with one another. For Veronika, however, it is also that thing which does not allow her to fulfil her sensuality on a purely bodily plane. Hence it prevents her from ever being able to attain a true equilibrium within herself. The soul is that which inflicts isolation upon mankind. Therefore, Veronika, by killing Johannes, has given him the impersonality of death. It is only with a soul-less Johannes that Veronika envisages the opportunity of union. She has followed the path of possibility which is the fully feminine one in the Musilian universe.

Since children and the dead are not yet anything or no longer anything, one can hope that they may yet become everything or have already been it. They are the perfect receptacles of total imaginative possibility. Veronika has cleared this path of possibility by ridding Johannes of his soul, his essential separateness. Yet the madness of Veronika's world becomes clear here, for by killing Johannes, she has also destroyed that very thing which was the only way to a confrontation with reality—a testing of the possibility within her. Without the test of the lucidity of day, the realm of unlimited possibility in which she lives becomes a realm which only leads inwards to destruction and madness. The separation which Claudine used to her own advantage by consciously coming to grips with her own dark core of femininity, Veronika is incapable of using beneficially, for she is not aware of the point where reality must be confronted, and where the inner must be exteriorized. Possibilities, Musil points out, are as yet unformed realities; but for Veronika the road of possibility leads only into the inextricable tangle of impossibilities and these form the totally inner and negatively-imaginative world of madness.

Through Claudine and Veronika Musil demonstrates what he sees to be the basis of femininity. In these two women he points out the unconscious hetaeric core of the feminine principle and how woman's closeness to this sphere allows her to be that embodiment of possibility which does not fear to perform the asocial or amoral act. The feminine, for Musil, is basically beyond good and evil : it is this which permits the feminine being to come to terms with her own being and to attain wholeness. Claudine is not afraid to proclaim that hold which her body has over her and to allow it to fulfil itself in an act which society would term 'immoral'. When the male, the being who represents that intelligence which governs the world of actuality, allows himself to be influenced by this feminine amoral and spontaneous force, a new world of possibility is born.

This feminine and unconscious force, however, must be tempered by a confrontation with reality, with masculine lucidity and control over form, before totality can be attained. If this confrontation is lacking, the inherently dark and destructive feminine power comes to the fore with annihilatory force, as is the case of Veronika. Hence an encounter and a union between the masculine and feminine principles is essential for a movement forward, for a 'Utopia' to come even partially into view. But inner harmony and with it totality, as Musil reveals, can only be attained by the woman, and here only in special cases, for woman's essential closeness to her physical, emotional and intuitive core equips her with a deeper insight into her own nature : a gift of her own femininity, when this is not allowed to corrupt itself by its own power.

THREE WOMEN

While in *Unions* Musil depicts femininity from the point of view of interiority as woman coming to grips with herself, in the volume entitled *Drei Frauen* (*Three Women*) he describes the effect of the feminine on the male world. In these three tales which bear the feminine titles of *Grigia, Die Portugiesin* (*The Lady from Portugal*) and *Tonka,* Musil never once presents the workings of the feminine mind unless it has already been sifted through that of her male counterpart. The importance of the feminine in these tales, however, is evident from the titles which Musil gives them and from the definitive influence which the three women have on their heroes.

It is pertinent to note the relationship between these three tales in the basic situation which they describe. In each a man comes into an uneasy association with a woman who represents a different culture and whose mode of expression diverges from his. The essential separation of the sexes is symbolized in this way and it lends an overtone of strangeness to each of the three relationships. Unified in theme, these three stories are also tied together in other ways and this inter-relationship seems to suggest that Musil intended the volume as a genuine trilogy. The first of the tales, *Grigia*, describes the hero, Homo, making his way to a remote Italian village which seems to be situated somewhere in a dark, primeval past where every woman is a hetaera bestowing her favours on any and all men. Fol-

lowing sequentially from this, the second tale, *The Lady from Por-*
tugal, takes place in a medieval setting of baronial and ecclesiastical
wars, isolated castles, belief in miracles, magic and the devil, all
suffused by the romantic light of courtly love. *Tonka,* the final tale,
brings the sequence up to the present and it is set in a modern German metropolis, where industry and science prevail.

The three women of these novella are essentially 'essays' moving
toward that completeness, that total definition of femininity, for
which Musil strives. The germ for *Grigia* lies in Musil's personal
war experiences on the Italian front. In his notebooks he describes
a setting which is almost identical to the one which Homo encounters in the primitive Italian village of the tale. This same section of
the notebooks contains reflections on the problem of fidelity and its
connection to religious feeling[1] which parallels almost word for
word those of Homo. Furthermore, the tale of the stranger returning from America or some other foreign locale and impersonating
the husband of several different women, finds its origin in this part
of the notebooks : its importance to Musil is evident in that he
repeats the tale once again in *The Man Without Qualities*. It would
seem that in Musil's mind there is some link between the experience
which Homo undergoes and that of the war. Indeed, the atmosphere
of being away from reality on some kind of strange, wild holiday
which is so prevalent in *Grigia* reflects Musil's feelings about war,
which he sees as an almost religious experience totally removed
from the bounds of everyday life. It might even be suggested that
the name Grigia, which the hero of the tale gives to his mistress, is
reminiscent of the colour of the Austrian army uniform. Like sol-
diers, banded together in an anonymous army, Grigia's 'greyness'
implies her lack of individual personality in this primal village.

Homo, the hero of the tale, is appropriately named for all mankind, and he succumbs to the temptation of following the ironically
named 'Mozart Amadeus Hoffingott', who would seem to represent
the Austrian emperor—Mozart Amadeus being Austria's quintes-
sential cultural product and Hoffingott suggesting her idealistic,
almost laughable spirit which can only lead to destruction. Following the call of the emperor, Hoffingott (who is fittingly in search
of a gold mine), Homo is plunged into a primeval environment
which is wholly outside the limits which civilisation has established
with such difficulty in the attempt to create order out of the chaos

[1] cf. *TB,* 172, *PD* 256.

of nature. War, like the search for gold, thrusts man into an irrational and primitive sphere of existence and this, for Musil, is somehow connected to the love experience which Homo undergoes. The
association between the feeling of primeval sexual lust which the
bare core of 'femininity' arouses in man and the experience of war
is well brought out in the passage where Musil describes the
drunken men listening to a gramophone record of a woman singing. (PD 239)

The effect of the singer's voice on the drunken men is depicted
in terms which suggest a woman in coitus and the madness of this
embrace brings the thought of war into Homo's mind. The passage
following upon this depicts a fly dying as it sticks to flypaper,
another favourite motif of Musil's, which once again suggests the
inescapable graveyard which follows upon war as men die like flies.

War, then, provides a powerful undercurrent to what otherwise
seems to be a simple tale of man and woman, and gives *Grigia* the
universality of a parable. Man entering upon war abandons all his
intellectual and rational powers and he loses his always somewhat
tenuous hold on consciousness and civilisation. What results can
only be destruction. Musil was always highly critical of the Klagian
philosophy which preaches man's return to the primitive and natural
state of matriarchy which Bachofen describes. In *Grigia,* he illus-
trates the danger which this return involves. In its linking of femininity, irrationality and war, this first of the novella is precisely a
criticism of Klages' anti-intellectual, back-to-nature (primary rather
than Rousseauistic) doctrine of mass enthusiasm.

The first fact which Musil presents about his hero's life is related
to the figure of Homo's ailing son, whose presence in the tale would
be almost irrelevant but that it serves to suggest the psychic disorder
within Homo himself, and within the relationship between his wife
and himself—his feminine and masculine parts. It is pertinent to
Homo's inner make-up that his wife, that aspect of femininity which
he has consciously learned to live with, goes with the child into a
state of convalescence—away to a spa. In his solitude and in the experience which he undergoes, Homo is the masculine counterpart
of Claudine. He feels the same incongruity as Claudine in the choice
one is forced to make between the one and the many, and Musil
thrusts him into that mythic and primeval past which formed the
core of Claudine's experience. Yet the effect of this experience on
the male is far different, for Homo abandons the light of conscious-

ness and totally loses himself in the world which he has entered.

Musil depicts Homo's journey into the primeval state of uncon-sciousness with great exactitude. The wallpaper on the wall of the room which marks Homo's first resting point, is a bewildering, labyrinthine maze. As Homo watches it, his hold on consciousness begins to slip away. In the prehistoric lake village where the com-pany makes its new home, each woman is a hetaera from Bachofen's swamp stage welcoming each man with her eyes and living in an atmosphere of continuous sensual desire. This becomes evident in the tale which is told about the village women welcoming any man as a long-lost husband; and again in Homo's confrontation with the Valkyrie-like peasant whom he questions about her virginity and who in response smilingly promises to give him, 'Alles! Alles!' (Everything!)

Homo senses the danger of giving in to this state where every woman is connected with the fertility of a nature capable of des-troying all that humanity has so arduously built up. This state may be natural to woman, as Musil shows in the story of Claudine, but for the man, willing to abandon his consciousness in it, it can only mean death—that death which is equivalent to a loss of intellectual awareness. Grigia, who is like the dry earth itself, embodies this hetaeric stage which is basic to the feminine and which links her totally to the irrationality of a nature both creative and destructive. Homo's dread before this omnipotent nature is evident:

> And one must not deceive oneself into believing that Nature is anything but unnatural: she is earthy, edgy, poisonous and in-human everywhere where man does not impose his will on her. It was probably this that tied him to the peasant woman and the other half of it was a never-tiring amazement at the fact that she so greatly resembled a woman. (PD 249)

Grigia is this fearful nature, but at the same time she resembles any ordinary woman. Homo's dread is linked with a fascination which will ultimately destroy him.

The relationship between love and death in the primitive state is clear in the various associations of the goddess, Aphrodite, with the god of war, Mars. Musil links love and death early in the tale in his description of the hetaerism of woman in the village and its relation to the old male peasant who looks like death. Both govern states which are irrational in the extreme. Homo, succumbing to his fascination for this state, loses all the powers which are proper to the masculine world and civilisation. The hero, like the men with him, no longer has control over words; and his intellect, like theirs, gives way to irrationalism and instinctual actions.

No longer master of himself in this hetaeric world, Homo feels that his affair with Grigia has happened to him almost as an accident over which he has no control and it has taken something away without replacing it. The old life in which he possessed the masculine principle of consciousness has disappeared together with his feeling of time and place. Because of this, Homo feels death—that ultimate stage of unconsciousness—approaching. He has lost all sense of reality. As Grigia entices him into that cave where his life is to end, Musil tellingly points out that he has lost all the 'civilised', that is, all the conscious man's need to light a match and explore his surroundings. At the very end of his adventure, Homo realises that all that has happened has only been in accordance with Nature itself which is governed by the unconscious and irrational female principle represented by Grigia.

In a sense, Homo's journey back into the primeval stage of existence, governed by the lust of hetaerism, has been a voyage back into the womb as well as forward into the tomb, for the womb is that place where man lies totally unconscious and within the power of the female body. The closer union which Homo feels with his wife in this hetaeric world is only natural : he has come to that area which properly belongs to femininity. Yet, as Musil shows, for man to lose himself in this world is disastrous, for the consciousness which is his basic quality is destroyed and with it that reality which man has created. Tempted by that possibility which the feminine, Grigia, represents, he has not had the strength to bring it into the light of day and turn it into a constructive principle. Hence only death can ensue as mother earth triumphs in her primitive aspect. Musil, who always insists on bringing any unconscious intimation into the light of day, shows the disaster which accompanies this triumph. The irrationalism of war, of the quest for gold, of hetaerism and the primitive state, can only destroy what man has built up. Ludwig Klages, with his enthusiasm for a return to a primitive state, always the object of adverse criticism in Musil's work, is answered by the voice of lucidity.

The Lady from Portugal marks the mid-point of this trilogy, not only because of its medieval setting, but because of the relationship

of man to woman which is presented in its pages. A perfect polarity
exists between Herr von Ketten and his wife, a balance which tips
toward the feminine side in *Grigia* and toward the male in *Tonka*.
This polarity is perhaps only possible because of the wholly fable-
like quality of the tale which permits the characters to exist almost
as abstractions of themselves, as symbols of that which Musil considers to be the most balanced and favourable relationship between
masculinity and femininity. With its miracles, devils, feudal wars,
and courtly procedure, this single fairy-tale of Musil's is the embodiment of what, ideally, the feminine brings into the masculine world
and the union which is thus achieved.

Herr von Ketten, who is only one link in the 'chain' of masculinity, is the representative of all that is intrinsically male in Musil's
vision of the human character. In joy, he glistens like the gold of
that wholly masculine principle, the sun. His power, Musil writes,
lies in his brow and his strength emanates from his forehead and his
eyes—the seats of the male intellect. He is the natural leader of men
and whether he uses violence or cunning to win his battles, he remains imperturbable and inexorable. His wife associates him with
the silent ferocity of the wolf and with the hard, impenetrable rock,
out of which his castle is formed. He is the male power complete
within itself.

Into this wholly male world comes the Portuguese lady, from a
distant land close to the feminine sea. She is that power which von
Ketten cannot comprehend. Like the moon, with which she is
time and again associated, she lies in polar balance to von Ketten's
sun. She brings into the cold, hard daylight world of the male, the
secrecy and otherness of the night. Musil has von Ketten appropriately visit her only secretly and at night, while he is occupied
with his feudal wars. Linked with the magical, mysterious and
spiritual power which is that of the moon, the Portuguese lady, like
her husband, is a being complete within herself.

> The figure sat there tranquilly in her rich gown with its skirt
> flowing down in innumerable rippling folds—a figure rising only
> out of itself and falling back into, like a jet of water in a
> fountain. And can the fountain's jet be released, be redeemed, ex-
> cept by a miracle or magic? And fully emerge from its self-borne,
> swaying existence? (PD 253)

Herr von Ketten wonders how he can set free this totally self-contained and elusive force—this 'femininity'—and bring it into relationship with himself by less than a miracle; for the Portuguese lady with her fine sensibility is a mystery to him, like the many strings of pearls which she wears. These pearls, again connected with the moon, are symbols of female sexuality, as well as of the spiritual realm, as Christ's parable reveals. And this form of feminine spirituality is totally foreign to the Herr von Ketten, who follows his enchantress like 'a poor lost soul'.

The drama which will bring these two separate forces into closer conjunction and will reveal the influence of the feminine, begins upon Herr von Ketten's return from the wars, when he is suddenly stung by a fly and falls into a smouldering fever. Not dead and not alive, von Ketten remains in a twilight state between awareness and unconsciousness for a long period. Symbolically his head shrinks, that seat of the masculine intellect, and he is now in a position to be worked upon by his female counterpart and the intellectual realms of miracles, magic and spirituality which she represents. Significantly he kills the wolf, that image of his past self, and waits for that event which will bring him out of his illness into a new totality. He cannot bring himself to use his old violent methods or his cunning to rid himself of the man whom he believes to be his wife's lover.

But the miracle does finally come in the unimaginable form of a kitten, who acts as a redeemer and, martyr-like, takes von Ketten's illness into itself. As the kitten dies, so does von Ketten's illness disappear, together with his lethargy: he performs that trial by ordeal which is demanded of the courtly lover if he is to win his mistress. Von Ketten, guided by the light of the moon, scales the stony heights which lead to the window of the 'moonlight enchantress' and he finds himself not only wholly cured, but also discovers that the other man has left with the rising of the moon.

Under the influence of the moon, and of the Portuguese lady from a world alien to the male's, a miracle has occurred. Musil points out its significance in the cryptic statement which his wife makes at the end of the tale: 'If God could become man, then He can also become a cat'. The Portuguese lady represents, for Musil, not that spiritually, that form of religion, which is institutionalised and which is depicted in this tale by the Bishop against whom von Ketten wages war; for that religion is actually a sickly and shrewd part of the male social sphere. Rather she is that mysterious freeing breath of spiritual possibility which, taken in, allows for the existence of what the outside world calls 'miracles'. She is, in the idealised world of the fable, the counterpart to the more existential Agathe, who is similarly associated with the moon.

With this embodiment of the feminine, the possibility of attaining the 'anderer Zustand'—the other condition of being—that mystical state of oneness and separateness between male and female, is given concrete reality. But the bright light of day which could test this flow of possibility in the Portuguese lady cannot enter the closed world of the fable and the tale ends with man and woman securely enclosed within the walls of fiction. In *Tonka,* the scepticism and lucidity of the daylight world of science arrive to test this otherness, and in the testing it is almost wholly destroyed.

Tonka is a composite figure, made up of the two women so far explored. In her Musil portrays the way in which the masculine eye of intellect will always, in a realistic and factual sphere, be incapable of comprehending the basic feminine otherness. The essential separateness of Tonka's nature is seen in her Cordelia-like muteness which cannot communicate the integral parts of her being in the words of the masculine world, but only in the language of the 'totality of things'. The anonymous 'he' of the story is the new scientific and empirical man of the twentieth century, who is interested only in questions with clear-cut answers; who rejects the emotions along with poetry, kindness and simplicity. Thus, only in his moments of intuitive insight when the garb of ambition and exactitude is shed, can the hero of the tale come to any communion with the ambiguous simplicity and complexity of Tonka, who takes into herself all that is basic to femininity.

Tonka gathers into herself both the qualities of Grigia and of the Portuguese lady. It is the male perspective which has changed and hence causes the drama to take a different turn. Like Grigia, Tonka is associated with that hetaerism which is the natural state of woman in the primeval world. This becomes evident in the point Musil makes of describing her background which is set on a stage of bawdy houses. Hetaerism, in the modern scientific and rational world governed by the male principle, by what Bachofen calls paternalism, is the proper sphere of the whore. But while in *Grigia,* the primitive society accepted the naturalness of this hetaerism, rational society looks upon it as a sin, a shameful way of life. Nevertheless, women, as Musil points out, although they feel the shamefulness of the prostitute's existence, also have something in common with it. Men, on the other hand, with their appreciation of reason and social obligations, cannot permit it. (PD 265) Tonka's aunt for example is quite willing to accept the visiting prostitute, cousin Julie, just as is Tonka, herself, for the breach between the woman and the hetaera is not large.

The hero of the tale sees Tonka's participation in this hetaeric world as mere innocence, but he feels something ambiguous in this innocence, when Tonka, at the age of sixteen, is still freely associating with Cousin Julie. This doubt concerning Tonka's link with prostitution rankles in the hero's mind and finds its culmination in his unwillingness to believe in her innocence and fidelity, after she has become pregnant.

Connected to Grigia in this ambiguous hetaerism, Tonka is further akin to this first of the three women in her identification with nature. The hero thinks, 'she has stayed like nature, pure and untouched', and later on he notes that she is like nature adjusting itself to mind. But this representative of the modern setting feels, unlike Homo, that nature consists of ugly little things and his attempt to make Tonka speak—to leave the muteness and the integral being which her folk-songs convey and to bring her into the realm of mind—result in her destruction. The tables have now been turned and man, dominated by intellect and science, can no longer leave himself wholly open to the influence of this nature, this feminine principle which is asocial and amoral.

This aspect of Tonka's character is linked with a further quality which ties her to the Portuguese lady. Twice Musil deliberately associates Tonka with the moon, the magical side of femininity which allows the coming of miracles, of unforeseen possibilities into the world. But, once again, in this rational universe so far removed from the fairy-tale of the Portuguese lady, the magical possibilities which Tonka holds in her being can only be denied. Musil, in one passage, clearly defines all that the feminine basically implies for him as it is summed up in the figure of Tonka. He also reveals how difficult it is for his scientifically-minded hero to come to grips with this femininity, precisely because the categories which shape the order of his mind cannot fathom this non-intellectual realm.

How inarticulate Tonka was! She could neither speak nor weep. But is something that can neither speak nor be expressed, some-

thing that disappears mutely into the mass of mankind—a small
line scratched into the pages of history—is such a life, such a
being, this snowflake falling all alone in the midst of a summer's
day, real or imaginary? Good, valueless or evil? One feels that
here traditional meanings have reached a limit beyond which they
cease to have significance. (PD 274-275)

Tonka is neither good nor evil, she is neither real nor imaginary.
Rather she is like a snowflake falling in the midst of a summer day,
that magical thing which lies at the utmost bounds of possibility,
while still remaining possible. Yet if one were merely told of its
occurrence, one would need faith to believe it. Furthermore, this
lone snowflake, like Tonka, introduces the not-yet, the winter which
is to follow upon summer.

This is what femininity, as such, represents for modern man in
Musil's vision. The poignant drama of Tonka reveals the turmoil
which an encounter with a being embodying this femininity can
cause in the mind of the rational man. As Tonka becomes pregnant
and diseased, the hero enters into a state of inner anguish, for he is
caught between two poles. It is noteworthy that Musil again introduces the motif of disease which has already been studied in the
two tales of *Unions.* Musil insists on illness as if somehow it were
a necessary part of the total equation of consciousness in the particular social period which he depicts. We find this same insistence
on disease in Thomas Mann's vision of the fully conscious artist tied
to the bourgeois milieu. Tonka's illness, here, incarnates the disease
within the hero's mind and the pain which is so intrinsically part
of the difficult path towards an attempted unity and wholeness. The
fact that Tonka's disease is a sexual one which taints man's birth
would seem to suggest that the hero's consciousness, at the end of
the tale, is similarly tainted, for he is, in effect, Tonka's child, a
creature formed by his memory of her. Considered more generally
this illness evokes the diseased attitude of the modern, rational man
toward all that is involved with sexuality.

When the hero first becomes aware of Tonka's pregnancy and
disease, he is caught in an insoluble opposition between the two
sides of his being. On the one hand, his rational, scientific mind tells
him that Tonka must have been unfaithful to him, since he was
away at the time of conception. On the other hand, Tonka's continual silence and ambiguous innocence leads him into dreams in which

he is almost capable of taking that illogical leap, that step of faith, and believing in what could only be a miraculous conception. He thinks to himself that in another time, perhaps the medieval sphere of *The Lady from Portugal,* Tonka's situation would have been hailed as miraculous and she would have been courted by great men. But unlike Herr von Ketten he is incapable of taking that ultimate step and allowing for the fullness of possibility. He is incapable of believing that 'If God could become man, then He can also become a cat'. Consequently his existence becomes a totally schizophrenic one, as in his day-to-day life he gropes further into the sphere of scientific discovery and exactitude; at night-time, in his dreams, he broods over the possibility of saying to Tonka, I believe in you. This final declaration, however, which could give the fairy-tale world of possibility into which Tonka gradually recedes, concrete existence, is never made. Tonka is left to the ravages of a 'deathly disease' which equally taints the hero. Man set in the modern world can neither consent to the amorality of hetaerism, nor to the magical possibility of a form of existence beyond logical comprehension.

After Tonka's death, the hero thinks to himself that what he has all this time been living with is not Tonka herself, but the embodiment of something that has called to him, the lure of the not yet, the breath of possibility. The significance of that integral feminine being which Tonka represents, however, only flashes through his mind and then disappears into his depths and into the quickly flowing stream of time. Only in this last tale, it must be noted, does time once again take on a linear, masculine direction. Although he has banished the feminine in him from his intellectual vision, the hero of *Tonka,* Musil suggests, is still a better man for his experience. Somewhere in his depths Tonka still exists together with the possibility that disease will eventually merge into its opposite, the wholeness of unity and self-realisation.

In the works which have yet to be studied, Musil attempts to bring this femininity and the possibility it is associated with, back into the world—into the light of day and the light of male intellect and consciousness. Musil, unlike the hero of Tonka, does not deny the hetaera in woman but attempts to bring it into perspective and unite its asocial and amoral qualities with the spiritual and magical elements which are also part of the feminine. Woman has the duality of being close to the earth and her body as well as maintaining a kinship to the realm of imagination from which all possibilities arise. To unite this to man's lucid intellect and sense of reality would be to achieve the ultimate union which could bring into being an earthly Utopia. The plays and *The Man Without Qualities* bring this 'not yet' into clearer focus and give it an intellectual definition.

THE PLAYS

In *Die Schwärmer* (Visionaries, or Enthusiasts), his first drama, Musil presents what is essentially the theoretical core of his final and greatest work. Each of the characters in the play is the embodiment of a network of ideas which lie at the centre of Musil's vision. Each is a type or a composite figure which will be more fully investigated in *The Man With Qualities*. The situation *of Die Schwärmer* is characteristic of Musil's work as it has so far been seen. The central problem of the play is once again the relationship of the sexes and the question of fidelity which arises from it. All the four characters of the play have known each other since childhood. Thomas, who is linked to Ulrich by his philosophy of 'possibility', has eventually married the majestically heavy Maria, conventional in her ideas about 'the good' and love. Regine, boyish, imaginative, anarchical, after a short marriage to another childhood friend, Johannes, who has committed suicide, has married Josef, an official in the Ministry of Education. (The connection to Agathe is evident here.) Anselm, a seducer, is also married. In his awareness that reality can only be perceived through emotions and intuitions, and in that Thomas insists upon his having been unmanned because he has given up masculine principles of intelligence and exactitude, Anselm has some ties with Walter in *The Man Without Qualities*. However, Anselm's marriage is only made known through Detective Stader's report.

When the play opens, Anselm has just lured an all-too-willing Regine away from Josef and the couple have found asylum in Thomas's home. The crux of the drama and its motivating force is that Anselm, in the course of the play, shifts his feeling from Regine to Maria, thereby asserting himself in his long rivalry with Thomas. He succeeds in inducing Maria to leave with him, after proving the depth of his emotions by burning himself with a cigarette and through a false suicide attempt. The pairs are then regrouped and Thomas and Regine find themselves together. What is pertinent here is the significance of the initial relationships between the characters and their regrouping, for by this movement Musil presents a fuller view of femininity and its role in the search for selfhood and wholeness.

Although, theoretically, Thomas and Maria would seem to be a couple capable of attaining a unity between themselves which would complete each of them in their own right, Musil reveals that this is not the case. Maria may have that feeling which Thomas essentially lacks, while Thomas abounds in that intellectual precision which could give shape to the formlessness of Maria's emotions, but there is a basic difference in their outlooks which cannot bring this potential into fullness. Wilhelm Braun, in an essay on *Die Schwärmer* points to the reason behind this failure : 'The marriage of Thomas and Maria fails because Maria's traditional, domestic values are frustrated by Thomas' failure to create a lasting and intense emotional relationship'.[1] Maria's search for fulfilment lies in the area of the conventional, in the area of *Wirklichkeit* (reality) and it is to this sphere that Thomas, who is still only a potential *Möglichkeitsmensch* (man of possibility) at the beginning of the play, cannot adjust. What Maria desires is the glibness of feeling expressed in flowery language (and Regine, it must be noted, criticises her for this taste) which Anselm, like Arnheim, is so ready to give, but which Thomas, with his lucidity and precision, cannot.

What Musil reveals is that Maria's ideas are false, because she is looking for a point of fixity, a stability within defined limits, which as Musil points out in his notebooks, is synonymous with death (TB 84). The ideal female characters in Musil's work must find themselves in a world which has no one fixed point. Maria, although she seems to give up her conventional values at the end of the play when she goes off with Anselm whom she now realises is already married, is really only taking that road which she feels will give her a greater emotional stability. The fixed point is still there in all the traditional romantic notions which she feels she will be able to concretise in the love which Anselm bears her.

It would seem at first glance that Maria challenges all that has so far in this chapter been described under the heading of femininity—for Maria is certainly not an amoral force who brings into the male world limitless imaginative possibility. Yet it must be remembered that the experience of the two women of *Unions* took place in a

[1] Wilhelm Braun, 'An Approach to Musil's "Die Schwärmer" ', *Monatshefte* 54, 156–170, p. 157.

timeless sphere of interior duration, and that of Grigia and the Portuguese lady in respectively primeval and medieval settings. When one arrives in the rational and modern world of *Tonka, Die Schwärmer* and *The Man Without Qualities,* however, a form of femininity wholly shaped in the image of the *Zeitgeist* comes into view. In *Tonka,* the representative of this type of the feminine is evident in the hero's mother; in *Die Schwärmer,* it is embodied in Maria. This feminine genre is essentially a version of the earth mother deformed by the world's movement away from nature, and shaped by what is the new natural state—society. The mother of the hero of *Tonka* is just such a new social woman. She disapproves of her son's relationship with Tonka because it does not conform to the social code's astringent division between classes. She incites him in his ambition to become a great figure in the scientific world and her life takes on a new meaning when her husband falls ill and she can relieve all her guilt by obeying that sense of duty and goodness—which are the rationalised remains of a Christian era—through nursing him. With this her life takes on a purpose, a direction which is approved by society. Modern society lauds the woman dedicated to goodness and charitable acts, but Musil looks upon her with an ironical air for she has falsified her own 'feminine' nature.

Maria in *Die Schwärmer* follows in the footsteps of this first of Musil's women defined by social standards in her role as mother. Anselm says to her 'you must sleep like the earth itself', and Regine likens her to a cow. Both images are reminiscent of Grigia, the first earth mother whom Musil describes. But Maria is no longer a *magna mater* indulging in hetaerism and she has lost the destructive qualities of this figure. Her hetaerism has been replaced by a false idealism, a desire to do good, 'frenetic good'. Her attitude to Anselm is always that of a woman going out to reform a little boy who does not quite know what he is doing. Although she is no longer destructive in the literal sense of the term, neither does Maria hold within her that sphere of imaginative possibility which is the gift of femininity to the male. Regine points out that what Anselm has committed with Maria is a 'cowardly flight into reality', for Maria in this play is the representative of reality.

There is a slight indication at the end of the play that Maria, by being thrown into contact with Anselm's amorality, has unkowingly taken the right step toward realising the falseness of her position and coming to terms with the core of her own femininity. It must be remembered that Anselm with his 'Verwandlungsfähigkeit' (transformational capabilities), his flexibility and his feminine involvement with 'Gefühl' (feeling), is in some ways that feminine force which Maria needs to encounter to achieve wholeness. Maria joined to Anselm becomes another of the 'visionaries' of the title of the play, although the success of this union is left as uncertain at the end of the drama as is that of Thomas and Regine.

It is Regine, however, who is more directly the embodiment of Musil's ideal woman of possibility. In her hetaerism with its asocial and amoral core, she incarnates feminine imagination and the will to make miracles occur. Regine, like Agathe, senses that basic split in the feminine character between what acts socially signify and their totally different inner value. She says to Stader who confronts her with the socially evil fact of her numerous adulteries, 'On the inside, one can be as holy as the horses of the sun god but on the outside, one is as your official documents have it. That is a mystery which your institute will never fathom'.

Totally asocial in her outlook, Regine possesses that integrity of self which allows her to indulge in hetaerism without suffering from the guilt which a paternalistic society imposes on the whore. She remains innocent and correctly tells Stader that this is a mystery which his rationalistic and scientific logic will never fathom. Her kinship with Anselm lies in this asocial and amoral viewpoint and, unlike Maria, with her conventional values, Regine recognises a purity in Anselm and the significance of his many lies. 'Lies assert themselves amid alien laws like a fugitive homesickness for dream-like familiar lands.' Lies, in their equivocality, are in essence one form of possibility, since they introduce into the world a dream, a wish for a place where man can be at home in the world. Regine says of Anselm as well as of herself—something which Maria cannot understand—'there are people who are truthful behind their lies and false before the truth'. Anselm and Regine are capable of living in the anarchic realm where defined values are non-existent, while still retaining their essential purity. They incarnate the idea which Thomas repeats several times in the play: 'One is never so much at home with oneself as when one has lost oneself'.

The alienation of these two characters, their inability to feel themselves at home in the conventional world of 'third persons' and their essential at-homeness in a world which is totally formless and hence filled with the possibilities of all that is 'not yet', influence Thomas to a great extent. It is by coming into contact with this abandonment of which Regine and Anselm are capable that Thomas becomes a true visionary, a full man of possibility. It is only then that his bent toward exactitude, scientific precision and hard-minded intellectuality is united with that formlessness and imagination which permits the coming of the 'Schöpfungszustand' (creative condition), the note on which the play ends.

So far one side of Regine has been explored, that side of her which is linked to Anselm and the anarchic, formless world of the hetaera. Her second side, that aspect of femininity which is related to Tonka and the Portuguese lady and which truly allows her to unite with Thomas in order to bring the 'visionaries' into being, must now be examined. It is noteworthy that Musil in his directions for the play says it must be composed equally of imagination and reality. With these words he sets the scene for that union between reality and imagination which is the proper harmony between what Regine and Thomas represent. He describes Regine as something formless, indefinable, both youth and woman and in possession of a dreamlike magical quality. The hermaphrodite concept is one which is very close to Musil and would seem to signify for him that mixture of male and female elements in a being which are prerequisites for inner wholeness and harmony. Boylike and yet woman, Regine would seem to contain in herself those possibilities for intellectual development and full consciousness which are the male's, together with those characteristics which are essentially female. The hetaeric aspect of her femininity has already been pointed out; that second magical quality must now be investigated.

Die Schwärmer opens precisely with this mention of Regine's secret strengths, those mysterious personal powers which link her to Veronika as well as Clarisse, although Regine does not travel the full path to that madness which is associated with dreams and imagination. These mysterious and miraculous powers of Regine's are related to her belief that she has been in close communication with Johannes since his death. They are further illustrated in the stories of metamorphosis which Regine relates about her childhood (PD 305, 359). Regine, however, has the strength of consciousness to realise that these miracles can find no concrete existence in the present reality. It is in this that she differs from Clarisse. Yet the imaginative faculty is strong in her, just as is her feeling for her childhood, and at the end of the play there is still something in her of the fairy who wishes to be able to bring good to people (PD 380) —although the magic formula of her youth has gone and the people in her life have been narrowed down to Thomas.

'For me, a thing is only true as long as I keep silent' says Regine, in a statement reminiscent of Tonka's muteness. Indeed, all the women in Musil who represent the sphere of imaginative possibility and spirituality have difficulty in expressing themselves, for inner thoughts once placed into the external world take on the form of lies. This is due to the basic impersonality of language and furthermore to the fact that the imaginative can only have a full existence in the mind when it is unaided by the precision of intellectual expression. Regine's wailing in the play is the only true expression of her inner world: when Thomas pictures their union in a dream, Regine once again speaks through a wail, no longer hysterical, but 'gentle and beautiful'. (PD 397)

It is in Thomas that Regine finds her true partner, for she is the embodiment of that possibility, that *not yet,* which must be given form by the exactitude of the intellect. Before the end of the play, Thomas can only theorise about the 'man of possibility' in an attempt to convince both himself and Anselm of their similarity. But Anselm, who is one small part of the man of possibility, answers Thomas with the statement that all he is saying is mere theory. Essentially, he is correct. Although Thomas is intellectually aware of possibility, he is not capable of acting upon it. It is only when he and Regine come together in that 'phantastische Hauskleidung' (fanciful housedress) which is an intimation of Agathe and Ulrich's pierrot costume on the night of their first meeting, that the man of possibility is given more than theoretical existence. It is the feminine who initiates those acts which are the forerunners of the *not yet,* for she acts outside the bounds of social convention and attempts to exteriorize her imaginative existence. But it is the man who must give these formless acts a shape, take that possibility which has been introduced and fashion it into a form of concrete reality. As his 'wild sister' says to Thomas, 'I have always had the comfort that if things really got quite out of control, you would be able to create order. You will make everything that I have done appear good and right' (PD 375).

Although there has been a confrontation between that pair who, together, could form an ideal working union, Musil, at the end of the play, presents no definite hope of the successful outcome of this union. The solitariness of the individual who is not at home in the world prevails and possibility is given no concrete existence for more than a fleeting moment. Thomas hesitates to act for one instant too long and there is a suggestion that Regine has run out in order to commit suicide. The visionaries remain only visionaries without finding an outlet in the world for their dreams. The wish for completeness remains something to be attained within the individual alone.

In the second play, *Vinzenz und die Freundin bedeutender Männer* (Vinzenz and the Friend of Important Men), a similar situation is described in a farcical mode. The characters are shorn down to their bare essentials. Except for Alpha, her husband Apulejus-Halm, and the love of her youth Vinzenz, we are shown only representatives of society defined by their profession. Alpha, the name which her husband has given her, suggests the first—the embodiment of that which is essentially feminine. As the critic Wilhelm Braun puts it, 'She is hazy and imaginative, has no borders or outlines and thus contrasts with her friends who are professional and sharply delineated'. Vinzenz is her male counterpart : cold and logical, and, like Ulrich, a mathematician. The two are linked to each other by their attitude toward possibility. They are both experimenters in life and they cannot be tied by anything. (PD 419)

As the title of the play suggests, the plot revolves around Alpha's relationship to Vinzenz and her relationship to the important men of the world who form her own private harem. In her Musil portrays most directly what he believes to be the feminine role in the world. Surrounded by the masculine forces of society—a merchant, a scholar, a musician, a politician, a reformer and a young man— Alpha exerts her influence on these men by talking to each specialist about the field of another. Her tactics are those which make the world shift its perspective so that each of her admirers is led to reflect about his position and see its limits. She acts as a disturbing critical force and attempts to widen each man's imaginative horizon.

This is most clearly brought out in the case of Barli, Alpha's most ardent suitor, who threatens suicide if she refuses to marry him. The values which Barli used to respect and which permitted him to become a rich merchant have disintegrated because of the light which Alpha has shed on them. As a result he can find no fixed definition in his life, no meaning on which to base his existence. 'One is never so much at home with oneself as when one has lost oneself', Thomas has said, and Alpha exerts her influence precisely in the direction which will force each man to lose himself and in this state to recognise himself. Alpha is the embodiment of imagination, of manifold possibility: coming into contact with any fixed idea or value, she shakes it to its foundation by the very act of revealing its limits. When Barli in his second, this time staged, attempt to kill Alpha and then himself, asks her for answers to his questions about life and demands that they have an immediate and logical significance, she is incapable of giving them. For in the imaginative realm, nothing is so simple, so direct. Alpha's intuitive grasp at answers leaves Barli's desire for masculine intellect and judgment unsatisfied. There is nothing fixed or inflexible, nothing limited about Alpha and even her femininity shades into a 'wonderful boy-like quality' as does that of all Musil's ideal women.

In Vinzenz, Musil creates a character who is a combination of Anselm and Thomas and the immediate predecessor of Ulrich. The perfect antithesis to Alpha, Vinzenz is the only man among her admirers who lacks the ambition and defined seriousness which would ensure his success in the world. Like the man without qualities, he sees around everything and everyone intellectually and is thus incapable of settling into any one mode of life or for any established truth. Every fact, every occurrence has its opposite for Vinzenz: 'If you maintain that the sun revolves around the earth, then according to the latest research you are no less wrong than if you say, the earth revolves around the sun. Mothers sacrifice themselves for their children, but they also sacrifice their children. Fire consumes and fire nourishes. Man makes order because he makes a mess and he makes a mess because otherwise he would have no need for order' (PD 433-434). In a paradoxical universe, nothing has a fixed or stable value, and everything is possible. Vinzenz is the perfect Musilian dialectician eternally positing opposites without ever achieving a solution.

Vinzenz's lying, like Anselm's and Regine's, is an experimental approach to life: lying, here, is not a denial of truth, but a wish, a possibility. 'But what is it to lie? To say of something you desire that it is the case, rather than that it ought to be the case? . . . The fantasy-liar is he whose lies agree with the facts!' A true possibilitarian, Vinzenz gives factual existence to his 'lies'. This is evident in his stage management of the play—the false murder attempt by Barli and the scene between Alpha and her girl friend, both of

which he plans. This is the concrete manifestation of Ulrich's desire
to 'live life as literature'. Furthermore, there is Vinzenz's fantastic
gambling scheme. All these 'lies' allow for wishes to be lived out
on an illusory plane and they provide the same sensations which
they would if they were real.

Intrinsically a criminal like Anselm in his amorality, Vinzenz,
Musil reveals, yet attempts to create some order in the chaos of the
world. His work is that of a statistician—and what is statistics but
the attempt to order the confusions and complexities of the social
sphere? But this attempt is a failure and the play ends with Vinzenz enunciating a code which is reminiscent of Anselm's. If one
cannot find a home in the world, one can only live through another
person. Thus the servant's position is the one Vinzenz chooses.
Once again the attempt at union and at concretizing possibility fails.

Nevertheless, in this farce, Musil comes one step closer to identifying theoretically the vision which will form the basis of *The Man
Without Qualities*. Alpha, in her imagination, intuition, flexibility
and lack of social scruples is the bare feminine archetype, the actual
embodiment of possibility; while Vinzenz, cold and intellectual, is
the theoretical possibilitarian and social criminal, the core of the
man without qualities. Given these two perfect counterparts, Musil,
in this farce first describes that 'other condition of being' which is
the actualization of possibility in the world, the mystical union
brought into the light of day through love and union between the
male and female (PD 421). But Vinzenz feels that this state of
mystical harmony between man and himself, woman and nature
cannot last—it cannot have duration except in art, in the fixed form
of a Bernini sculpture. Therefore he leaves the young Kathi and
when they meet again this union is no longer possible. Musil, however, will attempt a definition of this 'other condition of being'
once again in the union of Ulrich and Agathe. It is to *The Man
Without Qualities* that one must finally turn for a full understanding of Musil's vision.

THE MAN WITHOUT QUALITIES

The last twenty years or so of Musil's life were spent writing the
vast and complex work which marks the culmination of his art and
vision. *The Man Without Qualities,* however, remains an unfinished
book and one *defying* completion. Even if Musil had lived for

another ten years, it is doubtful whether he could have found anything other than a contrived and fictional end for his work; for in
his attempt to investigate objectively all sides of the modern dilemma
and to present the seeds of an operative solution to the human problem, he surpassed the bounds which even a man of his intellectual
strength could cope with. His book can have no 'ending' as such.
It can only terminate. This is now the general consensus among the
critics who have studied Musil's manuscripts and notes. Musil's
constant positing of dialectical opposites and his unwillingness to
enter upon a systematization of ideas seem to necessitate the writing
of a book which can provide no close.

Added to the threat of dissolution which haunts the first two parts
of the book in the form of the First World War, is the intenser
menace of Hitler and the Second World War which Musil had to
face in the last years of his life. The latter part of Musil's notebooks
are filled with thoughts about this disaster and his concern could not
fail to influence the writing of the 'final' part of *The Man Without
Qualities*. This perhaps accounts for the change of tone between
the first and second sections of the book, which are socially oriented
and written in the mood of a consummate ironist, and the section
'Into the Millenium', with its stress on the personal and mystical.
This section of the book which leads towards the experiment of the
'andere Zustand' was to find its culminating point in the chapters
Musil wrote in the last weeks of his life and which terminate with
'Breath of a Summer's Day'. But what next? There is sufficient
evidence to suggest that the experiment of 'the other condition of
being' is not a success, at least on a wider than personal basis. It does
not serve as a total solution to the human dilemma. Musil, having
portrayed the possibility of a mystical synthesis, would then seem
to return to the social sphere where the failure of any synthesis can
only lead to the chaos which is equivalent to war. *The Man Without Qualities* emerges as a presentation of the problems of a world
of endless possibilities and equally endless horrors. It remains the
total study of a troubled era of civilisation, whose problems cannot
be glibly solved. Musil can only present the germ of a redeeming
vision, one more possibility which he knows very well is not viable
in prevailing conditions. Before change is possible, man's entire
way of seeing and feeling both the universe and himself must be
drastically altered. What Musil describes in the last completed part
of his final work is the bare embryo of this new being.

In an interview with Oscar Maurus Fontana, Musil defines the way in which his work must be approached. He points out that he is far more interested in the public's investigating his ideas than his aesthetics, and adds that his final book is a search for an analysis, a dissolution of old values, and the suggestion of a synthesis for a world hindered by an archaic morality (TB 788). In keeping with Musil's directions, this study of *The Man Without Qualities* will concentrate on his material rather than his stylistics and attempt to define the nature of his vision, his 'suggestions for a synthesis'. Femininity plays a crucial part in this vision and provides an approach incorporating the central aspects of this encyclopedic work.

To give this study a coherent form, it is essential that the book be divided into those two parts already mentioned. The first section will deal generally with the social side of Musil's vision and his ironical depiction of the society women whom Ulrich encounters in his year of holiday from life. What remains then is the Utopian and personal part of Musil's vision—Ulrich's union with Agathe— which will form the second aspect of this study. But before the impact of the feminine on Ulrich and his counter-influence can be explored, one must have a fuller picture of this final Musilian hero.

Ulrich is the culmination of all of Musil's heroes from Torless to Vinzenz. He brings Torless' concern with imaginary numbers, with the 'unreal' able to function in a real context, into the adult sphere. Significantly he is a mathematician, for it is only the mathematician who, in a rational world, is permitted to work with the unseeable and still have an influence upon the ways of the world. Like the anonymous 'he' of *Tonka*, Thomas and Vinzenz, Ulrich is the modern man of science who attempts to apply the scientific principles of objectivity and intellectual exactitude to those areas of behaviour which are essentially opposed to order and precision.

Apotheosis of a relativistic universe, Ulrich, like his creator, can never settle upon any one fixed point, any absolute, for like Vinzenz he is capable of seeing the validity of any opposite view. As Walter, his polar opposite in the male world, says of him:

> You can't guess at his profession from what he looks like, and yet he doesn't look like a man who has no profession, either. And now just run your mind over the sort of man he is. He always knows what to do. He can gaze into a woman's eyes. He can exercise his intelligence efficiently on any given problem at any

moment. He can box. He is talented, strong-willed, unprejudiced, he has courage and he has endurance, he can go at things with a dash and he can be cool and cautious—I have no intention of examining all this in detail, let him have all these qualities! For in the end he hasn't got them at all! They have made him what he is, they have set his course for him, and yet they don't belong to him. When he is angry, something in him laughs. When he is sad, he is up to something. When he is moved by something, he will reject it. Every bad action will seem good to him in some connection or other. And it will always be only a possible context that he will decide what he thinks of a thing. Nothing is stable for him. Everything is fluctuating, a part of a whole, among innumerable wholes that presumably are part of a super-whole, which, however, he doesn't know the slightest thing about. So every one of his answers is a part-answer, every one of his feelings only a point of view, and whatever a thing is, it doesn't matter to him what it is, it's only some accompanying 'way in which it is', some addition or other, that matters to him. (MWQ I 103-104)

It is Walter who first gives Ulrich the apt title of the man without qualities, for although Ulrich has many characteristics none of these seem to belong to him, none are a definition of his being. This is due to the fact that Ulrich can take none of these qualities seriously and focus his ambition on it. Since these qualities remain external to the man, he is in a 'literal' sense a man without qualities. And it is the property of this paradoxical being that he can look out upon the world with a clear, unprejudiced eye and throw a new perspective on all that is established and taken for granted. It is to woman that this man without qualities appeals most highly, as Clarisse indicates in her response to what Walter believes is a negative description of manhood. 'I think it's very nice of him', she says and her statement will be echoed in various ways by the other women of the book.

The relativistic man of science *par excellence*, Ulrich has yet another side which he reveals only to himself and briefly to Diotima in the early parts of the book, and more fully in the section where he encounters Agathe. This hidden aspect of Ulrich, Musil indicates in one of his fullest descriptions of his hero, is a driving passion for some unknown element which will allow him to achieve totality and change the face of things. This second Ulrich is the visionary, the man of the 'not yet', who will be capable of allowing the influence of Agathe to work on him in the hope of achieving a mystical union and a wholeness in life. Musil makes the split in Ulrich between the cynical man of science and the Utopian visionary clear.

> In this moment two Ulrichs walked side by side . . . But while the one walked through the floating evening, smiling at these thoughts, the other had his fists clenched in pain and anger. He was the less visible of the two. And what he was thinking of was how to find a magic formula, a lever that one might be able to get a hold of, the real mind of the mind, the missing, perhaps very small, bit that would close the broken circle. This second Ulrich had no words at his disposal. (MWQ I, 204–205)

It is these two aspects of Ulrich which find their expression in the concept of 'Essayism' and that of 'metaphor'. This latter is particularly interesting in this context, for a metaphor is that perfect union between truth,—that is, the reality of fact—and falsehood or fiction. The ability to achieve a synthesis of these two elements outside the realms of art and dream would indeed mean that the Musilian Utopia had found root in life. It is this union between the two parts of a metaphor—between reality and dream or art, between understanding and feeling—that Agathe and Ulrich attempt to establish in the concrete world. This is what defines the Millenium. These two parts of the metaphor are linked with the masculine and feminine principles as Musil defines them. While the male provides the side of 'reality' through his intellectuality, the female provides the 'falsehood', the imaginative element related to art.

The figure of Moosbrugger, the rapist-murderer of the novel, is somehow linked to that of Ulrich and haunts the hero throughout the first two parts of the book, for Moosbrugger, in his mixture of madness and sanity is the parallel and reverse of the man without qualities. In his moments of madness, which he values above his sanity, Moosbrugger achieves that union of inner perceptions and outer happenings which is rarely attained by mankind. Moosbrugger is 'musical' to Clarisse, because he attains in reality that 'unity of being', which is only possible for others in music. Hallucination is his reality and Moosbrugger thinks in the manner of the metaphor —that synthesis between fact and dream. Parallel to Ulrich in this search for unity, Moosbrugger is yet the hero's reverse, for with him

—and this is where his madness lies—there is no concept of the limits of unequivocality. This criminal is incapable of logic, of rational thought. Hence his wholeness remains within realms which are inacceptable to society, while Ulrich, on his own, cannot attain unity precisely because of his strong intellectual side.

Yet Moosbrugger is an elemental force who mirrors the disintegration of modern man. Like Ulrich, he holds up to view society's archaic moral code which can judge him no more accurately than it can judge the hero. From one point of view, the murder which Moosbrugger commits is his expression of the frustration and alienation which a capitalistic social system forces upon him in its unwillingness to allow him to attain a position of prestige. It is murder which, if the majority of men allowed their aggressions to appear fully in day to day life, would result in mass homicide. As such, it is also a prefiguration of the war which stands ominously at the close of the book.

If society could dream collectively, Ulrich points out, it would dream Moosbrugger, for Moosbrugger is merely the distorted pattern of the common elements of existence. This suggests the mass homicide mentioned above. For Ulrich, however, this criminal further represents the basic anarchism which man needs to experience before he can create a better and different state. In this, Moosbrugger is somehow connected to Agathe with her social and moral imbecility. When Agathe tells Ulrich she would like to kill Hagauer, he answers her with a statement which not only explains her desire, but also Moosbrugger's position as a collective dream of mankind. 'One might almost say our evil wishes are the shadow-side of the life we really lead, and that the life we really lead is the shadow-side of our good wishes' (MWQ III, 100). Moosbrugger is the evil wish, the shadow side of life given actual existence, and he is important in defining that which must be and is yet to come.

There is a further and in this context more important relationship between Ulrich and Moosbrugger. Both men despise the prostitute, the hetaera in woman and the way in which Moosbrugger goes about explaining his hatred and acting upon it throws a new light on Ulrich and clarifies his own attitude toward the feminine. Musil describes Moosbrugger's murderous encounter with the whore in terms which suggest that this manifestation of femininity is really part of himself, his shadow side. Persistently the girl runs along beside Moosbrugger as if she were his shadow and nothing he can

do will scare her off. He thinks to himself that behind the woman
there is always the other man sneering at one and suddenly he is
faced with the idea that the girl looks like a man in disguise. Nothing he can ever do will rid him of her, for it is he, himself, who is
drawing her after him. Thus this 'caricature of a woman' as he calls
her, becomes identified with a splinter he once had in his leg and
which he cut out himself (MWQ I, 114). In the same way he tries
to rid himself of this woman with a weapon which ambiguously
comes from 'his or her pocket'. Musil is suggesting that the whore
is actually part of Moosbrugger himself and that his murder is a
symbolic suicide—an attempt to do away with the feminine in himself.

Hence there is more to Moosbrugger's murder than the obvious
explanation that what is sexually repressed must eventually find its
expression in a destructive act, for Moosbrugger is not merely ful-
filling his natural desires in a perverted way. By ridding himself of
the prostitute, he is not only ridding himself of his sexual urges.
This becomes evident in the later 'Moosbrugger Dances' chapter
where Musil specifically defines the reasons for Moosbrugger's murderous act.

> A woman you don't have is like when the moon at night is rising
> and rising up the sky, sucking and sucking at your heart. But
> when you've had her, you'd like to stamp in her face with your
> boots on. Why was it like that? He remembered that he had
> often been asked about this. Well, you could tell them: women
> are women and men. Because men chase after them. But that was
> another thing that the people who asked him could never manage
> to understand properly. They wanted to know why he thought
> that people were plotting against him. As though even his own
> body weren't in the plot with them! With women it was quite
> obvious, of course. (MWQ II, 115)

To Moosbrugger women are women *and men* because men chase
after them, men desire them. Hence in his killing of the whore,
he is killing that part of himself which desires woman and is
woman. The prostitute is symbolically a well-chosen victim, for as
the modern hetaera, she represents that primitive area of human
instincts from which an ever more domniant male civilisation has
attempted to escape. By doing away with the prostitute, Moosbrugger is also trying to do away with that part of the male which desires

her, that part of himself and universally of mankind which refuses to obey mind and is in a state of chaotic unconsciousness. In his own elemental way, Moosbrugger is searching for consciousness. This is reflected in his continual wish to be able to use words, professional and legal terms, which are the proper instruments of the male world. If he could only use words, he feels, he would be able to handle all that is happening to him.

Moosbrugger's attitude to femininity in its hetaeric aspect reflects that of Ulrich, and in his own primitive way he too is trying to come to terms with the problems that confront the hero. It must be noted that Ulrich's encounters with woman in the first two parts of the book have similar overtones, for in each of these encounters, once lust has given way, Ulrich is overcome with contempt for the objects of his desire. Pertinently, the first woman with which he is involved, Leona, is purely and simply a whore; and as he moves up the hierarchy towards Bonadea, Gerda, and finally Diotima (who in an unpublished sketch, succumbs to Ulrich), he systematically attempts to subdue the prostitute in woman and that part of him which submits to her. As he says to Agathe, his love for woman is really a hatred for all mankind: for Ulrich, too, woman is woman and man, and through his sexual reduction of her, he is attempting to refine everything in man which is primitive and irrational as he scales the difficult path to consciousness and total selfhood. Ulrich's disgust for the hetaeric core of humanity only turns to acceptance in his relationship with Agathe, and here, it is relevant to note, it is not the essentials which have changed, but the attitude toward them, for Agathe seen from the outside is as ordinary a woman as any other. Musil's perspective however, and with it Ulrich's has moved from the external viewpoint of social satire to the more receptive inward eye of the visionary.

Each of the women in the female hierarchy of the first two parts of *The Man Without Qualities* marks a step upwards in Ulrich's search for a unity in life. At the same time, each of these women is a comic heroine in her own right, embodying the essentially feminine and the divergences from this feminine—the falsities which her character has accrued in a world inevitably headed for destruction. Moving from Leona, to Bonadea, Gerda and finally Diotima, the path is relatively clear; it is only Clarisse and the final woman in this early hierarchy who looms over past, present and future, the Frau Major, who must be given special attention for they are intrinsically connected both in their being and in their effect to the ultimate embodiment of femininity—Agathe.

Some mention of Leona has already been made and since Musil handles her very briefly, one can follow his example and do the same. Her importance lies in that Musil chooses her to be the first woman whom Ulrich confronts. Appropriately she is a cabaret-singer and a whore, a hetaera, and she represents that primitive foundation upon which the feminine is grounded. Even in Leona, however, this feminine root has been perverted and her sexuality is diverted into an ambitious gluttony—a taste for special foods which for her signify a higher social standing. Faced with what she considers exotic and aristocratic food, Leona reaches a sexual pitch and then she responds languidly, but readily to masculine advances. The simplest and hence the most natural of the book's women, her primitive lust, her motivating principle, is expressed through an equally primitive desire for food and Leona does not stray far from the essential feminine. Yet even she, as has been seen, has a certain fascination for Ulrich, a certain quality not apprehendable by masculine intelligence alone. And although Ulrich gives her the animal name of Leona, he also likens her to a 'Juno', to a supremely feminine being, for Leona has an inexpicable something which was the property of godlike queens in past ages.

In Bonadea, Musil presents a Claudine seen from the point of view of society, for Bonadea, like Claudine, cannot control her desires, and yet is overcome by guilt every time she indulges in another nymphomanic adventure. Unlike this earlier woman, however, Bonadea does not arrive—except perhaps in a humorous sense—at any acceptance of her natural desires and at subsequent equilibrium. She is continually plagued by a conscience formed by social standards which yearns for a high intellectual tone in love. This is evident in her attempt to model herself after the high moral mode of Diotima, once she becomes aware of this supposed competitor for Ulrich's attentions. Bonadea is, however, essentially an earth mother, a primitive Aphrodite, caught in a world which does not approve of her primeval morality. Ulrich feels something 'maternally sensual' about her, and speaks of her 'maternal beauty'. In her truest moments, Bonadea is 'motherly', although again this motherliness finds its expression in a form of charitable idealism which is the age's image of the great mother.

From the social point of view (and it must be seen that Ulrich in some moments even with Agathe adopts the standards established by a paternalistic society), Bonadea's sensuality is a perversion of her normal state of goodness and moral concern, her social roles as wife and mother. Hence, Ulrich gives her the ambiguous name of 'Bonadea', the good goddess, 'because of the way she had come into his life, and also after a goddess of chastity who had a temple in ancient Rome, which by a queer reversal later became a centre of all debaucheries'. The name is appropriate because Bonadea herself sees her sensuality as a sickness, a disease which does not allow her to immerse herself totally in ideals of the good, the true and the beautiful.

In Bonadea, Musil's first attack on idealistic women is clear, for the woman who models her life on conventional and misunderstood ideals is on the false path and can never attain that integrity of self which is the only true measure of idealism. Bonadea is a captive of the tension formed between her own natural being and the standards imposed from without. She is the product of an age, itself the victim of an ineffectual morality and Ulrich, although he tires of her after their first few encounters, does not essentially understand her. He feels that somehow her desire for social distinction, her ambition, has got into the wrong nerve track and manifested itself as nymphomania. This is partially correct, but on the other hand it is also equally true that Bonadea's ambition for social distinction has placed her sensuality in the wrong perspective. Ulrich will only learn, after his experience with Agathe, to accept the 'naturalness' of the prostitute in woman; at this point he cannot accept this any more than the somewhat absurd Bonadea can. Hence Bonadea's relationship with Ulrich points out that neither of them has learned to see the body in its proper perspective, although both of them seek for control over it—Ulrich through his exercises; Bonadea in her attempt to master her uncontrollable sexual urges. It is not this which Musil finds worthy of satire, but rather the attempt to replace the body's natural desires and its fulfilment with vague and pointless idealism. Bonadea is merely the minor embodiment of this drive which finds its culmination in the somewhat more impressive figure of Diotima.

In this hierarchy of woman, the transition between Bonadea and Diotima is bridged by Gerda, whose role in the book is a much slighter one. Gerda who is a mixture of virgin and old maid is the perfect minor embodiment of the modern woman who neglects her body and sublimates her sexual energy into a false idealism. Her relationship with Hans Sepp parallels Diotima's with Arnheim on a lower plane, and both men lead these all-too-willing women into the vague realm of muddled ideals. Gerda is the butt of Musil's satire as well as of his compassion, for the women who turn outwards toward the sphere of attempted social change cannot but damage their integral nature. Hence, the perveretd asceticism and purity of Gerda's relationship to Hans leaves her sexual side dissatisfied. At the same time her inclination as a woman to indulge the 'moon' side of her nature—that is, her imaginative and spiritual faculties—draws her to him, away from the cold cynicism which is Ulrich's facade. For Musil, however, the woman who belies her nature by turning toward an externally oriented idealism cannot but remain at odds with herself, in a continual state of disharmony —and this applies to the more powerful Diotima, as well as to Gerda. The attempt to attain fulfilment and consciousness cannot be achieved at the expense of the body and unconscious hetaeric instincts. It is telling that when Gerda finally gives herself, more than half unwillingly to Ulrich, she lapses into semi-unconsciousness —what Musil calls a waking swoon—just as does Diotima in the unpublished rape scene.

Gerda's importance, however, lies not only in the fact that she is a parallel to Diotima. Musil uses her further to point out Ulrich's rapacious side, his link to Moosbrugger. Overcome by repugnance once he is finally confronted by Gerda in her semi-nudity, Ulrich nevertheless ruthlessly makes love to her. It is notable that his cruelty vis-à-vis the prostitute in woman becomes greater as he moves up the hierarchy of woman, up the dissociation between body, feeling and mind. With Leona this incipient cruelty manifests itself merely in his refusal to wine and dine with her in the midst of society and in his insistence on their meeting at his home. With Bonadea this streak of cruelty is slightly more apparent in his consistent coldness and refusal to satisfy her desires. With Gerda he is overcome by the ruthless desire of the 'conquering male', who is 'irresistibly attracted by the vacillation of a soul that is dragged along by its own body like a prisoner in the grip of his captors'. Finally, with an emotion that ties him inextricably to Moosbrugger, Ulrich 'found—not it is true the rapture of love—but a half-crazed rapture reminiscent of a massacre, of sex-maniacal suicide, a state of being seized and rapt away by all the daemons of the void, who have their habitation behind all the painted scenery of life'. Ulrich abandons himself to an anarchistic and chaotic state of irrationality. This state is reminiscent of suicide as well as murder because in it he destroys what is intrinsically his—consciousness—while at the same time trying to kill what has aroused irrationality—the woman, both inside and outside himself. The cruelty before passion is aroused and the repugnance which follows upon its disappearance, is linked to this attempt to murder irrational lust and the prostitute in woman, who represents this state. With Diotima, this joint murder and suicide reaches even greater proportions.

Ermelinda Tuzzi, the ideal woman of ineffable intellectual charm, the high-minded beauty, is dubbed by Ulrich the second Diotima, after the celebrated female philosopher of love. The ultimate in Musil's society women, Diotima reigns over society because of her simulated power over the masculine realm of words and intelligence —although Musil is quick to point out that these words are mostly derived from a memory of girls' school history books. Diotima's high-mindedness, her attempt to put as yet unfound ideals into action through the ineffectual 'collateral campaign' are all satirised by Musil, who creates her perfect counterpart in the merchant-philosopher, darling of all branches of society, Arnheim.

Subjected to a cynical husband, whose ideas about love-making are by any standards crude, the unsatisfied Diotima is led by Arnheim into the murky regions of soulful love and universal idealism. According to Musil, it is better to lead a formless life until the ultimate Utopia is obtainable than to live by false ideals. Diotima, however, like all the socially oriented women in the Musilian hierarchy who attempt to order their lives by muddled intellectual ideas rather than by the true demands of body and emotions, is doomed to disillusionment. She can find no equilibrium between her inner demands and the external workings of her life. Arnheim, professional master of the 'soul', leads her to a pitch of soulful communion, only to leave her in an unpublished chapter for the more basic appeal of Leona. Arnheim's vision of the soul and of the highest moments in man's existence seems, like Hans Sepp's, to lie in a union between half-defined emotions and muddy ideas. The prime victim of Musil's satire, he is even made to quote a passage from *The Temptation of Silent Veronika* concerning soul, because although he cannot understand it fully, it is considered very highbrow to be acquainted with this work. Led by this man of vague ideals and murky mysticism, who is the arch-representative of his society, Diotima cannot obtain

that hoped for union which she so greatly desires. In her more
honest moments, she admits that platonic love, even for a Diotima, is
not sufficiently satisfying.

Finally Ulrich's 'soulful ogress' turns away from idealist philosophers to psychological and physiological sex literature. The good,
the true and the beautiful are abandoned in favour of sex manuals
and the desire to reform Diplomat Tuzzi's sexual manners. In this
Diotima once again reveals the disequilibrium of the modern social
woman who tries to alter sexual behaviour from above, from the
head, rather than going to the 'solar plexus' of the dilemma, her
own hetaeric core and physical love. Unlike Claudine, Diotima is
unwilling to be just another woman and she is quite capable of
talking about woman's constant readiness for sexual excitement
without ever being personally involved in what she is saying. She
realises that her torments are due to her body's protest against the
contradictory instructions it is receiving from her soul, yet she is
incapable of abandoning herself, even momentarily, to her body.

In one sense, Arnheim and Diotima provide an ironic parallel to
Ulrich's relationship with Agathe, for both pairs attempt to find
union and harmony within the self through love. However, Musil
has no compassion for vague idealists and he realises that their union
is impossible within the existing social morality. There must be an
entire reappraisal of the core of man and woman before a union
can be successful and this can only take place if half-formed ideals,
founded in social falsities are destroyed by the cold light of intellectual exactitude. Arnheim and Diotima attempt not the possible, but
the impossible, for they are working within outdated social conventions and from tired ideals. As they stand they are not visionaries,
but 'philosophers of the soul', whose ineffectuality prepares the way
for disintegration.

Nevertheless, there is some kinship between Diotima and Ulrich,
if only in that they are both involved in a search for some element
which is missing from their lives. Cousins, their ability to communicate without the usual emphasis on social decorum is similar to that
freedom which becomes manifest in Ulrich's relationship with
Agathe. It is to Diotima that Ulrich first communicates his idea of
objective, impersonal love, of life lived as literature, and of the need
for reality to be abolished so that man can regain his possession of
unreality. Although Diotima rejects his ideas, it is notable that he
presents them to her in the first place for thereby Musil points out

that Diotima has that necessary hold on intelligence, that seed of consciousness, which is essential for the utopian condition to take root. In an important conversation with Diotima, in which he finally manifests the second side of his nature, Ulrich also reveals the difference between himself and Arnheim, which lies in their varying approaches to the utopian condition. Arnheim, Ulrich says, desires a second reality, a sphere in which he will not have to alter his essential way of life or his way of thinking, but will find the blossoming of these. Ulrich, on the other hand, suggests an unlimited upheaval, a recapturing of all that is basic to humanity together with a search for all that is imaginary. Diotima is caught between these two points of view, just as Gerda is uncertain whether to turn to Ulrich or Hans. Yet ultimately all the women in the book turn toward Ulrich, for his influence consists in setting them free from their social and personal obligations. A man without qualities, he allows them similarly to be without qualities and for an instant to gaze upon that part of themselves which is totally their own. As Diotima reveals, although she finds this lightness in herself suspicious, Ulrich's effect on one is that 'one became so involved in hundreds of kinds of awareness that one lost the awareness of responsibility and suddenly found oneself in a suspicious state of freedom'.

Sensitive to Ulrich's influence, Diotima is not, however, that 'other' for which Ulrich is searching. She is too fully a creature bound up in her own and society's lie, too fully a woman modelled on man's vision of the ideal. The only possible partner for Ulrich in his venture into possibility is a woman aware of her own femininity and indifferent to accepted standards of good and evil. In his sister, Agathe, Ulrich finds this woman. However, before an understanding of this final figure of femininity can be attained, it is necessary to look at Clarisse.

Clarisse is one of the most fully defined figures in *The Man Without Qualities,* for Musil portrays her from the interior as well as from the exterior. In some ways she resembles Diotima, for in her too, the root of femininity has gone askew and she is filled with the desire to exert her will on the world. Yet in her incipient madness, in her private anarchy of boundless possibilities, Clarisse is the dark side of the Agathe figure. She embodies one aspect of femininity—that one which can most easily turn to self-destruction.

Like Regine, Alpha and finally Agathe, Clarisse is slim and boy-like, but her hermaphroditism becomes a cult, a sign, as does everything in the significant universe which Clarisse inhabits. This is perhaps the clue to Clarisse's particular form of insanity, for Clarisse is caught between the instinctive and anarchic sides of her being— which we have seen to constitute one aspect of femininity—and the male side, which attempts to explain these while also exerting its will to act upon them. Clarisse's mind is a jigsaw puzzle filled with significant clues for constructing a universal order, which she herself interprets and attempts to give coherent form to. As a simple example : Clarisse intuits that Moosbrugger is an important piece of her puzzle, hence she invents a theory to explain this intuition, a theory strongly influenced by her own brand of Nietzsche and Meingast—the Klages-figure in the book; finally she sets out with such determination to concretize her theory, to see Moosbrugger and to create him in the image of the piece of her puzzle, that nothing can stop her. Clarisse's sexual energy is what gives her such strength, for in her this sexual energy has been transformed into sheer nervous momentum and will power. Frigid, she refuses to succumb to her husband Walter and to normal sensuality. Although her refusal is based on an assertion of the male elements within her and thus a thwarting of her own nature, her explanation for her rejection is strikingly acute.

Musil first introduces Clarisse in conjunction with her husband Walter and the pair are sitting in a typical attitude at their piano, sending forth streams of Wagner. The difference between husband and wife is immediately apparent as Clarisse, still twitching with the electric charge of the music leaps up to meet Ulrich, while Walter remains at the piano, soft, drained-out and forlorn. Clarisse's first word is the cryptic 'frog prince' which she thrusts both at Walter and his music. This word, as is evident from the dream which Ulrich remembers Clarisse to have described to him, refers to Walter's sexual advances which are repulsive to Clarisse and which are mirrored in the way he plays Wagner. For Walter, Wagner provides that 'other state' to which he can escape when reality becomes too oppressive and there he can luxuriate in vague sensual mists. Walter is a 'frog prince', furthermore, because he refuses to be metamorphosed by Clarisse's powers of will into the true prince which he contains in his depths—that is, he will not leave his soft sensuality to become that artistic genius, believer in everything lean and austere in art, which Clarisse originally saw in him. The entire struggle between them is made evident in this first phrase of Clarisse's. After a brilliant youth in which he showed promise in all the arts, Walter has taken the path of bourgeois security and accepted a minor civil service post. Clarisse, who feels she is a woman worthy only of genius and capable of redeeming a lost one, focuses all her interests on rebuilding Walter's abandoned genius. However, all of Walter's former ideas and ideals have made an about-face and he is now immersed in the sentimentality of the mediocre. He fears that Ulrich will encourage Clarisse's mad side, her attempt to live beyond good and evil, and he correctly links this fear with sexual jealousy: should Clarisse throw off the little social sense of restriction that she possesses, she would naturally fall into that feminine sphere of anarchic hetaerism. Hence, as security, Walter wishes to make her a mother, tie her down, as Clarisse says, to a child who will be Walter's own compensation for creative failure. And Walter envisages for them a simple life, filled with the sentimental joys of morning coffee together, listening to birds talking to the neighbours, and so forth. What Walter desires in his sentimental picture of the simple human life, as Musil points out, is to surpass in mediocrity the great mediocre mass of humanity, the backbone of life. The contradiction inherent in this does not seem to disturb him in the least.

However, Clarisse, with her Nietzschen ideals and her belief in her own transforming powers, will not allow Walter to rest in his sentimental effusion and his basically bourgeois principles. Before she will give him a child, she wishes him to be sound in soul and body, to be free and have triumphed over his inertia. With her belief, which parallels that of the early Regine, that she is in possession of mysterious powers which will allow her to accomplish great missions in the world, Clarisse feels that she can redeem Walter as she has already redeemed Meingast. To attain this transforming power and to change Walter from the effeminate sentimentalist into the ecstatic genius, Clarisse must give up her natural role as woman and take on the male's strength and duties. She is quite correct when she says to Meingast that she is a double being, but what Clarisse does not see is the destructive effect this refusal of her natural feminine sensuality can have. She refuses the hetaera in woman, because, like Ulrich, she realises that if she were to allow Walter to have his own way sexually with her, she would in fact be a sex-murderer; she would give him leave to abandon himself totally to chaotic sexual forces which are directly opposed to the precision and exactitude which Walter's sloppy soul needs.

In her 'mad' way, Clarisse attempts to redeem Walter from what she sees as self-destructive possibilities in him. Clarisse, furthermore, mirrors Ulrich and Musil's dissatisfaction with the status quo. In her asocial and amoral depths, basic to the feminine in her make-up, she senses the importance of Moosbrugger, who is an elemental force disturbing social inertia. The really great crimes, she points out, come about because they are tolerated, not because they are committed : one thinks of the war here of course. Thus far, Clarisse's critical analysis is correct. It is in the solution she seeks, that she lapses into a madness coloured by too much reading of Nietzsche. What society needs, Clarisse believes, is a redeemer who will shake it out of its lethargy and bring about a new state of being. Clarisse sees this redeemer alternately in Moosbrugger, Ulrich and Meingast, and with each of these men she sees herself as that power which will give them the energy necessary for redemption.

Moosbrugger interests her because, in her role as a faithful follower of Nietzsche, she sees him as an antichrist, beyond good and evil, a carpenter-cum-murderer who is musical. This musicality is an acute intuition of Moosbrugger's true nature on the part of Clarisse, because for her the musical man is the man without conscience, who when he moves from his place, takes it with him—a different way of expressing Moosbrugger's ability to unite his inner and outer worlds and to slide the borders of himself and the objective world into one another. This harmony, as Clarisse senses, is precisely what the world needs, but like all Musil's women, her lack of intellectual precision does not allow her to see that without exactitude and consciousness, this kind of harmony can be totally destructive. Clarisse's idolization of Meingast, the much criticised Klages of Musil's notebooks, further pinpoints this lack in her, since Meingast in his praise of the irrational and primitive elements in man, is directly leading the way to the devastating experience of the First World War.

In her attempt to exert her powers socially, Clarisse is the wild mad sister of Diotima, for like her she tries to apply ideals in a sphere where only total re-evaluation, beginning with the individual's relationship to himself, might be able to instigate change. This effort to work things out in a social sphere (made light of in Clarisse's proposal for a Nietzsche year), and to have the masculine side of her nature predominate over her more natural feminine side, is what causes Clarisse's breakdown. Her already precarious balance cannot take on the extra nervous strain involved in manifesting her energies and ideals outwardly. Furthermore, her natural sexuality can only burst out after long suppression by her male will in love for another ambiguous hermaphrodite—the homosexual in the convalescent home, whose rejection of her leads Clarisse into total madness.

Yet Clarisse, for all her emotional, mental and physical imbalance, embodies more clearly than any of the women thus far studied in *The Man Without Qualities* that realm of possibility which is feminine. This is especially evident in her intimation of Ulrich's true nature as a man of the 'not yet' and in her attempts to have a child by him, who will be the saviour of mankind. Her interpretation of the man without qualities may be a little too influenced by the collection of Nietzsche with which he presented her on her wedding day, yet essentially it is acute.

> A Man Without Qualities does not say No to life, he says Not Yet, saving himself up; this she had understood with the whole of her body . . . 'Perhaps every mother can become mother of God,' she thought, 'if she makes no concessions, is not false and does not strive, but brings forth what is in her very depths as a child' (MWQ, 172-173).

Clarisse has recognised that one must wait *in readiness* for the moment of high noon and only then, act. Before that all action is futile. Ulrich, for her, is the man, coiled in preparation, as he waits for the 'not yet'. In relationship to this man without qualities, Clarisse feels the integral woman coming out in her, that woman who makes no concessions to social mores, who lives beyond good and evil and who brings out of the depths of her imaginative existence, the divine child : the embodiment of the 'not yet' become actual. To do this the woman must take the man into herself. She must become mother and mistress and hence she is completed in the greater part of her Isis roles. She becomes the total being. Clarisse has recognised the essential position of femininity : the possibility of wholeness which is woman's as she takes man into herself and gives him rebirth in a son, the embodiment of a total consciousness and of all that is to come. Like Musil, who attempts to provide the seeds of a synthesis, she sees the epoch in which she lives as a transitional one, an age of John the Baptists, of precursors, who cannot make the final act of faith and hence put an end to irresolution (MOE 1201). This is essentially the position of Ulrich and Agathe in their union.

Yet for Clarisse, there is no union with Ulrich (although originally, Musil planned that either she and Agathe should go off together with Ulrich to an island, or after the hero's failed 'Journey to
Paradise' with Agathe, he would then join Clarisse on another
island), no chance to reassert her natural femininity. Rather, as she
returns to Meingast and Walter, the male side of what she proclaims
is her 'double being', takes stronger and stronger hold of her.
Woman is woman and man, Moosbrugger had declared, and Clarisse, as she wilfully grows into her masculine image and brings her
schizophrenia into dangerous realms of madness, decides to incorporate the masculine role of redeemer into herself and rid the world
of what she calls its 'body of sin'. Her insanity, Musil shows, takes
on the masculine expression of inventing a new language of sign
words which incorporate the duality of her own nature. Finally,
these words become purely symbols, as in an early sketch, Musil
shows Clarisse inventing an entire sign language on trees, grass,
sand and rocks in her island existence with Ulrich. In Clarisse the
imaginative and spiritual possibility of the feminine together with
its anarchic and asocial basis, goes astray as she becomes the prey of
her own distorted vision of the male in herself. Her madness, however, reveals the hidden but similar insanity of Gerda and Diotima
who divert their natural femininity into the masculine domains
of ideals and theory, without being properly guided by that arch
masculine principle of clear-headed intellectuality and lucidity.
Nevertheless, in her insane acuteness, her lack of conventional
values, Clarisse is the dark side of the Agathe figure, who completes
within the light of day what grows thwarted and sick in Clarisse.

The transition from the ironical focus of Books One and Two of
The Man Without Qualities to the daylight mysticism of the third
book is an interesting one. Gradually in the latter section of Book
Two Musil shows Ulrich's growing dissatisfaction with the first
half of his holiday from life and he sums up the duality inherent in
his character, the duality of mathematician and mystic.

His development had evidently split into two roads, one lying on
the surface, in the light of day, and one dark and closed to traffic;
and the condition of moral standstill that had settled down upon
him, which had been oppressing him for a long time (and perhaps
more than was necessary), could be explained only by the fact that

he had never succeeded in joining up these two roads (MWQ II, 352).

The dark and light sides of Ulrich's existence are reminiscent of a similar split in the hero of *Tonka,* also a man of science. These two tracks of life are apparent in his appeal for a general secretariat for 'precision and spirit'. On the one hand there is the mathematician, who brings a ruthless passion to bear upon reality and demands, according to his philosophy of Essayism and his sense of 'possibility and the fantastical' that the history of the world be invented and that one live the history of ideas instead of the history of the world. This is the half of Ulrich's personality which is anti-realistic and insists that man should grasp at everything that cannot be quite realized in practice, so that eventually he can reach a stage of living where he will be like a figure in a book with all the inessential elements left out. All this must be done with the precision and exactitude of a 'vivisector'. On the other hand there is the mystical shadow side of Ulrich which defies definition and which he can only express through the image of his relationship with the major's wife. Of this tendency in himself, Ulrich has merely had intimations and it is this side of his character—the seeker for unity rather than the analyst—which will be more fully brought out in his relationship with Agathe.

At the end of the second part of the book, however, Ulrich is at an impasse. He can find no solution to the duality inherent in his nature. He can envisage no union between the mathematician and the mystic in himself and he sees this split in terms of the strained relationship between literature and reality, between metaphor and truth, and one could add, the masculine and feminine modes of apprehension.

Metaphor, Ulrich defines as a 'combining of concepts such as takes place in a dream; a sliding logic of the soul (*die gleitende Logik der Seele*)' which has its equivalence only in the way things are linked together in the 'twilit imaginings of art and religion'.

Ulrich's experience with the Major's wife is that one concrete event of his life in which he actually partook of the 'sliding logic of the soul' and lived in a mystical state. Boundless love for a woman older than himself, who was less a woman than the embodiment of an idea, initiated the experience. Indeed, for Musil, the *'andere Zustand'*, the other condition of being that can only be brought about

by love. Through his love for the Major's wife, Ulrich was cast
into a state where inner and outer mingled, slid into one another,
and he felt totally united with the external world of his perceptions
and the inner world of dream. It is interesting that for this mystical
state to occur, Ulrich must be separated from his love so that she
exists within the mind's eye as the embodiment of the feminine
principle.

At the very end of Book Two Ulrich, on his way home in a state
half way between fulfilment and futility, and in need of new stimu-
lus, thinks of his experience with the Major's wife. Musil describes
his psychological state at this time as one perfectly suited to a meeting with Agathe and all that she represents; for the Major's wife provides an intimation of the mystical state and in her influence on
Ulrich, she fore-shadows the experience with Agathe. Following
upon his thoughts of the Major's wife, Ulrich encounters a whore
and for once he feels tenderness for the prostitute in woman. Possessed by none of his usual ruthless and predatory sensations when
confronted by the whore, Ulrich's mind is open to an acceptance of
the hetaera and the anarchic existence which she symbolises. From
the Major's wife, the soul, to the hetaera, Ulrich is presented with
the heights and the depths of the femininity which will find its ultimate embodiment in Agathe. By a logical process of association
Ulrich then thinks of Moosbrugger, and the unity of inner and
outer, of subject and object, which such a man must experience in
his moment of murder. From envy of the madman, because of his
delusions and belief in his role, Ulrich passes to the realisation that
he must put all this behind him. Moosbrugger is not stranger or any
less familiar to him than any other image in the world and Ulrich,
moving into a new state now, must leave his association with all
such things. What becomes clear for him is that now, at last, he
must live for an attainable goal or seriously come to grips with all
the possibilities which have haunted his existence. Overcome by a
sensation of freedom, he is ready to meet Agathe and to embark on
a different form of existence.

It is both ironical and fitting, that when he reaches his city home,
Ulrich should receive the news of his father's death and find Clarisse
awaiting him. Clarisse has come to make Ulrich 'father' to her conception of the redeemer of the world. Ulrich has been chosen to
fulfil this paternal role by Clarisse because he represents for her both
Devil and God : he is capable of giving a dreamed-of state, reality.

By telling him these things, Clarisse points out Ulrich's path for him and makes his own search for a decision easier. But Ulrich cannot unite with Clarisse because, although she too feels that mystical state in which she is in harmony with the external world, connected to everything like a 'Siamese twin', she does not have that 'order and unity of feeling' which is Musil's prerequisite for a valid new morality. With the mention of the 'Siamese twins' however, and all that this term signifies, Clarisse intimates the appearance of Agathe.

It is a noteworthy change in Ulrich, furthermore, that faced with another Gerda situation, he does not allow his rapacious instinct to overcome him. He has come closer to being able to accept the hetaera in woman and feels no need to manifest his one-time disgust. Ulrich, as he himself realises, is becoming different and this difference is somehow connected to what he calls an 'attack of the Major's wife'. The elusive moon woman in him, that part of humanity which is linked to imagination and belief, is coming to the fore and in a state of semi-sleep, Ulrich once again has a glimpse of that 'other state' which was his for one brief moment in his first love affair.

In this way Musil shows Ulrich in a state where the encounter with Agathe can have a formative influence, and he also prepares the reader for the change of tone to which he will be subject in the third part of the book. Presiding over this scene of change is Ulrich's dead father—the law-maker and upright social figure. Significantly, this image of the established and antiquated order is dead, so that the path leading into the Millenium and into what is socially a criminal existence is open. The man without qualities is free to embark on an adventure which presupposes the entire reorganisation of perception and life.

At this point, his sister Agathe enters his life. Agathe is the culmination of femininity for Musil. She is Isis to Osiris, her brother, husband and son, that element which can bring completion to the male being. Musil, realising that social solutions are unattainable in the complex modern world, turns to the personal and individual sphere, for a new Adam and Eve must be born before a totally different world order can be achieved. Ulrich and Agathe are the seeds of this new world, this Millenium. Since the dilemma of modern man lies in his fragmentation, his specialised, limited existence and hence his alienation from the external world of nature and objects, Ulrich and Agathe, to become new beings must attain unity and

wholeness within themselves and eliminate the opposition between
subject and object. To do this they must initially abandon conventional conceptions and modes of regarding themselves and the universe. This is why the incestuous relationship of brother and sister is
the psychologically correct one for Musil to choose, since incest is
one of the prime taboos of Christian civilisation, and acceptance of
it necessitates the entire reorientation of man's thinking and feeling
processes. From the point of view of society, Ulrich and Agathe are
criminals, and it is only the criminal who can disregard social mores,
move beyond good and evil into another state of existence. The conditions, the categories by which man lives must be redefined before
a new world can come into being. This is the role of brother and
sister.

However, Musil in using an incestuous pair[1] as a new Adam and
Eve, is not attempting to portray an incident of perversity, a criminal act in the narrow sense. As he points out in his notebooks : 'The
novel has been reproached for its perversity. Reply : the archaic and
the schizophrenic express themselves in the same way in art. Nevertheless they are totally different. Just as the incestuous feeling can
be perverse, so too it can be myth.' (TB 355) Musil is recreating a
myth—a myth of totality in its union between the two polar opposites in the world, the male and the female and two similarly opposed
masculine and feminine elements of the individual's make-up. It is
evident that the entire sequence of Ulrich and Agathe's relationship
can be interpreted as a Jungian search for total selfhood. From this
point of view, Agathe is Ulrich's discovery of his own female part,
the anima, and in coming to terms with this feminine within himself, he is fully realizing his own identity. Musil makes a Jungian
interpretation almost too facile. He has Ulrich say, 'Man is found
in two states, male and female', and that the ancient philosophers
often spoke of a male and female principle. Furthermore, he makes
Ulrich interested in the concept of hermaphroditism, that visible
union of male and female in one being, and has him reminisce about

---

[1] There is much disagreement among Musil's critics as to whether Agathe
and Ulrich actually do commit incest, since the chapter 'Reise ins Paradies'
(Journey into Paradise), where they join in a sexual embrace, is an early
sketch and one which Musil left unpublished. Nevertheless, even if incest is
never acted out within the completed parts of *The Man Without Qualities*,
sexual desire is evident throughout the relationship; and as the Sermon on the
Mount implies, intent is as good as the deed.

his desire to be a girl in his childhood, to live out the hidden half of himself.

Ulrich thinks that the core of unity of experience lies in the obscurely contrasting male and female modes of being which are everywhere mysteriously overshadowed by ancient dreams. Before Agathe even enters the book, Ulrich muses over the notion of the 'unknown sister' which he sees as one of those spacious abstractions for all those feelings which are not at home anywhere in the world. Hence, the path is clear for Agathe to be looked at merely as an extension of Ulrich himself, that other side of himself which first came clearly to the fore in the last chapters of book two. The fact that Ulrich first sees Agathe dressed in exactly the same Pierrot costume as he himself has chosen for their meeting; the later insistence on brother and sister being Siamese twins of different sexes; and Ulrich's feeling that his sister is himself all over again, transformed as in a dream all seem to be indications that Agathe is Ulrich's anima, or in non-Jungian and older terms, that soul which Ulrich has always wanted to unite to masculine precision. Their meeting could be looked upon as the alchemical fusion of opposites which produces the sought-after philosopher's stone.

But Musil is both too good an artist and too acute an observer of human complexities simply to allow Agathe to remain a feminine extension of his hero. Agathe, as Musil reveals, when he depicts her away from Ulrich, that is, outside the range of Ulrich's projections, is a full woman, not always in agreement with her brother. She too is a hermaphrodite, that is, in possession of certain masculine characteristics and is not purely a soul grasping for mystical communion with the elements. Agathe is a total embodiment of femininity : like Neumann's Psyche, she is in search of a consciousness of her own femininity as well as a union with the male being.

In his notebook Musil writes, 'Properly speaking, in *The Man Without Qualities* . . . the spiritual leadership must be given over to Agathe. The male is left with non-Socratic irony' (TB 552). This is the exact definition of what Agathe's role in the book is. Ernst Fischer echoes this thought when he says of Agathe: 'Everything in her is plastic possibility. What for him is merely the possible, she turns into reality; what for him were merely shadows, takes shape in her; what he thinks, she attempts to live.'[2] Agathe is not merely

---

[2] Ernst Fischer, *Von Grillparzer zu Kafka: Sechs Essays* (Vienna, 1962), p. 27. My translation.

an anima, a soul figure, but the initiator of those actions which can lead toward *existence* in the spiritual realm of selfhood and totality. Erich Neumann points out that the anima is only a partial aspect of the Psyche's directive totality. His explication of Psyche's role in relation to Eros and Lucius, to the masculine power, echoes the spiritual guidance which Musil attributes to Agathe and provides a bare outline for the events of the third part of the book.

> In Eros as in Lucius [here Ulrich], the development at every stage starts not from the activity of the masculine ego, but from the initiative of the feminine. In both cases the process for good and evil—is carried out by this feminine principle, in opposition to a resisting and passive masculine ego. And such developments, in which the spontaneity of the psyche and its living guidance are crucial determinants in the life of the masculine are known to us from the psychology of the creative processes and of individuation. In all these processes where 'Psyche leads' and the masculine follows her, the ego relinquishes its leading role and is guided by totality.[3]

If Ulrich's world with its insistence on scientific exactitude, lucidity, and as Musil points out, irony, is the ego world of daylight existence, then Agathe's world is that of totality, the search for unity, which is only possible through the sliding logic of the soul. It is evident that Musil wants her to have this symbolic value, but since he is dealing with literature and not purely with myth, Agathe cannot enter the book as a full-blown Psyche, that is, as a total feminine wholly aware of the components of her own femininity. Rather Agathe must be formed by the love which she experiences with Ulrich, and like Claudine, suffering and separation. Whether through her experience she achieves that ideal totality within the real world is not fully answered in the unfinished *The Man Without Qualities*, and it is doubtful whether Musil himself, who shares in Ulrich's irony and lucidity, would have brought such a total woman, a Psyche, into the light of day, far removed from the mythical realms of her predecessor and the equally mythical sphere of Claudine. It must be remembered, however, that Musil only claims to plant the seeds of a solution and so far his intention is clear. Agathe is the supreme embodiment of femininity within his fictional canvas and she enters the book with an accumulation of experience

---

[3] Erich Neumann, *Amor and Psyche*, p. 151.

and a level of awareness, which far surpasses that of the other women thus far examined. Ulrich's response to her makes this evident and she remains the only woman who can initiate a series of experiences which could lead to that unity and wholeness which both Ulrich and his creator long for.

Notably, the first thing Musil describes about Agathe as a being distinct from her brother's projections, is her attitude toward sexuality. In the chapter entitled 'Confidences' at the very beginning of part three, Agathe tells Ulrich of her decision to leave her second husband Hagauer. Ulrich, who dislikes the man intensely, wonders how she could have lived with him for so long and submitted to his sexual advances. As Musil points out, Ulrich is still far from understanding feminine psychology and he is still the victim of masculine prejudices concerning woman's submissive role in the sexual act. He cannot accept the idea of woman abandoning herself to any man whether she is emotionally involved with him or not. He bears the prejudice of a paternalistic society which sees the woman who succumbs to any number of men as a prostitute, an object of contempt. Agathe, on the other hand, has learned the lesson of Claudine and realizes that it is natural for woman to succumb with her body to the masculine embrace even though she may otherwise be totally uninvolved. She feels that 'this body of hers . . . was the only thing which belonged to her', and that 'men were complementary to one's own body, a completion of it, but no spiritual content' (MWQ III, 189). Thus, she can answer Ulrich with the words of the woman who feels no guilt about her hetaerism and who has consciously come to accept it : 'Surely a normal person isn't so sensitive to minor miseries.' (MWQ III, 32). And Ulrich, finally half realizing woman's closeness to nature and the naturalness of hetaerism for woman, if not for man, agrees with her : 'You're probably much more sensible than I am, if you look at these things in such a natural way. But a man's nature isn't natural. It's nature altering'.

It must be remembered that Agathe has already suffered the separation from a loved one which is, according to Neumann, the first step toward attaining a consciousness of her own femininity. Like Regine, Agathe has had a first husband called Johannes with whom she was deeply in love and with whom she had that first experience of the 'other state', just as Ulrich has had a glimpse of this state in his affair with the Frau Major. Separated from this husband through his death only a few weeks after their marriage,

Agathe was hurled from a state of unity in love back into the hard realistic world, where until she meets Ulrich, she only feels half-alive, half-awake. It is in this semi-sleep that she marries Hagauer and takes on a series of lovers who mean nothing to her, but satisfy her body. However, it is only through the love experience that woman is fully awakened to the world and to herself, so that Agathe whose formation begins with her relationship to Johannes, goes through a long period of semi-unconsciousness in her separation from him, where like Claudine, she is cast into her own natural hetaerism and forced to an awareness of it. It is only with her love for Ulrich that she is fully reawakened and her formation continues. She becomes herself. Agathe, as Musil allows her to call herself, referring to her closeness to the primitive in woman, is not a 'modern woman', for unlike Diotima and Clarisse, she recognises that there is nothing more important to her than the love experience.

In her closeness to hetaerism, Agathe is also a totally asocial being whose actions, if anything, are anarchistic. Ulrich merely provides verbal and theoretical expression for elements and feelings which have been part of her all along (MOE 729-730). It is she who initiates the acts which are based on conditions of perceiving and feeling alien to society and which do not conform to its limited standards. If Ulrich is the theoretician of criminality, Agathe is the criminal—at least in a technical, but non-violent sense—and it is only she who can give the longed-for Millenium, the necessary active impetus which will bring it into being. This is evident in the way in which she spontaneously puts a garter in her dead father's pocket and more explicitly in her altering of her father's will and her desire to kill Hagauer. Ulrich, although he can theorize about good and evil deeds and their irrelevancy to the actual moral state of the being who commits them, is struck by his sister's irreverence for their father, and worries, especially after the act becomes real for him, about the social implications of her crime. Essentially he does not totally disagree with Hagauer's imputation that Agathe is a 'social imbecile' and although Agathe worries about her deed when confronted with this aspect of it, she is not actually touched by the fact that she has committed a social evil, but rather by her brother's turning against her.

Like Regine, Agathe remains good, pure, even when she commits evil acts, for she lives beyond good and evil in a condition which is the basis for the coming of the Millenium. It is the spontaneity of Agathe's actions, stemming from a total faith in the good result of what she does, that sets Ulrich free. As the ultimate embodiment of possibility, Agathe has that faculty of belief necessary for any venturer into new realms. Ulrich as he watches her alter the will feels the full impact of this feminine influence on himself.

> Now it suddenly struck him that not only had Agathe somehow got from him what she had said about truth, but what she was doing in the other room was also something he had outlined. It was after all he who had said that in the highest state a human being could reach there was no longer any such thing as Good and Evil, only faith or doubt; that definite rules were contrary to the essential nature of morality, and that faith must never be more than at the most an hour old; that when acting in a state of faith one could not do anything beastly; and that intuition was a more passionate state than truth . . . And at this moment, regardless of her lack of conscience, he loved her, with the strange feeling that it was his own thoughts that had gone from him to her and were now returning from her to him, now poorer in reasoning but, like a creature of the wild, with an elusive odour of freedom about them. (MWQ III, 164)

Linked with Agathe's anarchism which gives her the freedom to act, is her faith in Ulrich and their union which will bring about an existence within the Millenium. In this she is akin to the Portuguese lady, to that side of the feminine which inclines to the spiritual and is willing to accept the possibility of the other without too much intellectual *angst* and doubt. This is the side of Agathe which is an antithesis to Ulrich's precision and exactitude. Yet again, merely to term Agathe as Ulrich's soul or anima is to disregard her own and hence Musil's disinclination toward this term. Unlike Diotima, Agathe is not comfortable with the word soul, for as Musil continually seems to wish to show, Agathe is a very ordinary woman. She is not capable of understanding Ulrich's intellectual flights and she consistently tries to bring him down, out of the sphere of abstraction which is naturally the male's. She does not, like Clarisse, think of herself in terms of a redeemer or even as any formidable power, and she has none of Diotima's ability to impress by her high-mindedness and her verbalisation of ideas. Agathe's whole power lies in that she is merely a woman who is close to her own emotions and body. It is because she has not attempted to form herself in the image of the male's ideal of femininity or along society's prescriptions and because she suffers from no desire to prove herself in the male world, that she is extraordinary.

Agathe's value lies precisely in the fullness of her emotions and sensations which are unformed, undefined and which occasionally give her an inkling of the possibility of living in a different state from the here and now. Furthermore, she is ready to believe intensely in the possibility of this other state although her only experience of it has been a brief one and one always brought about by love. Agathe describes her moment of premonition of the mystical state as an 'incomparable outpouring' of herself into her surroundings and simultaneously of her surroundings into herself so that a significant 'unity of the conscience with the senses' is achieved. Essentially this is a repetition of her previously expressed desire to live in complete accord with herself, for living in accord with oneself is also to live in accord with the world of objects, the external world. It is what Ulrich calls the Millenium and it is the possibility which he sees in Agathe, for bringing this Millenium into the light of day which attracts him to her. The work toward the Millenium, as Agathe realises, is for Ulrich a continual slow attempt to transform the super-natural into the natural. And Agathe is this otherness incarnate, the first step toward the Millenium. She is the culmination of that little girl—neither child nor woman—whom both Ulrich and his creator encounter on a tram and who serves as an epiphany of the possibilities inherent in the world.

The union between Agathe and Ulrich is in a sense an ideal one, for to Agathe's feminine belief, indefiniteness, and total reliance on emotions and sensations, Ulrich brings that ordering power and intellectual precision which is the male's. Brother and sister are fragmented halves of the Platonic whole, wishing to reincorporate the other half within themselves so that in their oneness they yet remain distinct and in their duality they are yet united. In different terminology, they are looking for that consciousness of themselves which allows an inner harmony and a fusion of the external world with the inner one.

However, although Musil shows in several instances that Agathe and Ulrich have attained a state of harmony within themselves and also that fusion with the external world which at first manifests itself only when two lovers are together and finally results in a sonorous communion of all things, the problem of duration has still not been solved. Musil is not a believer in absolutes, for they imply a rigidity which is closed to movement, and time necessitates movement. The Millenium, the 'other state', given concrete reality, cannot endure. It, too, must be continually re-examined. Similarly, consciousness of self must be perpetually redefined for the individual is subject to change. Hence, although it can be said that Agathe, in her union with Ulrich, has attained consciousness of her own femininity, and that form has been imposed through love on all that is sheer form-less possibility, this awareness too, must be repeatedly examined. In the same way, the mystical state achieved—which is essentially a moment of intense communion in a still centre—cannot persist without redefinition, for the world itself is in a state of perpetual flux.

This is why Musil intersperses Agathe's and Ulrich's moments of mystical consciousness and totality with moments of uncertainty and, especially in Ulrich, doubt. Agathe, as Ulrich points out, has very little sense of reality while he is continually confronted with the reality of the social world and the lucidity of the light of day. Thus in many ways, the path to consciousness and mystical union is easier for her, since the feminine is always closer to the core both of nature and belief. Femininity has an innate propulsion toward a state of unity. As far as the union between male and female goes, however, Musil cannot in all honesty give a fully optimistic conclu-sion to the book—or so it would seem from the fragments which are available—for the force of reality pervades it in the form of two world wars and the strength of this intrusion is such that it shatters even individual and personal attempts at creating a lasting 'other condition of being'.

Ulrich's and Agathe's relationship, for all its mythical quality, cannot escape the ups and downs which Musil's lucid awareness of daily reality imposes on it. From the first Ulrich is faced with a conflict between his intellect and his emotions, and a feeling that his love for Agathe is merely imaginary. Furthermore, his intellect forces him to recognise that the conditions of self-perception are such that one cannot truly see oneself from the inside, nor truly be in possession of oneself. Finally, even after such moments of mysti-cal communion as that within the chapters 'Breath of a Summer's Day' and 'Moonbeams by Day'—which in their very titles suggest the bringing of the mystical state out of the light of the moon, that is, out of the realm of feminine belief, into the light of day and hard-minded male lucidity—the certainty of maintaining this state and remaining together is not given to Ulrich and Agathe. It seems evident from this that Musil had not changed his mind between the writing of the early chapter 'Journey into Paradise' and the later mystical chapters. As he says in an interview with Fontana : 'But brother and twin-sister—the I and the not-I—feel the inner split, the inner disjunction of their togetherness. They fall out with the world. They flee. But this attempt to arrest, to capture experience, miscarries. Such absoluteness cannot be preserved. I conclude that the world cannot exist without evil, for evil brings movement into the world' (TB 786-787).

Even though this interview took place before *The Man Without Qualities* was envisaged in its final form, the book as it stands reveals that Musil's views on the absolute had not changed in the last days of his life. The search for an absolute, which Ulrich and Agathe undertake, is not something which can be successful in the temporal world of reality. The thought of separation is always with Ulrich and Agathe, and indeed, as Neumann has shown, separation is essential for the growth of consciousness, an awareness which needs constant redefinition. 'His mind filled with strange images. Agathe behind a railing. Or Agathe waving to him axiously from farther and farther away, wrenched away from him by the severing violence of alien fists. Then again, he himself was not only the abandoned and powerless one, but equally the abandoning and severing one . . . (MOE 1086).

Furthermore, even when Ulrich feels he has come to grips with the world for a second time through Agathe, he sees that he can never give up his intellectual side. Hence, as soon as the moment in which the 'other state' is lived out, passes, his doubts return. Agathe may be the initiator of a series of experiences which attempt to arrive at totality and in herself she may represent this totality. Nevertheless, her ultimate function for Ulrich is to change his *thinking* processes and he feels no need to know her in her femininity. The cleavage between emotions, imagination and belief—the feminine side of the human dichotomy—and the masculine intellect persists (MWQ II, 77). For Musil, to wish to establish the Millenium on earth, is to wish to reorganize mind and the way in which it grasps reality.

During his affair with the Frau Major which culminates in his relationship with Agathe, Ulrich has succeeded in changing the way in which man views the universe and himself. In his moments of mystical ecstasy, the separation between the world of objects and the world of subjects has been abolished and with it that category of space, 'apparent or real, a lifting up of the spirit of separation, yes, almost of Space itself'. However, as Ulrich realizes in the chapter 'Afterthoughts', this reorganization of the way in which one grasps reality is only possible in the 'other state'—an experience initiated by love and hence feeling. Totally relative and personal, feelings are opposed to that realm of truth which, for Ulrich, is connected to scientific exactitude and intellectual precision. Hence Ulrich cannot fully 'see' in the real world, for in all seeing some feeling is involved which causes one to go endlessly round the object without ever fully identifying it or understanding it. The separation between subject and object still exists in the world of truth and reality where 'space' cannot be abolished. Only in that mystical state initiated by love, which as he has realised cannot endure, is unity possible and that unity is incapable of being grasped intellectually and precisely.

Consequently, at the end of the chapter 'Afterthoughts', Ulrich embarrassedly finds himself having moved from his position as engineer of a new morality to a chevalier of love, a troubador seeking his lady. He is essentially dissatisfied with this change in himself, for he cannot resign himself to an abandonment of the intellect. Here, in these chapters so intrinsically caught up with debates about faith, Ulrich sees clearly enough that he cannot allow himself the 'leap of faith'—the *sacrificium intellecti* or Tertullian's 'Credo quia absurdum'. The split between love, faith—the realm of feeling— and awareness is too vast in him and it presents a duality which cannot be resolved. For a moment, Ulrich weighs the hope that a Christian transfiguration of the world through mystical love, that is, of a recognition of the 'neighbour' in oneself is possible. But he abandons this hope too. In what we have of the unfinished fourth part of the book, Ulrich is left with a fuller vision of experience, but with essentially the same inner debate, the same conflict between emotions and intellect, 'mysticism and reason'.

It is only Agathe, the feminine, who manages to find completeness and harmony to any extent through the personal experience of love and the mystical condition. The masculine tendency is toward analysis and constant redefinition of dialectical opposites; but femininity embodies the search for unity and the possibility of total synthesis. Agathe succeeds in bringing the absolute opposites of separation and unity together. Away from Ulrich or from the real world, she is yet at one with herself and her lover, for, the most 'illogical of women', her intellect does not rebel against an acceptance of love as the prime mover in the world. She is capable of subverting the conditions of the mind and grasping reality in a total and different way. Agathe functions according to the 'sliding logic of the soul': she is for Musil the incarnation of fiction, of art, and the revolutionary possibilities represented by this sphere. Only through the power of art or metaphor, can reason and mysticism be united.

However, even as a complete feminine being and the embodiment of manifold possibility, Agathe cannot provide a solution outside herself, one which has validity outside the sphere of the personal or the sphere of fiction. In the hard-minded intellectual universe based on the totality of 'real' experience, which is Musil's, femininity bears the seeds of a solution which as yet can only be incarnated within the individual woman.

3 Marcel Proust: Femininity and Creativity

Marcel Proust was born in 1871, the turbulent year of the Paris Commune, into a prosperous French middle-class family. His father, a public health official was also a renowned doctor; his mother was a cultivated Jewess, to whom Proust felt he owed his literary sensibility. He was a brilliant student as a child, but much troubled by asthma—a premonition of that neurasthenia which was to afflict and shape his entire life. At a young age he began his career of man-about-town and idle dandy which provided him with that range of characters who people his work: the gratin, the socially ambitious bourgeoisie, the wealthy financiers, the demi-monde and those artists who, at that period, were searching for new forms of expression. In 1905, the year of his mother's death, Proust embarked on a life of convalescence, punctuated by visits to sanatoria and marked by an ever-increasing retirement from society, resulting finally in his self-imprisonment in the famous cork-lined room. It was in these years that A la recherche du temps perdu took shape. Proust never ceased to revise and add to this work until, on 18 November 1922, he succumbed to a pulmonary infection. The many-factioned French literary world, which had only grudgingly acknowledged his stature some three years earlier, attended his funeral in large numbers.

A PSYCHOLOGICAL APPROACH

Proust's critics have often drawn attention to what they term Proust's 'feminine' nature. René Boylesve writes in Feuilles tombées, 'young, old, ill, and woman—a strange person.' Paul Souday adds to this with his description of Proust as 'above all an aesthete, a morbid man, almost feminine', while Harold March states that Proust 'thought like a man, felt like a woman, and acted like a child . . . There was much in him that suggested a feminine nature.' This femininity of Proust's is also attributed to the hero of *A la recherche du temps perdu,* Marcel, and would seem to lie in what P. H. Simon terms 'l'âme végétative et sensible'. Bruce Lowery sees this passivity in the majority of Proust's characters, 'They abandon themselves to the current of life . . . They submit to life more than they construct it.' A sensibility refined almost to the point of morbidity, together with a supine nature, would seem then, to be the chief components of what is described as the 'feminine' in Proust as well as in his major protagonist, Marcel. We have already noted that Henry James's principal heroines are characterized by this sensitivity, what Ruskin in *Sesame and Lillies* calls the 'tact or touch' quality of women. Furthermore Freud marks passivity as one of the chief elements in the make-up of the feminine principle and he is seconded in this by a host of later psychologists. It would appear from this that there is a certain validity in using the term 'feminine' in referring to Proust or Marcel when proof of a refined sensibility and a passive nature can easily be found throughout Proust's biography and *A la recherche.*

Given these feminine characteristics, it is surprising to note that Proust is often denied the capability of creating female figures. Justin O'Brien, in his article on Proust's transposition of sexes,[1] makes a case supported by many, for the fact that behind every Gilberte and Albertine there is a masculine Gilbert and Albert. This argument stems from a biographical inquiry into Proust's life and has as its major foundation Gide's record of a conversation between himself and Proust in which the latter's homosexuality is fully exposed:

> Far from denying or hiding his homosexuality, he exposes it, and I could almost say boasts of it. He claims never to have loved women save spiritually and never to have known love except with men.[2]

In a further journal entry, Gide writes:

[1] Justin O'Brien, 'Albertine the Ambiguous: Notes on Proust's Transposition of Sexes', *PMLA* LXIV, 5 (December, 1949), pp. 933–52.
[2] André Gide, *Journal* (Paris, 1939) p. 692. My translation.

This evening again we scarcely talked of anything but homosexuality. He says he blames himself for that 'indecision' which
made him transpose everything graceful, tender and charming in
his homosexual memories into 'à l'ombre des jeunes filles', in
order to nourish the heterosexual part of his book . . .[3]

This biographical evidence used to justify the theory of the transposition of sexes in *A la recherche* is of the kind which Proust himself attacked in *Contre Sainte-Beuve* and warned against in *A la
recherche* by stressing that it was not a 'roman à clef'. Although
Justin O'Brien makes a thorough textual study of all in *A la recherche* that would suggest that Albertine has more of a young man
(especially Agostinelli) than of a 'jeune fille' from a middle class
family, to accept his case is to deny a homosexual artist, like Proust,
the ability of creating a convincing male-female relationship. That
Proust was capable of doing so lies in a testimony such as Catherine
Carswell's. Miss Carswell points out in an article written before
the appearance of Gide's *Journal,* that Proust's women are in all
cases the 'reverse of shadowy' as long as Marcel is not emotionally
involved with them. 'Then as in life, the heart clouds the brain.'[4]
Furthermore, the sex of Odette, who is, in so many ways, similar
to Albertine and whose relationship with Swann foreshadows that
of Marcel and Albertine, never seems to appear dubious. As Harry
Levin suggests, to read Albertine as Albert 'raises many more questions than it answers'.[5]

To take the path of biographical inquiry is to narrow Proust's
vision; for Proust, with his feminine nature, was quite capable of
creating women. The portrait of Françoise provides an immediate
example. If there is dissension among the critics as to the sex of any
particular character, it can only suggest that Proust has intention-
ally created some sexually ambiguous figures. There are no ready-
made biographical explanations in the complex Proustian world.
After all, if the hero, Marcel, were not immediately equated with
Proust, it would be quite possible to see in this passive and highly
sensitive persona, a feminine Marcelle; and in 'The Confession of a
Young Girl' as well as in the figure of Andrée, Proust quite readily
transforms himself into a woman. In itself, this too, hints at the

[3] Ibid., p. 694.
[4] Catherine Caswell, 'Proust's Women', *Marcel Proust: An English Tribute*
London, 1923) p. 72.
[5] Harry Levin, *The Gates of Horn* (New York, 1963), p. 414.

type of literary ambiguity which ought not to be resolved simply by resorting to biography. It is to the point that, in what Edmund Wilson terms Proust's 'dream-novel', the demarcation line between the sexes should disappear.[6]

A study of femininity in the works of Proust and especially in *A la recherche* is thus complicated by Proust's wilful blending of the sexual principles. Unlike Musil, Proust does not give us that immediately apprehendable twin polarity of the masculine and the feminine; nor, in fact, the conflict or contrast between them. Nor does he objectively define what he sees as male and female characteristics. The Proustian universe is obviously different in this respect from the objective universe which the characters of Musil inhabit, since Musil's omniscient judgment is carefully located outside the lives he depicts. Both authors, no doubt, 'meditate' the data, but Musil's approach is crystallised by the 'he did' of continuous narrative exposition, while Proust's by the 'I feel' of intermittent epiphany. Therefore, with Proust, the 'he' of Musil becomes an 'I' intrinsically involved as the subject of the structure and events of *A la recherche*, and objective judgment becomes impossible in a world of ambiguities. Here one is less surprised to find no clear division between the sexes, no Agathe to draw out and polarize the totality of the feminine, no Ulrich to embody its masculine counterpart. Rather, the reader is faced by the dissolution of the sexes, first of all on the social plane as the fires of Sodom and Gomorrah destroy the conventional duality of man and woman; secondly and more significantly for this present study, as Marcel, developing into an artist, symbolically takes the feminine into himself. Given these shifts, the critic must find the coherent basis behind the ambiguity which, in this instance, gives value to the term 'feminine'.

If one were to find one stable symbol, some image which at once

---

[6] For the purposes of this study one could propose a further refinement on the much-debated question of the transposition of sexes. One could speculate that if Proust has chosen to make his Albert into an Albertine, this may suggest that he wishes to emphasise the 'feminine' qualities in the love partner as proposed to his basic, physical, sexual definition. The homosexual, as Proust makes clear in Charlus, can often be more overtly 'feminine' than the woman. He exaggerates femininity to the point of parody. As we have seen, femininity can be embodied in either man or woman. If Proust transposes the sex of Albert and makes his Albertine ambiguous, he may do so not only in an attempt to mask biographical data, but also because he wishes to stress the properties of femininity, distilled from their usual one-to-one relationship with women.

reflects the essence of *A la recherche* and almost makes its intent transparent, it would be that of the serpent devouring its own tail. This archetype, or the *Uroboros*,[7] to give its exact configuration, very much resembles the circular path of Proust's novel. It reflects that kind of self-containment wherein the narrator at the end gives us not a real 'end' but rather the beginning of the artist's creative task : an artist, we can assume, who will write this very book. As Erich Neumann describes it, the Uroboros stands at the beginning of life, before the ego has developed and established external contacts and at the end of life, when the mature man turns back to the self.[8] The Uroboros is thus the symbol of the original unity of primal creation as well as that final one of the mystical marriage of opposites, the *hieros gamos*. It is transpersonal in that it embodies both masculine and feminine. Furthermore, much like the pristine Maternal or 'Great Mother' sphere which Bachofen describes, it contains as well as shelters the nascent ego that grows out of the primal round of its womb. It is from this realm, where all things are fused and inextricably intermingled, that the young Marcel arises in the paradisal and maternally-dominated Combray, and to this sphere that he at last returns as he develops into the narrator who has found his self-realisation in solitude and art.

For the artist, the Uroboros also signifies that 'feminine' realm of the unconscious from which creativity itself springs. This is Goethe's realm of the Mothers and also, as we shall see, Proust's. Instances of involuntary memory, we observe, several times give Marcel the realisation that art is made not of the great ideas which he has constantly sought out, but precisely of those intuitive flashes beyond time. During these instants, the text reveals, Marcel *is* an artist. It is important to understand clearly that in this realm the actual sexual definition of persons as either distinctly feminine or masculine ceases to exist. It is as if the distinct person has dissolved, fallen back into the spell of maternal unconsciousness, so that it becomes possible for Marcel, as artist, to absorb the feminine into himself, to become a symbolic hermaphrodite. This final develop-

---

[7] The *Uroboros* is actually an alchemical symbol. Jung describes it as the 'tail-eating serpent' identified with the All-Seeing and with time. (*The Structure and Dynamics of the Psyche* (London, 1906), p. 196–8.) Erich Neumann defines it in *Amor and Psyche* (London, 1956), p. 82, as 'the circular snake, biting its tail, that symbolises the One and All'.

[8] Erich Neumann, the Origins and History of Consciousness (London, 1954), pp. 36–37.

ment in Marcel's history differs radically from Musil's parallel attempt to fuse Ulrich and Agathe in a hermaphroditic union which must withstand the test of reason and a clear daylight order. Not so in Proust: here the duality inherent in the lucid consciousness moves beyond consciousness to the total self with its multiplicity, its intuitions, it metamorphic possibilities. With Proust, the infractions of reality are overcome by the power of metaphor and art.

It is this motion from the 'serpent's head' to its 'tail', from the original paradisal state of Combray to Marcel as achieved artist, which, if traced, unfolds the real significance of the feminine for Proust. An equation here might reveal something of the meaning of this circuit. In this history of the artist becoming himself, insofar as Marcel comprehends that part of himself which is feminine and gives it concrete shape, he has facilitated his own birth as an artist. Or, to use the serpent image, the head contains the tail, that is, by narrating or concretizing the incidents of his own femininity, the narrator contributes to Marcel's growing awareness of himself as an artist. This does not deny the important fact that Marcel can continue to negate his possibilities as an artist until his role is suddenly revealed to him at the end. In this sense, *A la recherche* is not a *Künstlerroman* and the reader is not immediately aware of Marcel's artistic vocation as he is in the portrait of Stephen Dedalus. The point here is to lay bare the way the 'feminine' contributes to Marcel's final artistic revelation and how this 'feminine' is also of its essence.

THE MATERNAL UROBOROS

The ascendence of the maternal figure in Proust's work has often been noted. Harry Levin writes: 'It has been said that all of Kafka's work constitutes an epistle to his father. So we might say of Proust's novel, that it may be read as a letter to his mother.'[1] Howard Moss substantiates this by speaking of the 'pervasive maternal fog through which Marcel sees all sexual experience.'[2] Indeed the figure of the mother occupies the central feminine position in *A la recherche* as well as in *Jean Santeuil*. Together with the grandmother, she is one of the few major characters in the latter novel who is free from

---

[1] Levin, p. 440.
[2] Howard Moss, *The Magic Lantern of Marcel Proust* (London, 1963), p. 59.

sexual ambiguity and who remains stable in her position, suffering no surprising revelations of character. The pervasiveness of her influence makes her more than human and thus she takes on the aspect of the archetypal Great Mother.

In the beginning stands the maternal Uroboros, the refuge of all suffering and the goal of all desire for the nascent ego; the still centre of the child's universe. The child, with its as yet undeveloped individual consciousness, lies happily supine in a communal world where all its needs are taken care of and all responsibilities are lifted from its shoulders. In this world, over which the Great Mother presides, there is no separation between inner and outer, between subject and object; none of that distinction of opposites, that alienation of self from world which comes with consciousness. Time follows the natural rhythm of the maternal cycle, day and night, waking, eating, sleeping. This is exactly the paradise which Proust depicts as lost, the pastoral world of Combray, where the young Marcel lives in the stability of a family circle watched over by the maternal figures of the mother, the grandmother, Tante Léonie and Françoise.

In the uroboric stage of the ego's development, Neumann points out, everything and everyone is coloured by a mythical and emotional character and associated with gods, meanings and allusions.

. . . Originally thing and place belonged together in a continuum and were fluidly related to an ever-changing ego. In this inchoate state there was no distinction between I and You, inside and outside, or between man and things, just as there was no clear dividing line between man and animals, man and man, man and the world. Everything participated in everything else, lived in the same undivided and overlapping state in the world of the unconscious as in the world of dreams.[3]

This is the world of the magic lantern and of dream which Marcel inhabits in his childhood. Here subject and object meet in an imaginative unity as Marcel becomes the matter of the books he reads, 'a church, a quartet, the rivalry of Francis I and Charles V'; doorknobs blend into men; women spring magically from the curve of a thigh; and the mythical Genevieve de Brabant is incarnated in the actual Duchess of Guermantes.

[3] Neumann, *The Origins* . . ., p. 188.

To 'obtain' here, means to 'eat' for the uroboric phase is alimentary and not genital.[4] Meal times are highly important to the young Marcel and regarded with great avidity. He cherishes above all and enters into closest communion with those hawthorns which look 'eatable', because they have the colour of strawberries in cream cheese. It has been frequently observed that eating and digestion metaphors play a large part throughout *A la recherche,* especially in the description of sexual experience. 'In fact any kind of intimacy bringing with it knowledge of the other person's secret nature is imagined as physical assimilation.'[5] This would seem to suggest that the maternal world is very close to Marcel throughout his experience and that he never fully emerges from it.

Marcel's mother is the focal point of the Combray experience. The goal of all Marcel's desires, aptly concentrated in the 'goodnight kiss' ritual, is of course, his mother; the kiss at once calms him as its lack excites his anxiety. Thus, the mother also emerges as the cause of all Marcel's suffering in the Combray world. The rhythmical recurrence of this good-night kiss, marking the end of day and the onset of night, provides a stability which is embodied throughout the work in the figures of the mother and grandmother, whose values are fully defined and unchanging. As Germaine Brée observes in her acute description of this paradisal and uroboric phase: 'Happiness is the medium in which Combray unfolds'.[6] Saint-Hilaire 'embodies a communal order based on ritual and ceremony in which the present is prolonged in a mythical past rooted in mystery'.[7] 'The world as his mother and grandmother see it is simple, harmonious; values are absolute and unshakeable; the true, the good, and the beautiful exist in themselves'.[8]

The mother incarnates a further aspect of this stability for Marcel—a stability which otherwise evades him as he steps out of Combray into the world of lost time. As Leo Bersani points out: 'She has a timeless image of him; no matter what he becomes, he will always be for her the child to whom she will respond in the same loving way.'[9] This fixity gives Marcel's personality a continuity which exists beyond the constant fluctuation of his many selves in

[4] Ibid., p. 31.
[5] Leo Bersani, *Marcel Proust* (New York, 1965) p. 35.
[6] Germaine Brée, *The World of Marcel Proust* (London, 1967) p. 149.
[7] Ibid., p. 153.
[8] Ibid., p. 155.
[9] Bersani, p. 56.

the discontinuous world outside Combray; and as Marcel realises in the last pages of *A la recherche,* it is through his mother's eyes that he has always basically seen himself. 'I noticed that, when I wished to form an opinion of myself, I took the same point of view as she. Though in the long run I noted, as she used to do, certain changes that had occurred since my early childhood, they were changes which had taken place a long time before.' This is one of the several ways in which the maternal figure presides over Marcel's development until the very end.

Chronological time in *Du coté de chez Swann* is as vague as elsewhere in *A la recherche,* and in it Marcel appears at one and the same time as a child whose attentions are fully focussed on his mother and as a budding adolescent capable of indulging in fantasies centred round the idea that 'all women thought of nothing but love'. Furthermore, we have the thoughts of the narrator Marcel which come from a still different point in time. Since time here is the time of memory and not simply sequential, this section can combine both Marcel as child and the later thoughts which are not part of the child. This is part of Proust's technique which, by the subtle interference of narration, can let us know how, even in the child's eye, evil can coincide with paradise. Marcel can pass back and forth between a state of paradisal innocence which includes a feeling of wholeness, of oneness with nature, and also a later phase of development into consciousness and individuality wherein paradise is, at least partially, lost.

It must be remembered that the narrator of *A la recherche* states 'the true paradises are the paradises one has lost'; as soon as Marcel begins to function as a self-conscious individual slightly removed from the family group, he has taken one step out of paradise. Paradise is lost as consciousness begins to appear and the unified twilight of the uroboric unconscious momentarily clears to show the mother at one remove from the adolescent. As this separation is taken into account, together with Marcel's growing awareness, the paradisal world of Combray appears tinged with evil. The dark mother then takes her place beside the good mother, whose presence is 'lifegiving'.

As the adolescent moves from the uroboric state of total accord between himself and the world into a stage of developing consciousness, he becomes aware of a duality in the make-up of the mother figure. The mother emerges as not only chaste and virginal, but also as the prostitute, the hetaera, a sexually oriented being available to any man. From the child's world of unity where alimentary and digestive processes are dominant, the youth moves into this sexual sphere, and the mother becomes a love object for which one must compete. It is unnecessary here to go into the Oedipal ramifications of Proust's and Marcel's relationship to the mother. One can note however that Proust has the mother present throughout the book, while the father disappears from view. He shows Marcel's father's dislike of his wife's excessive attention towards their son, and delineates the young Marcel's desire to keep his mother constantly at his side, away from the father and other men. This competitive spirit and the incestuous relationship between mother and son is more explicit in *Jean Santeuil* where Jean, in his father's absence, delights in playing at 'man of the house' with his mother as wife.[10] In this earlier book, too, we find that after an argument between mother and son, the mother makes reference to their newly regained union in terms which suggest a Jewish wedding ceremony. Jean, in his anger, had broken a precious Venetian glass and this glass appears as the motif of the temple marriage.[11] The entire incident harkens back to a letter of Madame Proust's to her son after a similar quarrel between them: 'The broken glass will no longer be anything but what it is in the temple—the symbol of the indissoluble union'.[12]

What has more than Oedipal significance in *A la recherche* is the kiss ritual which brings the mother's figure peculiarly into focus. Still the object of the child's desire, the mother's kiss is preceded by a period of anxiety while the child waits for its calmative effect to put an end to his suffering. This kiss comes 'like a Host, for an act of Communion in which my lips might drink deeply the sense of her real presence, and with it the power to sleep'. However, when the kiss is not proffered because of the presence of a guest, usually Swann, Marcel thinks of his mother in terms which suggest that she is participating in a secret orgy closed to the small boy: '. . . That forbidden and unfriendly dining room, . . . seemed to me to be concealing pleasures that were mischievous and of a mortal sadness'. By juxtaposing the mother, here, with the mistress of Marcel's later life, Proust throws the mother figure into a hetaeric light and lays down the pattern of jealous love which will prevail throughout the

[10] Marcel Proust, *Jean Santeuil* (Paris, Gallimard, 1952). 3 vols. III, 285–289.
[11] Ibid. II, 315.
[12] Philip Kolb, ed., *Marcel Proust: Correspondence avec sa mère* (Paris, 1953) p. 103. My translation.

book. The absent mother takes on a role akin to that of the absent mistress participating in 'the inconceivable, infernal scene of gaiety in the thick of which we had been imagining swarms of enemies, perverse and seductive, beguiling away from us, even making laugh at us, the woman whom we love'. She merges into the hetaeric figure who indulges in this 'demoniacal feast' and tastes 'unknown pleasures', thereby revealing her terrible and destructive side as she throws the adolescent Marcel into agonies of sexual jealousy. The mother becomes for Marcel the sovereign enchantress who fascinates by her sexuality and fills the youth with painful blind drives.

Yet this hetaeric figure is the same as the redemptive and life-giving mother who proffers the calming kiss. The adolescent Marcel has apprehended the duality of the mother figure, as the narrator reveals in the description of the youth's turbulent sentiments. He has stepped out of the uroboric round into a world marked by the pattern inflicted by the kiss ritual: absence of the beloved which produces peace. This constant vacillation between suffering and its relief—both affected by the beloved—becomes the pattern of all Marcel's relationships with women. In Marcel's youth these conflicting states are the product of a single cause: the feminine in her initial manifestation as the Great Mother.

Consciousness—even in its dawning stage—Proust reveals, presupposes conflict and duality rather than fusion and oneness. As the narrator points out, Marcel has now left his idyllic childhood and is subject to emotions 'which his childhood has not known'. A split now develops in his own being making of him two people. On the one hand there is the daytime Marcel, the developing ego, the youthful hero who rejoices in the freedom of the ecstatic movements in a world one step removed from maternal domination. On the other, there is the night-time Marcel, still tied to the sphere of the Great Mother, the youth who agonizes over the kiss-ritual and needs this maternal communion before he can peacefully subside into the unconsciousness of sleep. Marcel is now divided into two unconnected parts. In the same way the external world becomes objectified and refuses to be assimilated by the subject without a certain effort on his part. Whereas in the earlier state of fusion Marcel could blend effortlessly into Golo, now he must work at making the hawthorn blossoms part of himself. The male ego has begun to move away from the unconscious realm of unity dominated by the Great Mother, and in this separation there is suffering.

Just as the maternal figure dominated the early paradise, she now rules over Marcel's later adolescent development in an aspect which absorbs the new quality of good and evil, joy and suffering. From here on Marcel's life centres on the blind drives we have mentioned; and these drives are beyond the control of his 'weak will'. As Neumann observes, these are the very 'blind drives' which make life run a predetermined course and together with passivity fall under the aegis of the feminine principle.

Uroboros and Great Mother are both feminine dominants, and all the psychic constellations over which they rule are under the dominance of the unconscious. Conversely, its opposite, the system of ego consciousness, is masculine. With it are associated the qualities of volition, decision, and activity as contrasted with the determinism and blind 'drives' of the preconscious, egoless state.[13]

The kiss ritual and the emotions it produces in Marcel condition him to a certain pattern of behaviour which is unchangeable. It is the key motif around which habit—itself central to Proust's psychology—has begun to concretize.

Thus the Great Mother stands over Marcel's nascent ego and his development into an adolescent. But, as Georges Cattaui remarks of Marcel, he is 'un enfant qui n'a point fini de naître' (a child who never ceases to be born).[14] With his vison of the human personality's discontinuity, it is essential for Proust to have Marcel incessantly reborn into new selves. And over each of these births, we shall see, the maternal figure presides in one of the many aspects which Proust gives her. As Marcel develops away from his mother and begins to focus his sexual desires on 'les jeunes filles en fleurs', the grandmother, who is essentially a desexualised version of the mother, takes ascendence.

Jung tells us that in the period of the differentiation of the ego, as the child breaks away from the mother, all the fabulous and mysterious qualities attached to her image begin to fall away and are transferred to the person closest to her, for instance, the grandmother . . . Not infrequently she assumes the attributes of wisdom.'[15] We

13 Neumann, *The Origins . . .*, p. 125.
14 Georges Cattaui, *Proust perdu et retrouvé* (Paris, 1963) p. 23.
15 C. G. Jung, *The Archetypes and the Collective Unconscious* (London 1922–1929), p. 229.

see that this is the case with Marcel's grandmother. Not sexual, but moral, she inculcates into Marcel certain values which remain with him until the end of *A la recherche*. It is her spirit who rules over the Marcel who ultimately finds something good in every heart—even in that of Verdurin's. Edmund Wilson sees the grandmother as a stable element within *A la recherche*: 'The narrator's grandmother may be taken as playing for Proust the same role that the speed of light does for Einstein: the single constant value which makes the rest of the system possible.'[16]

Proust has Marcel leave for Balbec with his grandmother. In this he draws attention to the growth of Marcel's ego consciousness away from the unconscious passive state of the Great Mother. 'The strengthening of consciousness is borne out by the laying down of . . . moral attitudes which delimit the conscious from the unconscious by substituting knowing action for unwitting impulse.'[17] It is telling that Proust has a woman take on what is usually the masculine role of laying down moral values. This would seem to suggest that his entire orientation is feminine and that the highest values in the world he creates will revolve around a refinement of sensibility. The grandmother, as the representative of stable morality in the novel, oversees Marcel's adolescence. It is she who reminds him of his responsibility, the necessity of work; who tries to keep him from over-intoxication which may harm his health. But above all, she inculcates in Marcel a respect for the supreme value of naturalness, both in men and nature and she immerses him in an atmosphere of sensibility where art, literature, and sensitivity to human relationships take precedence over everything else. Her morality is predominantly a feminine one.

No longer subject to the agonies of the kiss ritual Marcel now fixes his desires on the more youthful figure of the maiden, what Kerenyi terms the 'Kore' and Jung, the 'anima'. The Marcel of Balbec visualizes his separation from the Great Mother concretely:

> For the first time I began to feel that it was possible that my mother might live without me, otherwise than for me, a separate life. She was going to stay with my father . . . This separation made me all the more wretched because I told myself that it

[16] Edmund Wilson, *Axel's Castle* (New York, 1931). Fontana Library edition, London, 1967 p. 134.
[17] Neumann, *The Origins . . .*, p. 126.

probably marked for my mother . . . the first trial of a form of existence to which she was beginning, now, to resign herself for the future, as the years crept on for my father and herself, an existence in which I should see less of her, in which (a thing that not even in my nightmares had yet been revealed to me) she would already have become something of a stranger, a lady who might be seen going home by herself to a house in which I should not be . . . (III, 315-316)

Although Marcel visualizes his mother here as distinct from himself, he is nevertheless still intrinsically tied to the unconscious sphere over which the mother presides. Indeed, the maternal aura pervades the entire book, in that the kiss ritual with its attendant psychic states, developed in this early maternal phase, governs Marcel's actions throughout. More important here, however, is that Proust reveals how close Marcel still is to the matriarchal unconscious world by making him choose as a love object an entire group of young girls. In the sphere of the primitive unconscious, there is no individuality. Here faces blend into one another and humans fuse with nature. This fact is noted in *A la recherche* when Proust writes of 'those primitive organisms in which the individual barely exists by itself [and which] consists in the reef rather than in the coral insects that compose it . . .' The individual in this state has no existence outside the group and the young girls who capture Marcel's youthful imagination blend harmoniously into each other : 'And this want, in my vision, of the demarcations which I should presently establish between them sent flooding over the group a wave of harmony, the continuous transfusion of a beauty, fluid, collective and mobile'. The young girls are associated with natural forms such as the sea and birds, or superhuman mythological creatures, and they never descend to the level of factual reality until Marcel has grown into a phase where he can distinguish between them, can give them individuality.

Meanwhile they are reflections of the still unformed individuality which is his, a semi-unconscious state over which the maternal figure looms. As the older Marcel looks back on the earlier stage of his development, he notes :

My desire . . . concentrated now chiefly on one, now on another, continued—as, on the first day, my confused vision—to combine and blend them, to make of them the little world apart, animated by a life in common, which for that matter they doubtless imagined themselves to form; and I should have penetrated, in becoming a friend of one of them—like a cultivated pagan or a meticulous Christian going among barbarians—into a rejuvenating society in which reigned health, unconsciousness of others, sensual pleasures, cruelty, unintellectuality and joy. (IV, 179-180)

This unconscious community of young girls which is the focus of Marcel's imagination at this stage of his development recedes as he progresses on the road to adulthood and fuller consciousness.

Before he enters the 'age of facts', as Proust originally named the latter part of his work, and leaves adolescence and his grandmother behind him, Marcel embarks on one further youthful involvement. This time the object of his desires is the Duchess of Guermantes. Just as the little band finds its origins in the girls whom Marcel desires to see spring out from the banks of the Vivonne, so the Duchess is the last mythological creature to emerge from his paradisal childhood. Removed from the real world of facts—which is inevitably devoid of all magical implications—the Duchess of Guermantes is the focus of all Marcel's imaginings related to an ancient and feudal France.

Marcel's growth away from the harmonious realm of Combray and Saint-Hilaire where he had a first glimpse of the Duchess, is nevertheless a marked one, for now the Duchess no longer inhabits an enchanted castle, but the same plebian residence as Marcel. He is one step closer to the 'world of facts' in which the fully conscious ego functions. But in this transitional stage, the Duchess still retains for him a portion of the mythological aura which he saw in her in his Combray phase. Proust depicts, at great length, a scene at the theatre in which the nobility takes on the aspect of supernatural sea creatures. The sea has been transposed from Balbec into a Parisian locale, and the Duchess holds a central place among its mythical reigning deities.

Above all, the Duchess has the power of invoking, for Marcel, once more the paradisal Combray; for in this 'age of words', the incantatory magic of pronouncing 'Guermantes', or listening to Oriane's provincial intonations, is capable of bringing back 'The charm of the summer afternoons when I walked along Guermantes' way'. In the half-way house between childhood and the adult world, Marcel already possesses a highly developed sense of nostalgia, a feeling for the inevitable 'lostness' of paradise, which is to grow stronger as he grows older.

The break with adolescence comes with the death of the grand-mother, and in her wake we find the blossoming of that exotic and damned homosexual, the Baron de Charlus. At last, we see Marcel totally in the adult world of the 'age of facts' where evil is omni-present. He is, in this phase, an individual, completely separated from his mother and grandmother. The fact of death has given him a consciousness which testifies to his essential aloneness, for the beneficial aura diffused by the grandmother who has acted as a guardian angel has now disappeared. Marcel is no longer at one with the maternal world, representative of a stable and harmonious moral order. As an adolescent:

> I knew, when I was with my grandmother, that, however great the misery that there was in me, it would be received by her with a pity still more vast; that everything that was mine, my cares, my wishes, would be, in my grandmother, supported upon a desire to save and prolong my life stronger than was my own; and my thoughts were continued in her without having to under-go any deflection, since they passed from my mind into hers without change of atmosphere or of personality. . . . And when I felt my mouth glued to her cheeks, to her brow, I drew from them something so beneficial, so nourishing that I lay in her arms as motionless, as solemn, as calmly gluttonous as a babe at the breast. (III, 344-345)

Bersani points out that here 'Marcel, like an infant, finds the very source of his being in his grandmother's body; he is empty without a sufficient will to live unless he attaches himself to this body, in-corporates its strength.' He is still essentially in an early matriarchal phase and has not learned 'to give up an instinctive sense of con-tinuity between himself and the external world'.[18]

Through her death, the grandmother forces Marcel into a phase of his development wherein he alone is responsible for himself; and where he must incorporate into himself all that the grandmother has stood for. 'She had suddenly handed back to me the thoughts, the griefs which, from the days of my infancy, I had entrusted for all time to her keeping . . . I was already alone.' Thus, with the death of the grandmother, this 'child who never ceases to be born'

[18] Bersani, p. 33.

is born into another self—the Marcel of *The Cities of the Plain* and the Albertine volumes. We have so far seen Marcel pass from the uroboric stage of non-ego, from the paradise of the family unit at Combray, through to the ethical phase of the grandmother where sexuality is projected outwards, away from the mother figure. As Marcel enters *Sodome et Gomorrhe* we meet a new figure, the 'profaned mother'.

The profaned mother is a figure who often appears in the Proustian universe, from the early *Les plaisirs et les jours* (*Pleasures and Days*) into the last volumes of *A la recherche*. As many of his critics have observed, she exists as a projection of Proust's own guilt feelings toward Madame Proust. In his fiction she is embodied as the essentially good mother, who has been defiled by her children's wrongs, whether these take the form of direct conflict or an unconscious debasement of the mother's image.

'La confession d'une jeune fille' presents an early exploitation of this theme in the narrative of a young girl who causes her mother's premature death because of her lack of will and her delight in sensuality. Although the punishment which the girl inflicts on herself is highly disproportionate to the gravity of her crime, Proust intensifies his point by this exaggeration. It would seem that it is not so much the girl's sexual misdemeanours which are the cause of her guilt, but rather the bare fact that in turning her attention to another love object, she has betrayed her mother. Nevertheless, one cannot simply omit the point which Proust's biographical critics make. Since it is very possible that it is really Proust himself who is speaking here in the guise of a young girl, the sin which is committed is not merely sexual play between a man and a woman, but, for him, the much graver one of homosexuality. The desecration of the mother's hallowed image, however, stands central to any interpretation of the story—as it becomes much clearer in 'Sentiments filiaux d'un parricide.' Here one realises that the very fact of the child's existence is a profanation of the mother; for day by day, in his various selfish acts, he hastens her death and defiles her.[19]

After the death of the grandmother in *A la recherche*, Marcel's mother grows into the desexualised and chaste figure of the grandmother. This is a symbolic as well as a concrete change; for Mar-

---

[19] Marcel Proust, 'Sentiments filiaux d'un parricide', *Pastiches et Mélanges* (Paris, 1919) p. 223. There is no need to underline, once again, the Oedipal motif which is so strong in this tale.

cel's mother takes on the grandmother's appearance and carries with her everywhere the volumes of Madame de Sévigné—an equally profaned mother who lavished all her love on a notoriously ungrateful daughter. As a replacement for his mother as a sexual object of desire, Marcel now has Albertine, who continues the ritual of the kiss. Yet by this replacement, the mother is defiled, for the sacred communion between mother and son, represented by the kiss, now has as its high-priestess the hetaeric figure of Albertine:

> She used to slide her tongue between my lips like a portion of daily bread, a nourishing food that had the almost sacred character of all flesh upon which the sufferings that we have endured on its account have come in time to confer a sort of spiritual grace, what I at once call to mind in comparison is . . . the night on which my father sent Mama to sleep in the little bed by the side of my own. So it is that life, if it is once again to deliver us from an anguish that has seemed inevitable, does so in conditions that are different, so diametrically opposed at times that it is almost an open sacrilege to assert the identity of the grace bestowed upon us. (IX, 2)

The defilement of the mother figure in these late volumes is further emphasised by Marcel's mother's dislike of his mistress and by the fact that she has now lost all hope in his ever settling down to work. Marcel has failed to fulfil both his mother's and his grandmother's aspirations and his guilt for not making use of his time looms large in the anxiety of the Albertine volumes.

The profaned mother finds her principal symbolisation, however, in the figure of the homosexual, and Proust's personal guilt is in full evidence here. It is in the invert that the mother appears most fully deformed in purpose as well as in shape. Proust's description of Charlus, or any homosexual, entering a salon epitomises the fate of the profaned mother.

> When it is a Charlus, . . . it is always the spirit of a relative of the female sex, attendant like a goddess, or incarnate as a double, that undertakes to introduce him into a strange drawing-room and to mould his attitude . . . By virtue of the same law, which requires that life, in the interests of the still unfulfilled act, shall bring into play, utilise, adulterate, in a perpetual prostitution, the most respectable, it may be the most sacred, sometimes only

the most innocent legacies from the past . . . Not that there need be any connexion between the appearance of M. de Charlus and the fact that sons, who do not always take after their fathers, even without being inverts and though they go after women, may consummate upon their faces the profanation of their mothers. But we need not consider here a subject that deserves a chapter to itself : the Profanation of the Mother. (VII, 73-75)

Although Proust never actually includes in *A la recherche* this chapter dedicated to the mother, profaned either by her inverted or heterosexual son, it exists in different forms throughout the work. In the scene which describes Mlle Vinteuil and her lesbian friend spitting on the dead Vinteuil's portrait, for example, we find not only a transference of sexes, but an equally profaned parent. Vinteuil, it must be remembered, is after all a very maternal figure. He watches over his daughter with an enveloping protectiveness symbolised by his constant worry over whether she is clothed with sufficient warmth. Profaned by his daughter's lesbian relationship (just as Proust defiled his mother through his homosexuality), he ultimately dies because of it, as did the mother in 'La confession d'une jeune fille'. The fact that the desecration of Vinteuil's image takes place in Combray suggests the importance of this motif in Marcel's inner life, for all the major themes of *A la recherche* find their root here. Psychologically, it would seem that the child who imag-inner life, for all the major themes of *A la recherche* find their Marcel when Swann comes to dinner, punishes the prostitute which he senses in his mother by later profaning her. The guilt which stems from this early abuse of the mother then finds its partial justification in seeing the sullied maternal figure everywhere. Vinteuil is the narrator's and Proust's projection of this guilt.

As Marcel reaches the point in his development where he is about to be reborn into the figure of the artist, the many-faced maternal figure returns with her initial transpersonal aspect. With self-realisation and the homecoming to the unconscious—now truly a creative unconscious for Marcel—the maternal round is complete; and the Great Mother takes on the role of the arbiter of his salvation. What this signifies will be discussed later when Marcel, redeemed in his new vocation, is studied. Here it is only necessary to look at the last detailed appearance of Marcel's mother in the Venice sequence and see what her presence suggests.

The Venice sequence is described throughout in terms of Com-

bray; as Marcel remarks: 'I was receiving there impressions analogous to those I had felt so often in the past at Combray, but transposed into a wholly different and far richer key.' Saint Mark's is
compared to Saint-Hilaire, the canals to the Vivonne and at the
centre of Venice, as well as Combray, stands the mother. Venice,
which for Proust with his love of Ruskin was above all the enchanted city of art, thus becomes the transitional point between time
lost and time regained through art. Combray has not as yet been
recaptured through involuntary memory and set down in the fixed
form of the novel, yet it has found its analogy. The lost paradise of
youth is glimpsed again in Venice, the stepping stone into the paradise of self-realisation and artistic salvation.

Over this once again enchanted world stands Marcel's mother,
watching his actions from her elevated terrace and smiling with all
the goodness of a redemptive figure. The concretized version of the
symbolic and transpersonal uroboric mother, she can now serve as
a link between the world of lost time and redeemed time, but not
as its final embodiment. It is noteworthy that she disappears as a
character from the last pages of *A la recherche*, for here it is the
diffused atmosphere of a non-personalised reality which reigns, a
reality which is none the less feminine in its focus on creativity and
the unconscious.

Yet, the personalised figure of Marcel's mother in Venice can
still contain elements of the profaned maternal figure, as well as
embodying her new redemptive possibilities. As the narrator points
out, she is now filled with a patience toward Marcel which she
might not have had if her aspirations for him still existed. Her tenderness for her child has reached a new height; and she takes on,
for the now adult Marcel, a sacral and eternal aspect which conse-
crates her in her redemptive role. Marcel sees her as Carpaccio's
'Saint-Ursula': a veiled, aged, lady draped in mourning and sancti-
fied forever in Saint-Mark's.

Significantly, the Venice sequence ends with a choice for Marcel
between the mother in her tender and redemptive aspect and her
profanation by the possibility of indulging in sexual pleasures. On
the day that he and his mother are to leave Venice, Marcel notices
in the hotel register that the expected guests include 'Baronne Putbus et suite'. Immediately Marcel wants to put off the moment of
departure, for the Baronne Putbus' chambermaid has been recom-
mended to him by Saint-Loup and she has figured in many of Mar-

cel's dreams of sexual adventure. The terms used to describe the course of his sentiments at this time are revealing. 'Then, the sensation of all the hours of carnal pleasure which our departure would make me miss, raised this desire—which existed in me as a chronic condition—to the height of a sentiment and drowned it in melancholy and vagueness.' Leo Bersani pointedly asks: 'Why should Marcel's wish be smothered in melancholy and vagueness, which necessarily qualify the anticipation of pleasure?'[20] The answer would seem to lie in the conflict between sexual desire and what we call the profanation' of the mother through a sexual act, which, in fact, denotes her betrayal. This conflict is evidenced in Marcel's mother's refusal to take his demand for a prolongation of their stay seriously, and his subsequent need 'to rebel against an imaginary plot woven against me by my parents . . ., that fighting spirit, that desire which drove me in the past to enforce my wishes upon the people I loved best in the world, prepared to conform to their wishes after I had succeeded in making them yield.' Thus, the melancholy and vagueness which accompany Marcel's initial desire 'seem to anticipate his mother's resistance and his resistance to her . . . It is as if the subsequent struggle with his mother and the accompanying guilt were somehow part of Marcel's sexual pleasure.'[21] Indeed, a part of Marcel's sexual pleasure resides precisely in the idea that he is profaning his mother and punishing her; and this is accompanied by a feeling of remorse at the profanation which lies at the base of his melancholy.

Once Marcel's mother has left him behind, however, there is no more thought of the Putbus chambermaid, only a sense of desperation and a distintegration of personality which is outwardly projected and finds its reflection in the image of Venice suddenly reduced to its basic elements.

> Things had become alien to me . . . The town that I saw before me had ceased to be Venice. Its personality, its name, seemed to me to be lying fictions which I no longer had the courage to impress upon its stones. I saw the palaces reduced to the constituent parts, lifeless heaps of marble with nothing to choose between them . . . (XI, 320)

Away from the maternal gaze, stripped of his mother's attention,

[20] Bersani, p. 25.
[21] Ibid.

Marcel, like Venice, no longer posesses an identity. He becomes once again a helpless child, 'je n'etais plus qu'un coeur qui battait', an 'appareil vide', whose selfhood depends on the stability of the mother's image of him. David Holbrook defines this dependence of the so-called 'I AM' feeling as hinging upon the mother :

> In the 'mirror-role' of the mother—the way in which her response to her child, expressed in her face, is a way of establishing his sense of his own identity—what he sees in her face is himself; and this sense of being is the basis of a creative looking at the world.[22]

In his mother's absence, Marcel loses his sense both of his own identity and of the identity of the external world, a feeling which is duplicated in the opening pages of the novel in his awakening from sleep. And the birth of the self, after this extinction, can only take place through a return to the mother. The sexual pleasure which leads to a profanation of the mother gives way in this phase to a return to the mother in her redemptive role as the saviour of identity and selfhood. The tender gaze of the mother, now disembodied into her purest form, symbolically watches over *Le temps retrouvé,* as Marcel is born into his creative role.

Although it is the maternal figure which undoubtedly incarnates the most important aspect of the feminine in *A la recherche,* Marcel comes into contact with other figures of femininity who are significant in his formation. We will examine these respectively under the groupings of 'jeunes filles en fleurs' and 'prisoners'. It should be stressed here that we are, for the purposes of this study, interested in Proust's psychology of love only insofar as it reflects the nature of the feminine in *A la recherche.* The central focus lies on the place of the feminine in the formation of Marcel as an artist and the feminine aspect of this final position.

JEUNES FILLES EN FLEURS

The feminine figures Marcel confronted when he was under the dominance of his grandmother are initial manifestations of that form of the feminine which we can call the 'anima' and which finds its culmination in the Albertine of *La prisonnière.* Included in this aspect of the feminine are the many young girls who people the

---

[22] David Holbrook, 'R. D. Laing and the Death Circuit', *Encounter* XXXI, 2, 35–45 p. 39.

countryside of Balbec, Gilberte, and most significantly, 'les vierges impitoyables et sensuelles' of the little band.

> The anima, the 'Soul image' which the male experiences in the female, is his own inner femininity and soulfulness, an element of his own psyche. But the anima—as Jung pointed out from the very first—is formed in part by the male's personal as well as archetypal experience of the Feminine. For this reason, the man's anima figure, which has found its expression in the myth and art of all times, is a product of genuine experience of the nature of the feminine, and not a mere manifestation of male projections upon the woman.[1]

Marcel, in this phase, does not as yet have a fully defined anima figure. Occupying a position midway between the Great Mother, the unconsciousness of childhood, and the adult world where the anima represents the unique and fully achieved individual, the adolescent Marcel is fascinated by a series of potential anima figures which blend into one another. All of these girls are stamped with the imprint of his own imaginary projections. As the narrator says of the Albertine of Balbec :

> Since my first sight of Albertine I had meditated upon her daily, a thousandfold, I had carried on with what I called by her name an interminable unspoken dialogue in which I made her question me, answer me, think and act, and in the infinite series of imaginary Albertines who followed one after the other in my fancy, hour after hour, the real Albertine, a glimpse caught on the beach, figured only at the head, just as the actress who creates a part, the star, appears, out of a long series of performances, in the first few alone. (IV, 219)

Yet the characteristics which these projections draw attention to, serve to outline the essential nature of the feminine as 'anima'. We have already seen how the collective aspect of the little band reflected Marcel's own lack of individuality. It is now necessary to examine in what way the feminine figures of this phase influence Marcel in his development, and to distil from this the properties which Proust visualizes as feminine.

The principal quality which the budding girls possess in common

[1] Erich Neumann, *The Great Mother* (New York, 1955), pp. 32–33.

is that the fascination which they hold for Marcel lies not only in themselves, but in relation to some otherness. Unlike the mother and the grandmother, they are not total in themselves and cannot be loved in familiarity. They are the stepping stones to another life and exude the magic of the unknown. Gilberte is attractive because of her closeness to Bergotte and in Marcel's imagination she is always linked to 'the charm of all the fancies which the thought of cathedrals used to inspire in me, the charm of the hills and valleys of the Ile-de-France and the plains of Normandy'. Mlle de Stermaria is desirable because of the inaccessibility of the artistocratic life which she represents 'and its stock of heredity gave to her complexion, in which so many selected juices had been blended, the savour of an exotic fruit or of a famous vintage'. To capture the unknown essence of the Vivonne and the Méséglise way, Marcel needs to embrace a girl who has grown out of its soil.

Thus the way to unknown places, an unknown life, is through the feminine figure, and the little band, above all, exemplifies this. In its supreme health, its energy and activity, its sheer physicality, it represents all that is unknown to Marcel. What he sees in these budding girls is the eternal changeability of the sea: 'They were for me the mountainous blue undulations of the sea, a troop seen passing in outline against the waves. It was the sea which I hoped to find again, if I went to some town where they might be. Our most intensive love for a person is always the love of something else as well.'

Through the young girls of this phase Marcel is drawn to what is unknown and seemingly inaccessible. As the narrator points out: 'Once we believe that a fellow creature has a share in some unknown existence to which the creature's love for ourselves can win us admission, that is, of all the preliminary conditions which Love exacts, the one to which he attaches the most importance.' Thus love and the desire of women instils a curiosity in the adolescent which forces him to move out of his familiar world and relate to an unknown sphere. In this way woman becomes the instrument of change, of growth within the personality. She instils in the youth the desire to relate to an external object and hence expands his imaginative horizon. Of the early Albertine, Marcel says:

And it was consequently her whole life that filled me with desire; a sorrowful desire because I felt that it was not to be realised, but exhilarating, because what had hitherto been my life, having ceased of a sudden to be my whole life, being no more now than a little part of the space stretching out before me, which I was burning to cover and which was composed of the lives of these girls, offered me that prolongation, that possible multiplication of oneself which is happiness. (IV, 130)

Here Proust is invoking the transformative character of the feminine as we have already seen it both in James's Cinderella figures and in Musil's embodiments of possibility. In James, the central feminine intelligences are responsible for turning man inward, toward himself and engendering a process of spiritual growth. Musil, on the other hand, sees the feminine primarily as a means of freeing man from his social and moral conservatism and hence, pointing the way to a universe based on entirely new principles. With Proust, the transformative aspect of the feminine works on the male both externally and inwardly. Initially it draws the Marcel who lies supine in the enclosed world of the family, outward into a sphere where he is forced to make contact with the objective world. Ultimately, as we shall see in our study of the later Albertine, this only serves to turn him inward to the world of individuation and self-realisation. Neumann writes:

> The anima is the vehicle par excellence of the transformative character. It is the mover, the instigator of change, whose fascination drives, lures and encourages the male to all the adventures of the soul and spirit, of action and creation in the inner and outward world.[2]

The curiosity which the flowering girls engender in Marcel and which lures his personality into motion is based on several of their key characteristics. First and foremost is the mystery of their sexuality, their essential otherness as females. Proust renders this otherness so suggestively in Marcel's first encounter with a young girl, Gilberte, that it seems difficult to conceive how the critics could see in her a little boy. Gilberte suddenly flowers out of the Combray countryside, just as Marcel has often wished some dreamed-of woman to do. Closely related to the pink hawthorns, whose mystery the youth similarly tries to fathom, Gilberte becomes the first flowering girl. Her 'skin strewn with pink freckles' matches the pinkness of the

---

[2] Erich Neumann, *The Great Mother*, pp. 34–35.

hawthorns; and it is necessary to remember that in *A la recherche* flowers are continually associated with sexuality—the sexuality of the flowering girls of *A l'ombre* . . . of Odette's and Swann's 'cattleya', as well as with the more exotic and sterile sexuality of the opening pages of *Sodome et Gomorrhe*. As he does with the girls he encounters, notably with the young fishergirl in Carqueville, Marcel attempts to have Gilberte focus all her attention on him. 'I looked at her . . . with that look . . . which attempted to force her to pay attention to me, to know me!' By immobilizing her attention in this way, Marcel feels that he can possess her and the mystery of her sexuality. (Note the repetition of this process in Carqueville). But Gilberte merely answers him with an obscene gesture, which the young Marcel interprets as insolence, only to find out too late that it suggested the physical culmination of his desires.

This mysterious sexuality is also proper to the little band whom Marcel visualises as living in a realm totally different from his own. Extraordinary in their suppleness and grace, in their resemblance to Greek statues or sea birds, the girls of the little band are for Marcel the incarnation of an erotic freedom, far removed from middle class virtue. They seem to him the 'very young mistresses of racing cyclists' and from the vantage point of their otherness Marcel sees no possibility of being distinguished or recognised. He wonders at the mystery of the other sphere which they inhabit—that other world of the feminine.

> If she had seen me, what could I have represented for her? In the heart of what universe did she distinguish me? It would have been as hard for me to say as, when certain peculiarities are made visible, thanks to the telescope, in a neighbouring planet, it is difficult to arrive at the conclusion that human beings inhabit it, that they can see us, or to say what ideas the sight of us can have aroused in their minds. (IV 129-130)

Although Marcel half believes that he has penetrated this mysterious otherness in his later acquaintance with the little band, he does not really do so until the experiences of the Albertine volumes.

For Proust, the transformative character of the feminine is necessarily embodied in a youthful woman, for it is only she who contains that necessary fluidity of feature, that mobility and flexibility which makes of her a fugitive—a constantly changing creature :

Whereas adolescence is anterior to this complete solidification; and from it follows that we feel, in the company of young girls, the refreshing sense that is afforded by the spectacle of forms undergoing an incessant process of change, a play of unstable forces which makes us think of that perpetual re-creation of the primordial elements of nature which we contemplate when we stand by the sea. (IV, 287)

Induced to pursue this protean being, the male is himself transformed. In this Proust parallels Musil, for we have seen that Musil, too, found the supreme incarnation of possibility in the young girl whose features are not as yet fixed, and who thus leaves the path open to imagination and change. Proust concretises the protean aspect of the feminine by actually describing the various shifts in appearance and character which the young girls undergo. Their variability evokes surprise in Marcel and stimulates him to explore ever-changing facets of reality. What we find in the flowering girls is essentially what Beckett terms a 'pictorial multiplicity'. This becomes a multiplicity in depth only when Marcel leaves this stage of adolescence. Thus we see the external aspect of the budding girls constantly changing.

Gilberte in her first appearance has blue eyes which are then discovered to be black. At one moment she resembles Swann; at another Odette; at another a wholly different creature. The little band is even more variable, as each girl takes on the features of another to present an ever-changing panorama. As Marcel points out, the Albertine he first saw, he has never seen again, for like the fleeting instants of time, Albertine always presents a new face; and like a stationary object, her face 'shapes itself according to a totally different formation if we approach it from a different side'. Albertine's beauty mark shifts from her chin to her cheek to her forehead and her mood changes with her appearance. Similarly, Marcel becomes a different Marcel each time he meets or contemplates a different Albertine, who, as the supreme embodiment of the mobile fugitive, represents an unknown world, an unknown selfhood, and Marcel clearly sees her in this transformative role. As she changes, he changes; and contemplating her, he is placed in pursuit of a whole sphere of being which is other than himself.

Brought into contact with an unknown, with an external reality, Proust suggests that Marcel is still essentially on the road to a fuller selfhood; for the feminine in its transformative character is 'an image, a reversed projection 'a "negative" of our sensibility'. Proust sees the anima in women 'attuned to satisfying our senses and making our hearts suffer'. Activator of change, the transformative feminine is necessarily an activator of suffering. For Proust, it is through this very suffering that habit is broken down and the individual is forced to exist in a state open to stimulation and hence, renewal of the self. It is to the 'jeune fille' that the mature Marcel, imbued with the sense of his artistic purpose, will turn for his only source of company. For the feminine in her transformative character is essential to the imaginative life and its constant renewal.

> And indeed the pleasure that was given me by the little band, as noble as if it had been composed of Hellenic virgins, came from some suggestion that there was in it of the flight of passing figures along a road. This fleetingness of persons who are not known to us, who force us to put out from the harbour of life, in which the women whose society we frequent, have all, in course of time, laid bare the blemishes, urges us into that state of pursuit in which there is no longer anything to arrest the imagination. (IV, 132)

There is another feminine figure in the Proustian canvas who falls into the category of 'être de fuite'. This is the Duchess of Guermantes who holds, as we have already seen, a special place in the adolescent Marcel's imagination where she appears as a magical incarnation of an old aristocratic France. Representative of this particular form of the 'inconnu' the Duchess becomes the object of Marcel's constant pursuit, when he sees her in Paris on his return from Balbec.

This Paris is for Marcel an extension of the Balbec and Méséglise where every woman takes on the image of a hetaera and is prepared to satisfy his physical desires. He feels his heart bounding toward an unknown life and thinks:

> . . . The world appeared to me now a pleasanter place to live in, life a more interesting experience now that I had learned that the streets of Paris, like the roads round Balbec, were aflower with those unknown beauties whom I had so often sought to evoke from the woods and Méséglise, each one of whom aroused a sensual longing which she alone appeared capable of assuaging. (V, 72-73)

The principal actor in this drama of the Paris streets is the Duchess of Guermantes and she takes over the role of object of Marcel's longings—a role which neither Gilberte, Albertine or Gisèle have been able to fulfil. As Marcel transfers all his images of love to Oriane, she too becomes a fugitive, with supernatural associations. He wonders how he recognises this bird-like Egyptian divinity 'whose appearance changes daily'. But what Marcel seeks is the essential otherness of feminine sexuality behind this eternal flux: 'the invisible being who put all this into movement'.

Oriane figures as an 'être de fuite', a fugitive, not only for Marcel, but for Parisian society as well. The best of Parisian hostesses seek her often unattainable presence and regard her as the culminating figure at any social gathering. But Oriane is whimsical in her appearances as well as in her 'esprit'. In the midst of the Paris social season, she suddenly disappears and one learns that she has chosen this unheard of time for a visit to the Norwegian fjords. Or, she astounds the 'gratin' by failing to appear at a major gathering in order to go unostentatiously to the theatre and really see a play. In this she plays on the element of surprise and produces that stimulation which is a precondition of the transformative character.

Oriane's wit is similarly based upon this quality of surprise. While all of Parisian society is thinking one way, she will suddenly introduce another point of view and produce that shock essential to breaking down a stultifying habit, a perennial mode of thought. Although Oriane's need for novelty is of a superficial and frivolous character, well suited to her role as a social lion, she still points out how fundamental to the feminine the qualities of mobility and stimulation are. Her success as a hostess and as a transformative figure of Parisian society is based on her flexibility of mind and her ability to introduce surprise, to relieve boredom. As Proust remarks concerning her unexpected actions:

> People in society were stupefied, and, without any thought of following the Duchess's example, derived nevertheless from her action that sense of relief which one has in reading Kant when, after the most rigorous demonstration of determinism, one finds that above the world of necessity there is the world of freedom. Every invention of which no one has ever thought before excites the interest even of people who can derive no benefit from it.

The first aspect of Proust's vision of the feminine thus appears in a form we have already encountered both in James and Musil. The feminine in her transformative character embodies the properties of the fugitive—constant flux, a mysterious otherness representative of another mode of life—and as a fugitive, she is the prime mover and instigator of change. However, Proust presents a further facet of the transformative feminine character in that section of *A la recherche* which marks the end of adolescence and the entry into the 'age of facts'. We can designate this section by the general title of 'prisoners' for in it there appears a series of characters whose psychological formation is that of the captive. The feminine here emerges in the fulness of its anima aspect as the woman takes on a defined personality and resists the web of masculine projections.

PRISONERS

In the latter pages of *A la recherche* the prisoner appears in three major garbs. First of all he is the invert, notably Charlus, whose female character is chained to a masculine body and who subsequently becomes the slave of his homosexual desires. Secondly, he appears as the woman held captive by a jealous lover. Finally, the prisoner emerges as the lover himself, enslaved by his own jealousy.

Charlus' case is interesting because he contains both sexes in himself and thus the role of jailer as well as prisoner. A projection of Proust's homosexual side, he duplicates in certain ways the movement of Marcel's relationship with Albertine and throws a revealing light upon it. We first meet Charlus as the advocate of virility who chastizes the effeminacy of modern youth, and who yet contains in himself 'the most refined qualities of sensibility'. Marcel's grandmother is delighted to hear him talking of Madame de Sevigné with such refinement and she finds in Charlus 'certain delicacies, a feminine sensibility'. Indeed, a refined sensibility is always part of the 'feminine' although it is only found in the figures of the mother and the grandmother, the later Albertine, and Andrée, whose likeness to Marcel is often noted. This refined sensibility is, of course also evident in Swann, for as many of Proust's critics have suggested, Swann is a projection of Marcel, his alter-ego.

In Charlus, this feminine sensibility is not, as Marcel first believes, due to the influence of a mother, a daughter, or a mistress. Rather it finds its basis in the fact that Charlus is, in all ways except the physical, a woman; only the virility of his body disguises this essential femininity. During his first appearance in *A la recherche,* Charlus maintains this pose of masculinity and keeps his feminine nature tightly in reign, in bondage to his virile image. Finally, however, it breaks through and Charlus becomes more and more 'ladylike'. Beginning with the revelation of his homosexuality in the opening pages of *Sodome et Gomorrhe,* we see Charlus' female side taking ascendance and more and more openly demanding fulfilment in a masculine object. Ultimately his character, the masculine strength of will which kept his feminine side and his vice in check, is destroyed and he becomes the victim and prisoner of his blind sexual drives. His partial paralysis, his temporary blindness, all testify to his inner dissolution, as Charlus, even at the breakdown of his body, compulsively lures youths to indulge his diseased eroticism. The destructive unconscious side of the feminine duality has taken over with its command over instinctive drives. Charlus emerges as the prisoner of his instincts. Proust accurately outlines Charlus' secondary feminine characteristics as he portrays first his refined sensibility, then his tendency to hysteria and finally, the passivity of the feminine become diseased in Charlus' blatant masochism.

The pattern of homosexual love, which we need only dwell on briefly here, parallels that of heterosexual love. Both, for Proust, are illnesses based on that omnipresent jailer, habit, and are founded on jealousy. Happiness in love is psychologically impossible both for the invert as well as for the heterosexual. The fate of the invert is that, like a woman, he can really only love the heterosexual man. Since homosexuality is a disease for Proust, the homosexual can never be a 'whole' man and hence he cannot constitute an ideal love object. This places the invert in interminable pursuit of an unattainable ideal and he is forced to settle for half-measures—for the invert or the prostitute, in whom, lying to himself, he believes to have found his ideal lover. Similarly, Marcel seeks the perfect embodiment of his ideal woman, an ideal which is unattainable in reality, and, having found a woman, tries to recreate her in the image of his dreams. Both types of love result in suffering, or rather the oscillation between boredom and suffering : the first when the lover is present, the second when his or her absence throws the lover into jealous agonies. This, of course, only accounts for part of the impossibility of happiness in love, but it is the aspect which concerns us most directly here.

As we shall see more fully in the relationship of Albertine and

Marcel, however, there is one difference between homosexual and heterosexual love. Morel, who plays Albertine to Charlus, does not possess the transformative character of the feminine. Fugitive and bisexual, like Albertine, he does not, however, turn Charlus back to a re-examination of his own essence. Rather he leads him to the path of destruction and total dissolution, as Charlus is more and more fully enslaved by his own vice. The bisexual character, or the hermaphrodite, in Proust's vision is doomed if he attempts to exercise his bisexuality in a carnal sphere. For in this he becomes literally a slave to his obsession. Robbed of his liberty and of the possibility of inner growth, he falls victim to the spiritually annihilatory fires of Sodom and Gomorrah. It is in the *physical* expression of his bisexuality that the homosexual differs from the hermaphrodite, for this latter exists as a symbolical expression of an inner unity of masculine and feminine qualities.

The direction which the 'prisoner' theme will take can be seen in the Charlus figure : first of all, the feminine element is found imprisoned by the power of the masculine will; subsequently there is a reversal and the male becomes the slave of his own attempt at imprisonment. Proust, it would seem, is suggesting that there is something in the make-up of the fugitive female which will not allow her to be imprisoned, to be captured. He provides two examples of love-relationships, prior to that of Marcel and Albertine, which lay down the pattern subsequently to be enlarged on. It is worthwhile glancing at these, for even though they do not present the full scope of the final relationship, they reveal certain key aspects of the feminine in the fullness of her transformative character.

'Swann's Love' lays down the well-known pattern of Proust's psychology of love as the constant alternation of boredom and despair. Boredom is the effect of habit, the outcome of the loved one's presence and security in the knowledge of her affections. Suffering comes with the absence of the loved one and the consequent breakdown of habit through jealousy. Swann, like Charlus, is one extension of the narrator's personality. This is evident in the rhythm of jealousy and appeasement which his love takes on, a rhythm we have already seen in the young Marcel's relationship to his mother. Odette, similar in so many ways to Albertine, is in breadth, rather than depth, the most fully drawn woman in the Proustian canvas. Portrayed from multiple points of view and from various points in time, Odette is the *dame en rose* who excites the boy, Marcel; the transvestite portrayed with love by Elstir in the portrait 'Miss Sacripant'; Swann's Zephora; the mysterious and fashionable mother of Gilberte; the militant anti-Dreyfusite; Madame de Forcheville, useful mother-in-law to Saint-Loup; and finally mistress to the Duc de Guermantes. Through all these metamorphoses there lies a certain continuity, for Odette retains the basic character of the cocotte, the hetaera—whom all men desire and who succumbs willingly to all men.

The drama of Swann's jealous love for Odette appears essentially as the narrative of an attempt to captivate a fleeting and multiple object. It unfolds in the telling atmosphere of the Verdurin salon—just as Marcel's love will, in part—where a jealous vigilance over the members of the little clan is exercised by the 'patronne', Madame Verdurin. Odette, like Albertine, is a fugitive with a Sapphic side to her nature and a great tendency to falsification. Her presence is essential to Swann once he has acquired the habit of seeing her regularly. Odette, however, has a more elementary character than Albertine in that she is a professional demi-mondaine and Swann 'sees in every man a possible lover for Odette'. In her mobility, Odette presents faces varying in degrees of attractiveness; but Swann, like Marcel, seeks the enigmatic essence of the feminine behind this changing facade : 'The knowledge that, within this new and strange chrysalis, it was still Odette that lurked, still the same artful temperament, artful and evasive, was enough to keep Swann seeking, with as much passion as ever, to captivate her'.

Swann's attempt to make Odette a prisoner is essentially an attempt to shape an ever-shifting external reality into a fixed and stationary imaginative object. His constant jealous vigilance testifies to the impossibility of this task; for Odette has not only a facade changing in the present, but a past which shapes her and which continually alters in Swann's mind as he learns more about her. As Germaine Brée observes, in the Proustian universe the 'attempt to hold idol and idolator within a closed, timeless space from which change is eliminated'[3] is impossible. Instead Swann becomes the prisoner of his own jealous habit.

This jealous vigilance of Swann's is, however, an interesting one. Aimed at circumscribing Odette by gaining a total awareness of her actions, it is essentially a curiosity about the unknown. Swann, at the Prince de Guermantes' gathering does, in fact, state that jealousy

[3] Brée, p. 202.

is an incentive for people who are not naturally curious, to manifest an interest in others and more specifically in another's life. Odette's mystery is frequently likened to the equally fleeting mystery of the little phrase of Vinteuil's Sonata. Thus Swann's curiosity about her becomes an attempt to fathom art. For Proust, the essence of the feminine is somehow inextricably linked to the essence of creativity. And Swann, although he parallels Marcel in his jealous habit, in his voyeuristic spying, and in the entire pattern of his love, does not, as Marcel will later, discover in what this mystery lies.

Nevertheless, Odette's effect on Swann is a telling one. She too is an 'anima' figure for Swann, and in her role as jailer, she transforms him. Proust's original description of Swann's love habits casts him as a Don Juan figure. He constantly desires different women and, unlike Marcel, actively embarks on a process of conquest. These conquests, however, are purely physical, and as soon as he tires of a certain woman's sensual gratification, he moves on to another. In the Swann of this phase, emotion and physical desire are totally disparate. Through Odette, emotion and sexuality are reunited in Swann. He is reborn into a youth, for Odette is capable of making him suffer and suffering in Proust is always the precondition of entering upon a new self : 'Perhaps it was to that hour of anguish that there must be attributed the importance which Odette had since assumed in his life. Other people are, as a rule, so immaterial to us that, when we have entrusted to any one of them the power to cause so much suffering or happiness to ourselves, that person seems at once to belong to a different universe, is surrounded with poetry . . .'

Related to the painting which Swann loves, Odette is imbued with emotion and hence, a sense of poetry. But although Swann projects this poetical light on Odette, she remains the instigator of his projection. A prisoner, Swann yet benefits from the effect of the transformative character of the feminine :

> For Swann was finding in things once more, since he had fallen in love, the charm that he had found when, in his adolescence, he had fancied himself as an artist; with this difference, that what charm lay in them now was conferred by Odette alone. He could feel reawakening in himself the inspirations of his boyhood, which had been dissipated among the frivolities of his later life, but they all bore, now, the reflection, the stamp of a particular being; and during the long hours which he now found a subtle pleasure in

spending at home, alone with his convalescent spirit, he became gradually himself again, but himself in thraldom to another. (II, 29)

'Un amour de Swann', then, introduces in *A la recherche* the full scale of transformative possibility which resides in femininity. Odette forces Swann to relate to an external object and she also turns him back to himself, to the inwardness of introspection. It is here that femininity is first linked to art; that jealousy and vigilance reflect the curiosity of the male about the essence of the feminine; and that the pattern of suffering anxiety and appeasement in love is set down. The jailer becomes the jailed and benefits from his imprisonment. And the desire to possess wholly, to enslave another being, is shown to be impossible. Odette, domesticated as we see her in *A l'ombre* . . . has not as yet given up her secrets. It is only Swann who has lost his curiosity and with it the possibility of becoming more than a dilletante.

In the relationship of Rachel and Saint-Loup, we find another partial exploration of the prisoner theme. This time the transformative aspect of the feminine character appears in a slighter, more superficial light. In essence, however, the pattern is repeated. Proust does not present the entire scope of this love affair and when Saint-Loup first appears in the novel, he is already the prisoner of Rachel and his own jealousy. Victim of 'the general disease called love', Saint-Loup sees in the hetaeric 'Rachel-when-from-the-Lord' all the mystery of the unknown—the 'other' which is woman.

This woman . . . was for him all the love, every possible delight in life, whose personality, mysteriously enshrined in a body as in a Tabernacle, was the object that still occupied incessantly the toiling imagination of my friend, whom he felt that he would never really know, as to whom he was perpetually asking himself what could be her secret self, behind the veil of eyes and flesh. (V, 211)

Marcel, at first, sees in this object of all Saint-Loup's affections only the two-penny prostitute of the 'maisons de passe'. But Saint-Loup, as Proust reveals, has not chosen an unworthy figure to embody all his illusions of the mysterious feminine. Rachel is a unique and fully individualized anima, who has moved Saint-Loup to those projections which so alter his character. In her role as an actress, she embodies the mobility, the possibility of metamorphosis, which is proper to the feminine. And it is with Rachel, the actress, that Saint-Loup falls in love. Placed at the mysterious distance of the stage, Rachel becomes the most total and unattainable of female figures; and Proust appropriately conveys her essence in the prime symbol of feminine mysteriousness—the moon : 'At a proper distance . . . rose like a crescent moon a nose so fine, so pure that one would have liked to be the object of Rachel's attention, to see her again as often as one chose, to keep her close to one . . .'

Like Odette and Albertine, Rachel also possesses that ambiguity of sexual tastes which makes her essence even more impenetrable to the male. Proust portrays her attraction to the effeminate dancer at the theatre and Saint-Loup's growing jealousy as she lauds the dancer's delicate movements. ' "Do they do those tricks with women too, those nice little hands?" she flung to the dancer from the back of the stage . . . "You look just like one yourself. I'm sure I could have a wonderful time with you and a girl I know".' This hint of complicated lesbian practices will become an agony for Marcel later on—for the male dancer is, in many ways, a woman. But this is also an important hint at what Proust will define as the basic hermaphroditic or bisexual being; that is, in this saltimbanque figure of the dancer (and we remember that in Picasso's work, the saltimbanque is representative of the artist), Proust gives us a glimpse into the artist's real nature. He describes the dancer, this 'artiste', as a figure from another world—one anterior to present civilisation. He is a stranger to everyday preoccupations and pursues his ecstatic dream like some alien being amidst ordinary men. Above all, the dancer is totally free from the laws of nature and society, and like a butterfly, he introduces a touch of repose, a touch of freshness into the theatre crowd. A sylph from a primitive world, this hermaphroditic creature embodies part of the mystery of the artist, as well as that of Albertine and her lesbianism. However, he is also part of the theatre world of Rachel and the enigma which she remains for Saint-Loup, her prisoner.

Rachel's effect on Saint-Loup is, as Proust points out, nevertheless a beneficial one, for she possesses the transformative character of the feminine. In great detail, the narrator outlines how, through Rachel and his love for her, Saint-Loup is metamorphosed into a better human being :

For many young men of fashion who would otherwise remain uncultivated mentally, rough in their friendships, without gentleness or taste—it is very often their mistress who is their real master, and connexions of this sort the only school of morals in which they are initiated into a superior culture, and learn the value of disinterested relations. Even among the lower orders (who, when it comes to coarseness, so often remind us of the world of fashion) the woman, more sensitive, finer, more leisured, is driven by curiosity to adopt certain refinements, respects certain beauties of sentiment and of art which, though she may fail to understand them, she nevertheless places above what has seemed most desirable to the man, above money or position. . . . With her feminine instinct, with a keener appreciation in men of certain qualities of sensibility which her lover might perhaps, without her guidance, have misunderstood and laughed at them, she [Rachel] had always been swift to distinguish from among the rest of Saint-Loup's friends the one who had a real affection for him, and to make that one her favourite. She knew how to make him feel grateful to such a friend, show his gratitude, notice what things gave his friend pleasure and what pain. And presently Saint-Loup, without any more need of her to prompt him, began to think of all these things by himself . . . His mistress had opened his mind to the invisible, had brought a serious element into his life, delicacy into his heart. (IV, 109-112)

Here the social and the archetypal roles of woman meet. No doubt Rachel makes of Saint-Loup a better man, but this is merely a simple way of observing that much literature since Stendhal has underlined the transformative effect of the feminine upon the male. For the full scale of these feminine powers, we must turn to Albertine.

Through the figure of Albertine, Proust analyses in depth all the possibilities of the feminine character. Albertine is for Marcel 'at one and the same time a mistress, a sister, a daughter, a mother'. Because *A la recherche* is the subjective world of Marcel's vision, Albertine can only be studied in her relation to and influence on the hero. Unlike Agathe, she develops little in her own right. Nevertheless, once she leaves the adolescent, unindividualised world of Balbec, Albertine takes on a certain unique personality which comes into conflict with Marcel's will and imaginative projections.

When she first comes to Marcel's room in Paris, he notes that 'she has finally acquired a face'. The profile of the young girl outlined along the sea has now become a full face. This first Parisian encounter defines her as a young woman with a certain fund of intelligence and a large store of sensuality. She relates to Marcel in a way which marks her individual womanhood, for, having satisfied Marcel's carnal desires, she proceeds to weave emotions around the kiss and make of it the beginning of a romance. In this she is distinct from Marcel's imaginative projections, although he continues to spin a web of illusions around her person; for 'We are all sculptors. We are anxious to obtain of a woman a statue entirely different from the one she has presented to us'. Albertine, however, as her pictorial multiplicity becomes a multiplicity in depth, constantly evades the outline of Marcel's scuplture. The world of Combray and Balbec, where a certain unity between inner and outer existed, has become the fallen world of facts where conflict is central. It is on this foundation that the drama of the captive unfolds—a drama which will lead to Marcel's metamorphosis into the 'moi' of the artist.

Proust's metaphor of the prison describes the attempt made by one individual wholly to circumscribe and possess another being. This attempt is bound to fail in the world of facts, for to encompass another being fully necessitates the possibility of living within his or her consciousness—an impossible task. There is no total possession outside the world of the imagination. Marcel, in his attempt to imprison Albertine, embarks on an impossible voyage which, nevertheless, provides his fullest experience of the feminine, of the other.

The relativistic universe of constantly shifting objects and perspectives which Proust describes, has as its prime embodiment this Albertine, this 'fugitive being'. Marcel's relationship with her consists of trying to pierce through the secrets of her multiple selves and to hold this reality stationary so that it cannot change again. He sees that he can only do this by holding Albertine captive: 'About Albertine, I felt that I should never find out anything, that, out of that tangled mass of details of fact and falsehood, I should never unravel the truth: and that it would always be so, unless I were to shut her up in prison (but prisoners escape) until the end'. This is, in effect, the course which Marcel's love affair takes.

Marcel imprisons Albertine and attempts to possess her thoughts and the shifting multiplicity of her life. A difficult task, this necessitates the possession of all of Albertine's past memories and future activities. To possess her fully, Marcel must capture and hold still every moment of her life; and this attempt emerges essentially as an effort to imprison 'time', to stop the fleeting moment. Thus the fugitive Albertine becomes the Goddess of Time, implacable and mysterious, like immemorial oceans. To touch her is only to touch a surface, an envelope whose interior reaches toward the infinite. As goddess of time, Albertine also rules over habit, its making and breaking as the moments pass. Her presence, cruel, pressing and constricting, incites Marcel to explore the past—and one facet of his role as artist.

'Déesse du Temps', Albertine is furthermore the goddess of place. Through her, Marcel directly experiences all the places in which she has figured as an actress—Balbec, Paris, his room. Thus love, with Albertine, becomes for Marcel 'space and time made sensible to the heart'.

But it is Albertine as captive, captor and as woman who exerts a transformative influence on Marcel that interests us most directly here. To examine this aspect, we must look at the Albertine-Marcel relationship which unfolds in much the same way as the other love affairs in *A la recherche*. Marcel, initially indifferent to the Parisian Albertine, gradually gets into the habit of seeing her in Balbec; and when she cannot be seen, his jealousy and hence his love is aroused. Jealousy, and with it the omnipresent suffering, is augmented in Marcel's case by the suspected lesbianism of Albertine. This lesbian-ism, which is never fully verified in the shifting perspectives of *A la recherche*, is interesting because it throws a further light on what exactly jealousy signifies for Proust and the place of sexual ambi-guity in his vision.

Marcel is first made to suspect Albertine's lesbianism when Cot-tard remarks on the way in which she is dancing with Andrée and suggests that the two girls are indulging in Sapphic pleasures. Mar-cel is deeply pained at the thought and by Albertine's highly sensual laugh, through which she seems to be conveying some secret and voluptuous thrill to Andrée. This laugh rings out like the first and last strain of some unknown, unvisited ball—a ball reminiscent of the voluptuous feasts the young Marcel envisages his mother as attending.

It is the mystery, the unknown aspect of lesbianism which makes Marcel suffer and is the basis of his jealousy and love for Albertine. Jealousy, as we have thus far seen it in *A la recherche*, is essentially a curiosity, an obsession about the way in which another being lives and feels. Insofar as it brings the person out of himself and forces him to make contact with another object, it is generally beneficial. Marcel's jealousy is this curiosity heightened to an imaginative level; and it is focussed specifically on the woman, who, for the male, is the creature most like and yet most different from himself. Because of her likeness, he is capable of relating to her. Yet in this relation, she manifests herself as something constitutionally other and is thus shrouded in mystery.

The way in which Albertine's lesbianism heightens her feminine mystery is that Marcel must in effect become a woman to know her fully. Although 'being' in Proust is sharply etched by physical desire, what he is really after is the far more ideal desire to know, that is, to possess the other's distinct person. Proust uses physical desire as a technical procedure : it is a metaphor for the far greater desire for total knowledge of the other. Sexual appropriation is used as a short-cut to total possession of another's consciousness. As Bersani states : 'He locates the mystery of personality in the way a sexual desire is felt.'⁴ This is why Marcel's physical desire is so often translated in terms of his acquiring a woman's attention, that is, of making her focus her consciousness on him.

If Albertine is a lesbian, then Marcel's attempt to capture her must be frustrated : frustrated, because her attention, that is her whole physical preoccupation, seeks pleasure where Marcel cannot follow. Marcel cannot imagine the pleasure which Albertine gets from another woman. And this is the crux of the whole jealousy-psychology of love. Marcel's love here reaches a material limitation, since, by not being a woman, he cannot duplicate Albertine's pleasure. Secondly, and especially, Albertine's pleasure, her 'woman's' pleasure, is simply unimaginable to Marcel. Thus he suffers profoundly from what cannot be imagined, that area where the mind as voyeur cannot penetrate. Hence, Albertine's enigma is doubled and Marcel's jealousy, his curiosity about what constitutes femininity, is heightened. This fascination which Albertine exudes is precisely what leads Marcel to suffering and hence to recognition—essential steps in his development into an artist.

What is called aesthetic curiosity would deserve rather the name of indifference in comparison with the painful, unwearying curiosity that I felt as to the places in which Albertine had stayed, as to what she might have been doing on a particular evening, her smiles, the expressions in her eyes, the words that she had uttered, the kisses that she had received. No, never would the jealousy that I had felt one day of Saint-Loup, if it had persisted, have caused me this immense uneasiness. This love of woman for woman was something too unfamiliar; nothing enabled me to form a certain, an accurate idea of its pleasures, its quality. (X, 247)

Marcel, after Albertine's death, can contradict this limit by imagining what he himself might do in that condition, and here no doubt Proust's biography as invert lurks in the background, but it does not dissolve the basic dilemma. The fact is, it need not be a sexual dilemma, but the dilemma crystallized by sexual experience of the essential limits of *all* experience. Lesbianism, thus, is only the sexual metaphor for Marcel's curiosity about the essence of this unknowable otherness, what we have called 'femininity' which, in itself, suggests a still more mysterious realm and one which we can only hope to designate in the last part of this study.

Lesbianism, or more generally, homosexuality, might also hint at a form of social criticism in that the invert's disregard of moral norms harks us back to a paradisal state. This paradise is the child's, for it is only in this early state that outgoing sexuality need not be specified or directed to any one sex. In the golden state, innocence is sex, not as aim, but as total state of being. That Proust briefly connects this state with Lesbianism and more directly with the hermaphroditic dancer rather than with male inversion is perhaps the effect of his own guilt at being a homosexual. Here one can only suggest this line of enquiry, leaving it open until the analysis of the hermaphrodite later on.

We come back to the point that Marcel's jealousy is essentially curiosity and a desire for a vaster knowledge. Woman may be the stimulant of love, of joy and pain, but it is not her usual characteristics which stir Marcel, but some invisible moving essence within her :

For that matter, the mistresses whom I have loved most passionately have never coincided with my love for them. . . . One would have said that a virtue that had no connexion with them had been attached to them artificially by nature, and that this virtue, this quasi-electric power had the effect upon me of exciting my love, of controlling all my actions and causing all my sufferings.

⁴ Bersani, p. 59.

But from this, the beauty, or the intelligence, or the kindness of
these women was entirely distinct. As by an electric current that
gives us a shock, I have been shaken by my love affairs, I have
lived them, I have felt them : never have I succeeded in arriving
at the stage of seeing or thinking them. Indeed I am inclined to
believe that in these love affairs, . . . beneath the form of the
woman, it is to those invisible forces which are attached to her
that we address ourselves as to obscure deities. It is they whose
goodwill is necessary to us, with whom we seek to establish contact without finding any positive pleasure in it. With these god-
desses, the woman, during our assignation with her, puts us into
touch and does little more. (VIII, 378-379)

It is the nature of the 'forces occultes', of the 'obscures divinités'
in women, women's otherness, which Marcel is curious about and
whose mystery he wishes to penetrate. This is the vaster reality of
the feminine principle rather than the actual *womanhood* which
resides in the female person.

Once Marcel is assured of Albertine's lesbianism by her mention
of her friendship with Mlle. Vinteuil's anonymous Sapphic partner,
his curiosity and jealousy reaches unprecedented heights and he
must make of Albertine a captive. His pain at Albertine's revelation,
he feels, is a punishment for his unkindness to his grandmother, his
hastening of her death. On the complex level of symbolical self-
introspection, Marcel's diagnosis is acute. In this twilight realm of
half-myth, fact, and neurotic fears, the combination of events can
only suggest what Marcel believes. By the death of the protective
grandmother, Marcel is thrust into an adult world where 'sin' is
omnipresent. Relating to an external reality, no longer harmonious
with the inner world, causes constant suffering. The grandmother's
death has launched Marcel into the conscious world of guilt and
guilt's logic.

More significantly, Marcel seems to believe that his pain is also a
punishment for his youthful voyeurism—his having spied through
the window at Montjouvain and seen the Sapphic rites of Mlle. Vinteuil and her friend. Voyeurism is basic to the structure of Marcel's
inner life : not only does it focus his behaviour upon the possession
of others through his visual faculty, but it lets us make the important connection between curiosity, desire and knowledge. This voy-

eurism finds its culmination in his constant vigilance of Albertine—a vigilance which makes him as much a prisoner as jailer. As Albertine's life becomes for Marcel a schedule of events, an inquisition into 'her use of time' (for only by factually tracing the minute by minute progression of another's life, does Marcel believe one can pierce through his dissimulating surface), he becomes the captive of his own vigilant curiosity. Watching over the daily progression of Albertine's life, he is 'more a master, that is to say, more a slave,' for he is chained by his obsessive curiosity which forces him to concentrate his attentions wholly on Albertine.

This following of Albertine's actions is, nevertheless, essentially beneficial from one point of view, for in doing so, Marcel attempts to experience the life-processes of another being. As Bersani remarks, making a different point, this vigilance of Albertine is perhaps a 'sexual parallel to Marcel's staring at the hawthorns in the Combray church, attempting to imitate "the action of their blossoming" in order to penetrate their essence, and finding the metaphor in himself that "repeats" the form of the flowers.'[5] During his Combray phase, it was nature and woman which Marcel found so intimately fused, but now in being faced by female resistance and in employing himself to overcome this mystery, he discovers himself as an artist. In effect, Marcel, at least partially succeeds in penetrating Albertine's 'essence', as he abandons the active and masculine role of jailer to become the captive feminine. Though never distinctly solving the riddle of femininity—for this by its very nature is an impossible task—yet by succumbing momentarily as a woman might to this mystery which encompasses all nature, Marcel is prepared for the artist's hermaphroditic role, that is, for the artist's dual intimations about experience. Before we examine Marcel in his feminine role, however, it is necessary to look back for a moment on the nature of Albertine's captivity.

Keeping Albertine under constant surveillance, Marcel attempts to appropriate the world of another being. The only time he can do this fully and to his own satisfaction and maintain a calmness of spirit, is when Albertine is asleep. Then the conflict with the loved object ceases, Marcel is turned back to himself, and his imaginative projections can wholly encircle an unresisting being. Asleep, Albertine is fully passive and partakes only of the life of the plants. Moreover, her consciousness gone, she ceases to be an ever-changing fig-

[5] Ibid., p. 61. This refers to I, 112.

ure, a fugitive. Marcel can now watch her as he watched the hawthorns at Combray.

> By shutting her eyes, by losing consciousness, Albertine had
> stripped off, one after another, the different human characters
> with which she had deceived me ever since the day when I had
> first made her acquaintance. She was animated now only by the
> unconscious life of vegetation, of trees, a life more different from
> my own, more alien and yet one that belonged more to me. Her
> personality did not escape at every moment, as when we were talk-
> ing . . . I had that impression of possessing her altogether, which
> I never had when she was awake. Her life was submitted to me,
> exhaled towards me its gentle breath. (IX, 85)

Unconscious, Albertine is totally possessable. Taking into herself
all the characteristics which her life as a woman has imposed on her,
she becomes the embodiment of the pure feminine principle, an
earth mother who gives Marcel 'a sensation of calm, which appeases
in the way nature does'. This feeling of possession is strengthened
in Marcel when he watches Albertine awake, come to consciousness
in his own room. Throughout the book, Marcel, upon awakening,
takes his identity from the familiar objects of his various rooms.
Here, he feels he possesses Albertine more completely when the
identity she takes on is supplied by him and stems from the same
objects as his own. Projecting, Marcel seems then to believe that
Albertine must be a familiar being, very like himself, and he succeeds momentarily 'in expelling all mystery'.

Albertine asleep allows Marcel to turn back to that self within
him which seems to be constant throughout *A la recherche*. And
this 'moi' is essentially an infantile, narcissistic one out of which all
illusory figures arise and to which they return. As Albertine sleeps,
she loses that individual personality of the 'other' and becomes
merely the incarnation of a dream. Marcel then reverts to his youth
and indulges in masturbation fantasies.

There is a link between all the suggested masturbation scenes in
A la recherche and it lies in the image of the prison. The child,
Marcel, confined to his room—a prison that he cannot escape from
to run to his mother—creates a woman like Eve born from Adam's
rib, from the position of his thigh—a woman formed by the pleasure
he is on the point of gratifying and who, he imagines, is offering

him this gratification. A woman arises from a thigh and this same thigh placed over the sleeping Albertine in the prison of the Paris room, results in a similar pleasure. Albertine is the dreamed of woman, in her sleep just as acquiescent as an imaginary figure and just as much part of Marcel. In fact, the image, if we replace rib for thigh, is strikingly Adamic. It leads back to Combray and Paradise, but also forward to the type of Genesis-creativity wherein things are fixed by the naming of them; that is, it points to the artist. Again, locked in the 'small Combray closet, perfumed by irises' (note the link, once more, between flowers and sexuality), the young Marcel masturbates to the fantasy of a woman arising from the 'Roussain-ville dungeon'. This imaginary woman, linked with a prison, again suggests the sleeping Albertine.

The 'moi' of the infantile Marcel is therefore a narcissistic one which finds its love object and its satisfaction in itself. We have already noted how Marcel's sexual desires are satisfied as soon as another person fixes her attention on him. This, in itself would seem to suggest that Marcel contents himself with being his own love object. But this infantile narcissistic world is a prison which cannot allow Marcel to relate fully to the external world. It is this prison from which Marcel must escape before it becomes possible for him to re-create the world in the light of art. The conscious Albertine, as opposed to the sleeping one, by refusing to fix her attention solely on him and to conform to his fantasies, forces him out of this infantile 'moi'. A constant fugitive, she breaks the barriers of this particular prison of the self and transforms him into a liberated Marcel, capable of creation. And this becomes a tangible fact when Albertine really flees. By fleeing, however, Albertine paradoxically gives Marcel one key to the feminine mystery. What she has left him is passive suffering, and it is exactly this passivity which resembles femininity itself. At last, Marcel is in the woman's position, the usual social one, when she, and not the male, is the 'left-one'. Proust thus shows one of Marcel's 'moi's' actively experiencing a feminine position. Left behind, Marcel is forced to a re-examination of himself. This is where the study of the ambiguity of sexes in Proust takes on more than biographical significance.

Albertine, throughout her capitivity, has played the feminine to Marcel's commanding jailer. Incorporating the mother figure into herself, she has evoked the same jealousy and given the same appeasement as Marcel's mother in Combray. Trieste and the Combray dining-room are linked for Marcel in an unaccountable air of hostility:

> It was Trieste, it was that unknown world in which I could feel that Albertine took a delight, in which were her memories, her friendships, her childish loves, that exhaled that hostile, that inexplicable atmosphere, like the atmosphere that used to float up to my bedroom at Combray, from the dining room in which I could hear talking and laughing with strangers . . . Mamma who would not be coming upstairs to say good-night to me. (VIII, 370)

And again: 'I kissed her as purely as if I had been kissing my mother to charm away a childish grief which as a child I believed I would never be able to eradicate from my heart.' (VIII, 375)

The rhythm of the mother-son relationship has been transposed to the rhythm of the lovers. This, in itself, would seem to imply that Proust desires to make Albertine a woman and not a disguised homosexual lover. It is only the woman who can incorporate the maternal role. The homosexual lover is, rather, an extension of the male: in his love object he is seeking for himself and in this other male, he loves himself. As Freud tells us, inverts 'proceed from a narcissistic basis and look for a young man who resembles themselves and whom they love as their mother loved them'.[6] Marcel may have narcissistic tendencies, but Proust reveals how this pattern of narcissism is broken up by the very fact of a heterosexual relationship. In Albertine, Marcel seeks a duplication of his mother's love for him and not an object whom he can love as his mother loved him. And Albertine in her captivity is the archetypal woman, both mother and mistress, sister and daughter, and linked with the feminine domain of nature.

Her femininity is further enforced by the element of passivity in her which Proust stresses, when he speaks of 'her great faculty for submission', her obedience, her 'great force of passivity'. Indeed, Albertine takes on the role of a wife, domestic and familiar, and totally obedient to the will of her husband Marcel, as Marcel's mother is always shown to be towards his father; and Marcel imagines the future calm and domesticity of their life together. This aspect of the Albertine-Marcel relationship almost parallels the one Proust describes between Monsieur and Madame Santeuil. Obedient

---

[6] Sigmund Freud, *Three Essays on the Theory of Sexuality*, ed. James Strachey (London: 1962) pp. 10–11.

and respectful, Albertine treats Marcel as a stern master. And Marcel, as jailer, finds himself taking on an authoritative and paternal air in many instances: 'Indeed, like those plants which bifurcate as they grow, side by side with the sensitive boy which was all that I had been, there was now a man of the opposite sort, full of common sense, of severity toward the morbid sensibility of others, a man resembling what my parents had been to me.' This overtly masculine side of Marcel is rarely stressed in *A la recherche*. By emphasizing it here, Proust seems to be suggesting that the experience of maleness is also important to the formation of the total artist, something which is rarely brought into relief in the book, since Marcel is after all a man. The distinction between masculine and feminine is well marked in this instance, but as always with Proust clear polarities give way to ambiguity.

As Albertine takes into her own hands the action of leaving Marcel, of fleeing, she literally steps into the masculine position. Traditionally, it is the male who seduces and abandons and leaves behind him a whimpering woman. The Don Juan, whom we have already glimpsed in the early Swann, here looms fully into view in the figure of Morel. Morel, as has been observed by Proust's critics, is the masculine version of Albertine. Like her, he is a fugitive and an invert. A male, he yet indulges in lesbian activities, as the letter from Lea points out. Morel's most enthusiastic pastime consists in deflowering virgins and then leaving them—and it is suggested that he has often done this, not only in the case of Jupien's niece. He is essentially a Don Juan who materially embodies the homosexual aspects which usually lie latent within this figure. Albertine, with her abandonment of Marcel takes on one aspect of this masculine role. She now acts out the masculine side of the lesbian duality. Her oft-intimated closeness to Morel is concretised in Aimée's reports and she steps into the position of the female Don Juan, seducing young girls into the ways of Gomorrah and then turning them over to Morel.

But Morel is also an extension of the masculine side of Marcel, another possible 'dédoublement' (a dividing into two) of his being, as the similarity in their names would suggest. Portrayed from the outside, Morel appears as a hateful character, but essentially he objectifies many of Marcel's qualities. He is the product of the masculine side of Marcel's family—the bachelor uncle, whose mysterious relations with cocottes Marcel idolises in his youth. Like

Marcel, Morel is a neurasthenic and hypochondriac, with artistic inclinations. And seen in an objective light, Marcel's romantic dreams of possessing the young women of Balbec and Combray are not so different from Morel's crass statements about seduction and abandonment.

Thus Albertine, as she abandons Marcel, takes with her the masculine extension of his character, and leaves him, *at least momentarily,* supine and in the feminine position. Always captive to the curiosity of what constitutes femininity and its heightening in lesbianism, Marcel is now forced to relate truly to the other and to break the bonds of his narcissistic prison. For a moment, he becomes a woman; and this femininity is incorporated into him as he lives over his entire life with Albertine in memory, until she finally becomes part of him.

Albertine is thus the initiator of an important two-fold movement in Marcel. Firstly she is the instigator of an outgoing movement, the incarnation of Marcel's desire for the other which we have shown to be essentially a heuristic development. Next, she focuses Marcel's attention on memory, which is the first step on the return to the self, transformed in its fuller self-realisation. Albertine's mystery, the enigma of her femininity, follows her to the grave together with her grey presence as a captive. Dead, she re-emerges as the fabulous desirable bird of the sea-shore : and Marcel must consecutively relive his jealousies and joys until finally Albertine is lost in 'oubli'—forgetfulness. Albertine has redirected Marcel to the life of memory and of the self.

By the suffering she has caused, by the experience she has given Marcel of femininity, Albertine kills the old self in Marcel and watches over the birth of the new. 'Nothing, I told myself, but an actual extinction of myself would be capable (but that was impossible) of consoling me for hers. I did not realize that the death of oneself is neither impossible, nor extraordinary; it is effected without our knowledge, it may be against our will, every day of our life.' (II, 722) Albertine transforms Marcel and reveals to him the possibility of change in depth within the individual. Furthermore, she shows him the relevance and the constant existence of the past in him by her connection to Montjouvain and by her maternal aspect. Her redemptive role is completed. Marcel has been forced to relate to an objective reality and to suffer from the breaking of a habitual response. He has been given a full experience of femininity. Now, a mere forgotten presence, Albertine hovers over his metamorphosis into a new self—the self which will in turn give birth to the artist.

THE REDEEMED HERMAPHRODITE

Albertine, like all the inhabitants of Sodom and Gomorrah, is doomed. Yet of all the hermaphroditic beings in this world only the artist remains imperishable. It is the peculiar quality of his dual nature which allows him to be redeemed. The kind of femininity which Marcel has absorbed into himself, that is, the forms of his grandmother and of his 'anima', Albertine, survives essentially in his memory. In this light, femininity has contributed to his development, and insofar as memory has a profoundly preservative quality, Marcel is allowed to emerge from Sodom and Gomorrah. Both Albertine and his grandmother die, but their elements have passed into Marcel and have made of him a hermaphrodite, embodying both feminine and masculine properties.

It is important to see in this how, for Proust, the feminine mystery is so implicitly related to the creative mystery. This creativity itself has a dual aspect: firstly, it is that which allows the self to develop; secondly, that which leads to art. In the first or expanding phase of the self, growth is really transformation brought about by femininity. In the second, or in the creation of art itself, creativity finds its shape in the intuitive, primal sphere of the Great Mother, that is in the unconscious. And, thus, through a fusion of both, Marcel is redeemed through art in the figure of the hermaphroditic artist, and some order is given to flux. The mystery which he has always tried to penetrate, Proust shows us, is intimately related to femininity: as he develops, Marcel comes closer to deciphering this mystery the more he realises that its key lies in creation itself.

The three principal artists of *A la recherche* all stand in an important relationship to women, who are in some way the crystallising principle of their art. Thus throughout the novel, creativity is connected directly or indirectly with femininity. Bergotte, Proust tells us, finds in women the inspiration for his art. His generosity towards young girls is prodigious and he excuses himself 'because he knew that he could never create as well as in the atmosphere of feeling himself in love'. Bergotte's love for young girls lies in their ability to make him suffer and hence in their stimulation of him which results in the production of a work of art:

And even if this love leads to disillusionment, it does at least stir, even by so doing, the surface of the soul which otherwise would be in danger of becoming stagnant. Desire is therefore not without its value to the writer in detaching him first of all from his fellow men and from conforming to their standards, and afterwards in restoring some degree of movement to a spiritual machine which, after a certain age, tends to become paralysed. (IX, 244)

Because of what we have termed their transformative character, women enable Bergotte to create.

Elstir, too, owes the crystallisation of his artistic powers to the feminine. His 'nouvelle création du monde' only comes when he has met 'ma belle Gabrielle' who incarnates the most intimate part of himself, his ideal vision of beauty. Although the Marcel of Balbec finds in Madame Elstir a very disappointing woman indeed, he recognizes her importance for Elstir, once he has seen the master's mysteriously embodied in a concrete, tangible form.
hold constant communion with his own imagination, now somehow mythological works. Gabrielle's presence is what permits Elstir to

The relationship Proust depicts between Vinteuil's art and his women is more central to Marcel's development than that of the other two artists in *A la recherche*. Vinteuil's music reverberates throughout the work and it is the leitmotif for Swann's love of Odette as well as the prime example for Marcel of what can be achieved in art. Yet the great composer Vinteuil is, in reality, the little music master of Combray who dies of a broken heart when his beloved daughter enters into a Sapphic relationship. The agony of Vinteuil's life is what permits him to produce the overpowering Septuor wherein pain gives way to an 'ineffable joy which seemed to come from paradise'. Ironically but fittingly, it is his daughter's Sapphic friend who transcribes Vinteuil's otherwise incomprehensible notation and brings this joy to the world at large. Vinteuil suffers through women and creates out of this suffering a work which surpasses his agony. Finally, this work is redeemed by the very instruments of his suffering. Just so Marcel's 'mal' (pain)—Albertine—is also his remède' (cure).

Albertine is intrinsically linked to Vinteuil through her lesbianism. In the Verdurin salon, Marcel imagines her voice blending with the notes of the Septuor in a sublimity which unites her to him. Her lesbianism is the cause of Marcel's agony, just as his daughter's was for Vinteuil. Yet in the notes of the Septuor, Marcel finds a greater joy than in Albertine and the 'only unknown it had ever been granted me to encounter'. We have already seen Marcel speaking of this 'unknown' in relation to Albertine and although he would seem to contradict this here, Proust appears to be suggesting a link between the two forms of the unknown. And indeed, Albertine with her lesbianism is one of the fundamental moving powers in Marcel's development toward the joy of creation. Not least significantly, it is because of her that he hears the Septuor at the Verdurin salon—the Septuor which shows him the powers of art and the fact that there may still be something ahead of him to be experienced. Creativity in Proust's vision is inextricably linked to femininity.

Proust seems to emphasise this by placing at the beginning and at the end of *A la recherche* two feminine personifications of the artist. At the head of our uroboric serpent, we find Tante Léonie, the artist as observer. Hypochondriac and neurasthenic, Tante Léonie spends a good portion of her life in her room, much as Proust did in his cork-lined chamber. Marcel, at one remove from the revelation of his artistic vocation, similarly secludes himself in his room with his prisoner, Albertine. The artist's room is, however, a room with a view and Tante Léonie's life revolves around the faculty of observation. From her window, she watches the life of Combray unfolding around her. Marcel, it would seem, inherits this vigilant quality from her and it is expressed in his voyeurism as well as in his surveillance of Albertine. With the ingenuity of the invalid, Léonie each day invents new reasons for staying in her room and she exerts authority over her household in various crafty ruses which Marcel watches himself duplicate. Furthermore, it is Léonie's material heritage which Marcel squanders in the lost time of sexual desire. The couch, which she has left him, becomes the central furnishing of a 'maison de passe' (a brothel). A large jar is sold to enable Marcel to buy flowers daily for Gilberte. But it is only by experiencing lost time to its fullest extent that Marcel is able to redeem time at the end of *A la recherche*; and it is the figures from the world of lost time who populate the canvas of the book he is about to write. Germaine Brée correctly remarks that the periods of Marcel's life 'not dominated by a feminine figure are those which fall into oblivion and are never recovered.'[1]

[1] Germaine Brée, p. 204.

At the tail-end of the uroboric serpent stands the feminine personification of the artist as maker—Françoise. Servant to Léonie, she appears as the link between the vigilant invalid and her revivication in the creative narrator who composes *A la recherche,* for it is Françoise who is to help Marcel in his artistic vocation. The round is complete as, with Françoise, there is a return to the stability of Combray, and all the dreams of childhood; for the figure of Françoise stands at the imaginative base of Proust's as well as Marcel's vision. She incarnates the values of old France, the picturesqueness of its language. Her sadistic cruelty and her loyal goodness present both poles of *A la recherche.* Her long experience of Marcel and everything concerning him makes her an ideal partner in his venture. Moreover, Françoise is the maker of the vital material element—food—just as the artist creates food for the imagination. An expert in the art of the particulars needed to produce a general effect, Françoise is truly the counterpart of the narrator of *A la recherche* :

> As all the unpretentious persons who live close beside us acquire a certain intuitive comprehension of our work . . . I would work near her and almost in her manner . . .
> Moreover, since individualities (human or otherwise) would in this book be constructed out of numerous impressions which, derived from many girls, many churches, many sonatas, would go to make up a single sonata, a single church, a single girl, should I not be making my book as Françoise made her *boeuf à la mode* so much savoured by M. de Norpois, the jelly of which was enriched by many additional carefully selected bits of meat? (XII, 416-417)

Thus Françoise, the feminine as maker, becomes the personification of the writer's craft.

Marcel's epiphanies about time and selfhood, which open the path to his creative work, are similarly linked with feminine figures, for, as we have already mentioned, it is only the time presided over by a woman which is ultimately redeemed. Gifts of involuntary memory, these moments of revelation allow Marcel to live wholly in a 'moi' of the past. By the yoking of this past self with the present self, there is a release of joy similar to that which Marcel feels upon hearing the Vinteuil Septuor, for in this moment Marcel is liberated from the movement of time which leads only to death. He tastes 'un peu de temps à l'état pur'—a little time in its pure state.

The sensations which transform Marcel into a past self are almost all linked with women. His first epiphany, that due to the madeleine dipped in herb tea, carries him back to his childhood and the world of Tante Léonie. Fittingly, the personification of the artist as observer gives him his first taste of that involuntary memory which will finally move him to take up his pen and write. The second important moment of revelation comes when he is tying his shoe lace in Balbec and his dead grandmother comes back to him with the full force of actual existence. There is the grandmother who, we have already noted, is central to Marcel's development into an artist. At the final Guermantes social event, Marcel experiences a series of these significant moments. As he walks on an uneven step, Venice comes back to him and the self of Venice, we remember, is under the dominance of the mother figure. The stiffness of a napkin against his lips brings back Balbec, the Grand Hotel, and with it the band of young flowering girls outlined on the seashore. *François le Champi* throws Marcel back to the night when his mother stayed in his room—the night which marked the breakdown of his will. Finally in the closing passage of the book, Marcel notes how the sound of the bell and the footsteps of guests reinstate him in that distant self of the past when this bell signified Swann's departure and the fact that his mother would soon be coming upstairs. Thus the book comes full circle in the figure of the Great Mother.

When Marcel's epiphanies are not linked with woman, they yet suggest her in their relation to nature, which is for Proust, as well as archetypally, a feminine element. Just as time, flux, in its constant transformation is feminine—note the figure of Albertine—so place, nature and stability, constitute the obverse side of the feminine principle. Every phase of Marcel's life is associated with a feminine figure and through her with a place, an aspect of nature.

And, to tell the truth, (as in those calendars the postman brings us when he wants his Christmas box) there was not one year of my life that did not have the picture of a woman I then desired as its frontispiece or interleaved in its days; a picture sometimes the more arbitrary that I had not even seen her . . . I imagined her beautiful, I fell in love with her, I created an ideal being, queen of the provincial countryside where, I gleaned from the *Annuaire des Châteaux,* her family owned an estate. In the case of women I had known, that countryside was at least a double one. Each one of them emerged at a different point of my life, standing like protective local divinities first in the midst of the countryside of my dreams, a setting which patterned my life and to which my imagination clung; then perceived by the memory in the various places where I had known her, places she recalled because of her association with them; for though our life wanders, our memory is sedentary, and, project ourselves as we may, our memories, riveted to places from which we are detached, remain at home . . . (XII, 362-363)

Woman, in Proust, as antique deity of place, triggers the memory of 'having been', of the original unity now lost, but hauntingly rendered as the possibility of *stable* and *localised* being. On the primal level woman is also 'homecoming'; she *is* home in the most literal sense of the term—shelter, first abode, and the original contact with nature. Thus, the feminine element is necessarily closely related to Marcel's epiphanies, for through them he realises that there is a certain stability and continuity of being. The lost paradise of Combray, of the first abode, returns to him in his first epiphany, that of the madeleine. The final epiphany is homecoming, the return to the mother and unity of being.

It is important to realise that these epiphanies do not constitute the creative process for Proust, but that they are the inspirational source of Marcel's newly-found will to create. What these epiphanies make Marcel realise is that there is, after all, a certain continuity of the self:

I was terrified to think that it was indeed that bell which rang within me still, without my being able to abate its shrill sound . . . So that ringing must always be there and with it, between it and the present, all that indefinable past unrolled itself which I did not know I had within me. When it rang I already existed and since, in order that I should hear it still, there could be no discontinuity, I could have had no instant of repose or of non-existence, of non-thinking, of non-consciousness, since that former instant clung to me, for I could recover it, return to it, merely by plunging more deeply into myself. (XII, 432)

This continuity of the self, which Marcel discovers in the final pages of the book, has already been suggested to him by the pain which

Albertine's mention of her relationship with the Vinteuils caused him. By stressing this continuity Proust makes it clear that the Marcel who takes on the artist's task contains within him all his past.

The major experiences of his past are, however, centred around the women of the book. Marcel, therefore, has taken these feminine figures unto himself. His grandmother, the maternal element, is as we see in the shoe-lace passage, very much part of him, as is her love of and closeness to nature. He says of her that in moments of distress she has 'given him back to himself', because she is 'himself and more than himself'. Thus she appears as one of the many 'moi's' of Marcel and she is 'larger' than him because she also exists in her separate womanhood. Albertine's place is a similar one: 'It was in me that the possible actions of Albertine unfolded themselves . . . It was in my heart, at a great depth and difficult to extricate, that Albertine's double resided.'

With these figures of femininity within him, Marcel emerges as the symbolic hermaphrodite—not the doomed hermaphrodite who seeks carnal satisfaction in the worlds of Sodom and Gomorrah, but the hermaphrodite redeemed in the figure of the artist. Proust would seem to agree with Coleridge's dictum that all great minds are androgynous. Harry Levin suggests that 'the ideal novelist might well be a kind of spiritual hermaphrodite, combining this man's scope with that woman's sensitivity.'[2] By endowing his masculine hero with feminine characteristics and by actually showing the process of Marcel's taking of the feminine into himself, Proust suggests that, for him as well, the ideal artist is androgynous.

Marcel emerging as the hermaphoditic artist completes the circle of the novel and re-enters the similarly hermaphroditic, uroboric sphere of childhood and unconsciousness. This is his homecoming, his return to the world of the mothers, where the 'eternal feminine' presides. Archetypally, the world of the hermaphrodite is akin to the paradise lost of Combray. Here love extends to nature as well as people and union of opposites is possible; constant metamorphosis of self and objects occurs without pain.[3]

[2] Harry Levin, *Refractions* (New York, 1968), p. 256.
[3] Hermann Hesse in *Steppenwolf* (Penguin Books, 1965, p. 195) provides a noteworthy description of the magical aura of the hermaphroditic world: 'Without so much as having touched her I surrendered to her spell, and this spell itself kept within the part she played. It was the spell of a hermaphrodite. For she talked to me about Hermann and about childhood, mine and her own,

Proust's 'dream novel', the novel which Marcel sets out to write, is the home, par excellence, of androgynous characters, for in the unconscious world of dream, male and female blend and constantly shift positions : 'And I entered a state of slumber which is like a second room that we take, into which, leaving our own room, we go when we want to sleep . . . The race that inhabits it is, like that of our first ancestors, androgynous. A man in it appears a moment later in the form of a woman. Things in it show a tendency to turn into men, men into friends and enemies.' The world of dream, like the child's world and the world of the *'premiers humains'*, those unfallen creatures who contain both sexes in a state without strife, is androgynous. Within that world there is that ease of transformation which Marcel experiences on the opening pages of the novel and that sexual ambiguity which we have already met in the saltimbanque-dancer.

For Marcel, this dream realm has the full clarity of conscious, waking reality : 'I was alarmed nevertheless by the thought that this dream had had the clear precision of consciousness. Would consciousness then, reciprocally, have the irreality of dream?' *A la recherche* presents us with both the clarity of the dream world and the irreality of the waking world. The androgyne is however, only properly at home in the unconscious—or the unconscious realm of childhood, the *'premiers humains',* and the artist—for outside this dream-like sphere, he partakes of the *race maudite* (the damned race), and is swallowed in apocalyptic fires. For Proust, only the artist can travel freely between both worlds and retain his androgynous character. Like the hermaphroditic dancer already mentioned, his home is in that other primitive realm of the unconscious, and yet he can live in daytime reality through the function of his art which mystifies and liberates. Thus Proust, the man with the feminine sensibility, finds his salvation in art; and just so, Marcel, the symbolic hermaphrodite, is redeemed and liberated from the killing stroke of clock-time by his creative role.

Transformed by his experiences with women in the world of lost time, and taking into himself the feminine character, Marcel

---

and about those years of childhood when the capacity for love, in its first youth, embraces not only both sexes, but all and everything, sensuous and spiritual, and endows all things with a spell of love and a fairy-like ease of transformation such as in later years comes again only to a chosen few and to poets, and to them rarely.'

returns to the uroboric sphere of the mothers. The hero who seeks stability and indestructibility, the conquest of death by the liberation from time, and the transformation of personality, finds his final home in the feminine realm of the unconscious—the sphere of creativity, where the fusing power of metaphor and art reign supreme. Marcel, captive to his curiosity about what constitutes femininity—which is part of the larger sphere of the 'inconnu'—finally, in his last epiphanies intuits the nature of this mystery. It consists of the abandoning of intellect and consciousness and with it, doubt and duality, and re-immersing oneself in the unconscious, where unity and guilt-free harmonious selfhood are found. Here the fear of death and the remorse over lost time are conquered:

> That explained why my apprehensions on the subject of my death had ceased from the moment when I had unconsciously recognised the taste of the little madeleine because at that moment the being that I then had been was an extra-temporal being and in consequence indifferent to the vicissitudes of the future. That being had never come to me, had never manifested itself except when I was inactive and in a sphere beyond the enjoyment of the moment, that was my prevailing condition every time that analogical miracle had enabled me to escape from the present. Only that being had the power of enabling me to recapture former days, Time Lost, in the face of which all the efforts of my memory and of my intelligence came to nought. (XII, 216)

The way to the heart of the mystery is not through conscious memory or intelligence, but rather through an abandonment of action and immediacy. The mystery lies in the very process of freeing oneself from consciousness and permitting the involuntary to occur. Marcel, always vigilant over others and himself, finds the essence of things in a relaxation of the conscious mind. This suggests a return to the paradisal state of childhood where joy is prevalent precisely because the dualities imposed by consciousness do not exist. Without duality, there is no doubt and hence no pain. But one can only discover this by experiencing the agony of a vigilant adult consciousness. Time lost leads to selfhood and time regained; and femininity rules over the beginning and the end.

From the realm of the mothers, Marcel states that genius is 'instinct': 'At each moment the artist must listen to his own instinct, which is what makes art all that is most real, the most austere school of life and the true last judgment.' Instinct, ruled over by the feminine spirit, is the only 'true' reality and 'The ideas formed by pure intellect have only a logical truth, a potential truth; the selection of them is an arbitrary act. The book written in symbolic characters not traced by us is our only book . . . Only the subjective impression . . . is a criterion of truth . . . The subjective impression is for the writer what experimentation is for the scientist, but with this difference, that with the scientist the work of the intelligence precedes, and with the writer it comes afterwards.' Intelligence, that quality which Musil has attributed wholly to the male and which archetypally is part of the masculine sphere, is only secondary to the artist. Proust reveals that it is in the feminine realm that the artist finds his home and it is from this sphere that his creativity is derived. Thus, we can account for the feminine properties attributed to Proust in the first part of this study, as Proust presents his own *apologia* in the form of *A la recherche*. Marcel is necessarily a hermaphroditic creature, for it is only as such that he can awaken to his creative task and describe the full scale of human experience.

In this study an attempt has been made to point out the significance of the feminine in Proust's vision and how this femininity is intrinsically related to Marcel's development into an artist. There is an important two-fold motion, dependent on femininity, which ought to be stressed here, once again, since it illuminates Proust's whole psychology of the artist's coming to being. Firstly, there is the need for the outgoing movement, the desire for the 'other' which we have shown to be essentially a heuristic development. This is mirrored in the figures of the 'jeunes filles en fleurs'. Secondly, after the external harvest is completed, it is memory which makes up the accounts. What Proust shows, however, is not 'emotion recollected in tranquillity', nor is it orthodox philosophy wherein sense experience always precedes knowledge. This negative foil, in fact, gives us a glimpse of the complex 'dédoublement' and reversal which Proust's thought entails.

One can proceed in this fashion : the complete trajectory begins in habit and ends in habit, that is, from the primal habit wherein the self is an undifferentiated being fused to totality by the mother and where the habit of security is continuously nourished by the mother. This phase of self is shattered; the security is lost, half wilfully, half imposed, so that guilt is the ambiguous outcome. The break with the first self, however, can only be seen to be really beneficial at the end, when reflection on it becomes possible. In various ways, Proust reinforces this secondary phase of self-alienation by events from Swann's life, Saint-Loup's, Charlus' and especially Marcel's experience. The self has been projected outwards and in so doing it has become strange *to itself*.

It is important to stress 'to itself', since the knowledge which is being forced upon the self at this juncture ultimately accumulates to the benefit of the self and to self-transformation. To this extent Proust's world is selfish; what we learn of others belongs to us, to one's self, since this is finally all we shall ever possess of the real world. In the third phase, it is memory which alone gives self back to self, as the experienced world slowly shrinks back to the original nodal point of the journey, 'moi'—the 'moi' however, now transformed. The feminine is again instrumental here, for as we have seen in the case of Albertine and the grandmother, it is this which instigates memory and makes up the substance of memory. Furthermore, since memory, in its full sense, is for Proust essentially involuntary, it belongs in the realm of the unconscious, which we have similarly seen to be feminine. In this last phase of memory, the 'dédoublement' is reinforced by those early virtues of Marcel's aunt: self-sufficiency, retirement—all the items of the aunt's solitude where the world is reduced to the rumours her maid reports —become transfigured into the ideal locality of the artist who can now reconstruct the world and 'save' time.

Some Closing Reflections

Femininity. What can now be said of its essential properties? What are the configurations the myth of femininity has taken on in the creative imagination of James, Musil and Proust; how is this central to an understanding of each one's vision and particular dilemma?

In James, the feminine appears as that aspect of being which is responsible for turning man inwards to a moral examination of himself. As such it governs all that is 'personal' in life: the possibility of individuation and truly 'felt' relationships. Femininity achieves this because of its essential flexibility, what can perhaps more precisely be defined as a creative openness to the full force of life. It is the basic principle of the Jamesian 'free spirit', undetermined by prejudices or pre-organised systems of any kind and unwilling to settle for the limitations imposed by an absolute or a systematization of life. Thus, femininity emerges as the basic prerequisite for 'intelligence' which for James would seem to be a spiritual rather than an intellectual quality. It is this feminine or spiritual intelligence which determines the individual's possibility for attaining to 'consciousness': the ability fully to see and hence fully to be.

In Musil's sharply etched intellectual universe, the polarities of the masculine and feminine principles are clearly delineated. Exactitude, precision of mind, the intellect which functions according to scientific or empirical observations are masculine qualities. Femininity is all that is not defined by the limits of cognition or intellectual modes of apprehension. Thus, femininity is the mystifying 'other'; on the one hand, the poetic, imaginative and spiritual, on the other, the anarchic and irrational ways of being and seeing.

Since it constitutes all that cannot be understood in terms of intellect alone, it comprises, for Musil, the entire realm of possibility: the possibility of living in the other condition of being—*der andere Zustand*—of introducing poetry into life, of living life as literature. Femininity is for Musil the root of all transcendental experience. While the masculine intellect tries to *understand* life by partitioning aspects of experience and making distinctions, the feminine attempts to *live* life and to attain unity and wholeness within a personal sphere. Hence, femininity introduces into a relativistic world of specialisation, the possibility of attaining totality.

In Proust the feminine emerges as a fundamentally transformative principle and thus a creative one. As in Musil, the feminine here is the 'other', the unknown, and as such it exerts a magical pull which draws the being out of himself toward ever-expanding imaginative horizons. Protean, the feminine effects a constant renewal in the being who is fascinated by it; and like memory it turns the invidual back to himself. Thus growth in the individual is brought about by the transformative power of femininity. This is essentially a creative function. But femininity is equivalent to creativity for Proust in a second and purely artistic fashion. It is the dominating principle of the creative unconscious: that realm from which stem the intuitive flashes of insight out of which art is made.

These three descriptions of femininity emphasise individual particularities of vision in the three writers. Nevertheless, a certain constancy emerges in this depiction of femininity. In all three writers the feminine is something removed from intellectual and rational spheres. As such it embodies something 'other' and at the same time it reveals what can be attained by pursuing the other. This otherness, which is femininity, is the personal, imaginative or spiritual side of existence and it contains the seeds of unity of being and of harmonious existence. It is the principle which reigns over the interiorization of life as well as all transcendentalism.

For James, this feminine aspect rules over the inwardness of existence, which challenges any social system defined by material absolutes, and it permits a seeing of the 'invisible', a full consciousness of the subtle sphere of spiritual and moral relationships. For Musil, the feminine defines that area of life which is beyond intellect and beyond all accepted social norms. Femininity forces man to re-evaluate his conventional modes of apprehension and being, and hence introduces in a godless world the possibility of the mystical 'other state of being'. In this other state true interiorization takes place as the limits between subject and object cease to exist. This is Musil's higher unity of being or total selfhood. Finally, for Proust, once again the feminine is all that is removed from the sphere of ideas and intellectual analysis. It comprises the intuitional sphere of life which permits past time to be transformed into presence, and which give birth to the creative artist—the sole inhabitant in the Proustian universe of Musil's 'other state'.

Thus it can now be seen how femininity not only occupies a central position in the works of these three writers, but also how it suggests an analogy for each one's particular artistic dilemma. If what have been described as the components of the Jamesian myth of femininity—inwardness, personalism, a free spirit, flexibility—is valid, then it becomes clear how femininity is analogous to James's own artistic focus. James's art is directed at examining the inner make-up of man, rather than his relation to 'the pistol, the pirate, the wild and tame beast'. He is not interested in sociological and idealogical generalisations, but rather in the relationship of his principal character to himself, in the subtleties of moral choice and personal relations. Free of any didactic purpose, James allows his characters to develop 'freely' as they would in life and he entertains no preconceptions on how they will turn out. As he says of the writing of the *Ambassadors* :

> Never, positively, none the less, as the links multiplied, had I felt less stupid than for the determination of poor Strether's errand and for the apprehension of his issue. These things continued to fall together, as by the neat action of their own weight and form, even while their commentator scratched his head about them; he easily sees now   that they were always well in advance of him.[1]

Inwardness and flexibility are the prerequisites for fully seeing, the highest function in James's ethical structure. We have already seen how femininity is a means to this end; how it is only the feminine character or the one influenced by femininity who attains this in the Jamesian universe. Similarly James's art is primarily a visual one. It has a voyeur-like quality and emphasises the 'seen' object, character or situation. It further insists on the 'demonstration of this process of vision'. Seeing is also the basis of James's law of successive aspects which permits the narrator to see all subtleties from all

[1] Henry James, *The Art of the Novel* (New York, 1934), p. 315.

points of view. Thus the feminine, in its possibility of being 'finely, intensely, acutely aware', points out the artistic path to follow for the implementation of both vision and technique.

In James's writings we find no evidence of any difficulty which he may have encountered in determining the importance of art's place in the whole of life. He seems totally convinced of the validity of his artistic purpose and unhindered by doubts as to whether the creative or imaginative mode of seeing and being may not be the best. Similarly, no difficulty confronts him in accepting all that he describes the feminine to be. He fully empathises with the feminine outlook and accords it the highest place in his artistic ethos. With Musil, on the other hand, we find a basic dissatisfaction with art and this equips him with an irony unknown to James. This irony is double-edged. It circles a rational view of society and the scientific universe with doubts; and at the same time it casts doubts upon the paramount place of imagination in reality. Musil is haunted by the split between the scientific or rational mode of life and the imaginative, artistic one. Hence with Musil, such a perfect equivalence between femininity and the focus of his vision cannot be found. Nevertheless, to understand the feminine in Musil is to understand his particular artistic and human dilemma.

Musil attempts, in his final, but unfinished, work, the ambitious and perhaps impossible task, of providing a solution for the problem of the *condition humaine* in his time. For a solution to emerge, he sees that the individual must totally re-evaluate and reorganise his modes of perception and hence his life. This cannot be done by scientific, rational and intellectual means alone, which for Musil constitute the masculine pole of life.

Thus Musil sets out, one might say is driven, to investigate the feminine mode of being and seeing. He penetrates to the depths of the feminine and finds at its core anarchic and amoral elements which would be essential to a revolution in cognitive processes and hence in life. He also finds in femininity an imaginative mode of perception which for him constitutes 'spirit' or 'soul', a poetic or mystical way of apprehending, which recognises the possibility of magic and miracle. The feminine, then, emerges as that source in which the possibility of total human reorganisation lies. It is in femininity that the impulse to that 'other condition' can be found.

'To live life as literature', as Ulrich suggests, is essentially to bring this feminine element back into the mainstream of life, from whence it has been expelled by a rationalistic, paternalist civilisation. In art, in literature, Musil recognises that this feminine, imaginative element of 'spirit' is central. It is the essence of art, of fiction, to attempt to understand and portray that which is incomprehensible in terms of intellect alone. In fiction, this feminine principle with its full scale of irrational and imaginative possibility can be organised, can be formed by the masculine intellect. Musil clearly shows us, especially in his earlier short stories, that literature permits a synthesis of the two principles, at least in the single individual.

But life poses another set of problems and in *The Man Without Qualities* Musil is concerned with the *totality* of life. Ulrich's attempt to apply masculine intellect to organise the feminine principles of irrational or imaginative possibility may or may not succeed. We do not know; the novel remains unfinished. Perhaps— and we are strongly led to believe this in what we have of the novel —Musil's wish to manifest a marriage of spiritual possibility and intellect, of 'exactitude and soul' is hopeless. The problem which Musil presents is nevertheless a fruitful one, more urgent now than ever. Can art, which aspires to present a totality of experience, provide a synthesis of these two opposite poles, both of which must be part of life? For Musil the answer in the final analysis would seem to be no. In Proust and James a synthesis does seem to be offered.

Musil is too strongly entrenched in intellectual and scientific modes of thought to allow the feminine 'sliding logic of the soul' to take over completely and lead the way to a lasting synthesis. First of all, he recognises the danger inherent in the irrational and anarchic qualities he describes at the core of femininity. Uncontrolled by reason or intellect, this aspect of femininity can lead on one level to the madness of a Moosbrugger, or on a more universal plane to the Hitler hysteria. Musil had good grounds for despising the Klages cult of an enthusiastic return to matriarchal ways. Secondly, the imaginative or 'spirit' qualities inherent in the feminine can on a realistic plane lead to the idealization of superstition—an equal threat for mankind. Finally, in life, the synthesis of masculine and feminine principles, the openness in separateness of the mystical state which is the seed of the solution which Musil would like to present, cannot exist for more than an instant, as it can on a purely fictional plane. Reality exists within time, not outside it, and hence any ideal state is subject to change as conditions change. Thus Musil cannot, even within his art, allow the synthesis or the solution which he posits to last.

Neither can he permit the feminine element to triumph completely in leading the way to a harmonious state on more than a personal level. In herself, woman can achieve a synthesis of masculine and feminine principles and thus attain a fullness of being, together with a reorganisation of her own conditions of being. But this is a personal achievement which has no repercussions on the social plane.

Femininity thus provides us with an insight into Musil's artistic as well as human dilemma. If life could be lived as literature, then the possibility which Musil depicts as peculiar to femininity would come to fruition. It could join with the masculine ordered and intellectual ethos to create a harmonious whole. But since this is impossible in life, it becomes, for Musil, impossible in literature as well. The final note which *The Man Without Qualities* strikes is the one of intellect, of daylight lucidity. Musil's vision, in the last analysis, is a 'masculine' one, for he cannot permit art to triumph over life, spirit over reality, imagination over intellectual modes of apprehension. He cannot allow a synthesis between masculine and feminine—and one instigated by the latter—to occur. In this he stands apart from James and Proust, both of whom are more keenly interested in the problems of artistic form and experience, and, especially with Proust, in the make-up of the artist himself.

Yet Musil has occupied the central position in this study, precisely because he so clearly presents the polarities of the masculine and the feminine, of what is, within his vision, social reality and fiction. He investigates the feminine element in depth and clearly delineates the possibilities which it presents. He succeeds in demystifying the 'other', while Proust and James are content to work with the suggestiveness of the mystification. In his imaginative leap, his attempt to provide a synthesis, Musil uses the feminine. But finally, he cannot fully give in to it. Musil opts for life, the responsibility of a social vision, rather than the purity of art.

The difference between James, Proust and Musil is one between art which seeks to offer a solution on a *personal* level and one which attempts a social or universal solution. The latter may be beyond the capabilities of art; and Musil demands something from art which it may not be in art's power to deliver. Proust, however, can find the resolution of his personal problem—lost time and the discontinuity of the self—in art. Femininity is thus of the essence of his vision, for by equating it with a creative unconscious force, it becomes the power by which the real situation is transformed into metaphor or art. Proust fully believes in the metamorphic possibilities of the creative process. We have already seen how the feminine contributes to Marcel's development into an artist. On the one hand, the feminine is instrumental in bringing about each birth of a new 'moi' in Marcel. This for Proust is essentially a heuristic development, as Marcel is drawn into ever-expanding fields of imaginative experience. On the other hand, Proust shows us that this femininity is concretely the realm of the unconscious from which creative powers stem. It is in this intuitive sphere that Marcel's final revelations originate and these give him the inspiration to begin on his artistic ventures.

Proust has none of Musil's difficulty in believing in a union of intellect and spirit, of reason and imagination, of order and chaos— the dialectically opposed poles of masculinity and femininity. The hermaphroditic being who contains within himself these two poles can dwell in reality in the form of the artist. But this can only happen because, in Musil's terms, the artist is essentially more at home in the feminine realm of the 'sliding logic of the soul', in the realm where a fusion of opposites is possible because of the lack of strictly defined intellectual categories. Where distinctions merge, where flux begins and ceases—this is the realm of the feminine.

*   *   *

Bibliography

Since the extent of the critical literature on James, Musil and Proust, as well as on femininity, is so vast, I have merely listed primary sources here.

HENRY JAMES

The Novels and Tales of Henry James New York Edition 24 vols, London 1907–9.
The Reverberator London 1949.
The Sacred Fount London 1954.
The Sense of the Past New York 1917.
The Ivory Tower New York 1917.
The Complete Tales of Henry James ed. Leon Edel, 12 vols, London 1962–4.
The American Novels and Stories of Henry James ed. F. O. Matthiessen, New York 1956.
Henry James's Autobiography ed. F. W. Dupee, London 1956.
The American Essays of Henry James ed. Leon Edel, New York 1956.
Notes on Novelists London 1914.
French Poets and Novelists New York 1964.
'Saint-Beuve' *The North American Review* CXXX Jan. 1880, pp. 51–68.
The Painter's Eye London 1956.
The Art of the Novel: Critical Prefaces by Henry James Introduction by Richard P. Blackmur, New York 1934.

The House of Fiction ed. Leon Edel, London 1957.
The Notebooks of Henry James ed. Leon Edel, New York 1961.
The Letters of Henry James ed. Percy Lubbock, 2 vols, London 1920.

ROBERT MUSIL

Der Mann ohne Eigenschaften in *Gesammelte Werke in Einzelausgaben* ed. Adolf Frisé, Hamburg 1968.
Prosa, Dramen, Späte Briefe in *Gesammelte Werke in Einzelausgaben* ed. Adolf Frisé, Hamburg 1957.
Tagebücher, Aphorismen Essays und Reden in *Gesammelte Werke in Einzelausgaben* ed. Adolf Frisé, Hamburg 1955.
The Man Without Qualities 3 vols, trans. by Eithne Wilkins and Ernst Kaiser, London 1965.
Theater, Kritisches und Theoretisches ed. Marie-Louise Roth, Hamburg 1965.

MARCEL PROUST

A la recherche du temps perdu ed. Pierre Clarac and André Ferré, 3 vols, Paris 1954.
Chroniques Paris 1927.
Contre Sainte-Beuve suivi de nouveaux mélanges Paris 1954.
Jean Santeuil 3 vols, Paris 1952.
Les Plaisirs et les jours Paris 1924.
Pastiches et mélanges Paris 1919.
Remembrance of Things Past 12 vols, trans. by C. K. Scott Moncrieff and vol. 12 by Stephen Hudson. London 1964.

GENERAL TEXTS ON FEMININITY

Backofen, J. J. *Das Mutterrecht* Stuttgart 1861.
   Mutterrecht und Urreligion ed. Rudolf Marx, Stuttgart 1926.
Mutterrecht und Urreligion ed. Rudolf Marx, Stuttgart 1926.
Beauvoir, Simone de. *Le deuxième sexe* 2 vols, Paris 1950.
Chasseguet-Smirgel, J. *La sexualité féminine* Paris 1964.
Deutsch, Helene. *Neuroses and Character Types* London 1965.
   The Psychology of Women 2 vols, New York 1944.
Freud, Sigmund. *The Complete Psychological Works* 23 vols, London 1953–66.

Graves, Robert. *The White Goddess* London 1961.

Hays, H. R. *The Dangerous Sex* London 1966.

Jung, C. G. *The Collected Works* 1953–.

Jung, C. G. and C. Kerenyi. *Essays on a Science of Mythology* New York 1963.

Neumann, Erich. *Amor and Psyche* London 1956.

  The Great Mother London 1955.

  The Origins and History of Consciousness London 1954.

Weininger, Otto. *Geschlecht und Charakter* Wien und Leipzig 1904.

Index